Between Peasant and Urban Villager

American University Studies

Series IX
History
Vol. 128

PETER LANG
New York • San Francisco • Bern • Baltimore
Frankfurt am Main • Berlin • Wien • Paris

Michael J. Eula

Between Peasant
and Urban Villager

Italian-Americans of New Jersey
and New York, 1880-1980

The Structures of Counter-Discourse

PETER LANG
New York • San Francisco • Bern • Baltimore
Frankfurt am Main • Berlin • Wien • Paris

Library of Congress Cataloging-in-Publication Data

Eula, Michael J.
    Between peasant and urban villager : Italian Americans of New
Jersey and New York, 1880-1980 : the structures of counter-discourse /
by Michael J. Eula.
        p. cm. — (American university studies. Series IX, History ; vol. 128)
    Includes bibliographical references.
    1. Italian Americans—New Jersey—Cultural assimilation.   2. Italian
Americans—New Jersey—Ethnic identity.   3. Italian Americans—
New York (State)—Cultural assimilation.   4. Italian Americans—New
York (State)—Ethnic identity.   I. Title.   II. Series.
F145.I8E9   1993   305.85'10747—dc20   92-12074
ISBN 0-8204-1864-1   CIP
ISSN 0740-0462

Die Deutsche Bibliothek-CIP-Einheitsaufnahme

Eula, Michael J.:
Between peasant and urban villager : Italian Americans of New Jersey
and New York, 1880-1980 : the structures of counter-discourse /
Michael J. Eula.—New York; Berlin; Bern; Frankfurt/M.; Paris; Wien:
Lang, 1993
    (American university studies : Ser. 9, History; Vol. 128)
        ISBN 0-8204-1864-1
NE: American university studies/09

The paper in this book meets the guidelines for permanence and
durability of the Committee on Production Guidelines for
Book Longevity of the Council on Library Resources.

© Peter Lang Publishing, Inc., New York 1993

Printed in the United States of America.

We should acknowledge that life itself is
not logical but is full of elements that
cannot be weighed on the scales of reason.

Antonio Gramsci, "'Anjisa'
by Andreyev at the Carig-
nano," *Avanti!* (1920)

CONTENTS

III. RELIGION AND THE STRUGGLE AGAINST DOMINATION

Preface

STRUCTURES, DISCOURSES, AND THE RHETORIC OF WORKING CLASS CULTURE

This book began inadvertently. Ironically enough, it was initiated in a graduate seminar entitled "History and Theory." Along the way, after a chance reading of the radical historiography on the American south, I was captivated by the notion of continuity. Were the African-American sharecroppers really that much better off than their slave predecessors? Did Reconstruction really make that much of a difference by the end of the nineteenth century? Thinking seriously about these questions kept bringing me back to a simultaneous interest in Italian-Americans. How different were third and fourth generation Italian-Americans from their peasant ancestors of the nineteenth century? Had settlement in urban New Jersey and New York really changed them? What has the experience of migration meant for subsequent generations?

Thus began a project culminating in this book. Scholars have done a magnificent job of portraying Italian migration and its demographic consequences in the nineteenth century and beyond.[1] Labor and social historians have been equally successful in depicting the daily reality of

Italian-American life. Nonetheless, I quickly detected the gap in a scholarship generally emphasizing questions and analytical techniques which often overlooked the richness of cultural territories characterized by endlessly creative forms of cultural resistance. Numbers of bootblacks, physicians, and cigar makers served to describe much and yet explain relatively little. Discussions of social mobility, fertility patterns, and rates of home ownership left me dizzy with statistical tables, computer printouts, and economic models presenting the exterior world at the expense of the people in it. If one wants to comprehend the historical reality of working class life, Italian and otherwise, then one must also set out for the cultural terrain of the "subaltern" class described decades ago by Antonio Gramsci.

I am therefore attempting to recreate the world of Italian-American workers as seen and felt by them in New Jersey and New York over a century-long period. It is a universe which begins in the Italian south of the nineteenth century, a traditional society characterized by a culture in which social mobility, if it occurred at all, was so slow as to remain almost undetectable. The emotional lives of the peasants were accordingly forged within the restrictive social relations of a conservative society. When the peasants left that world for New Jersey and New York, those same emotional patterns came along "in the baggage" to a liberal, capitalist United States. Thus my point begins to emerge—that in a pattern evident throughout this region the peasants continued to contextualize their lives as they had done in rural Italy, for class subordination remained a central reality of everyday life. Over time, the limitations of the class structure combined with demographic concentration to produce a working class culture replete with emotional characteristics similar to those evident in the Italian south.[2]

My use of "culture" is thus in need of elaboration. Culture in this instance refers to an arena of struggle. In that sphere Italian peasants, and then Italian-American workers, engaged in practices, and constructed ideas, which enabled them to take on an equally complex and pervasive Anglo-American middle class culture. Early on, Italian-American culture—or what Richard Terdiman has called in the case of France "counter-discourse"—is clear. Language, public rituals, and a variety of daily behaviors all stand in overt opposition to the language, public rituals, and daily behaviors of the region's Anglo-American middle class. As we move further into the twentieth century, that counter-discourse becomes harder to see. By the 1920s the dominant culture of those in power succeeded in becoming dominant precisely because it became orthodoxy—can we conceive of an America not characterized by the values of the Anglo-American middle class? Thus on the surface, Italian-Americans begin to assimilate in the years after World War One. At least on the surface.

But lurking just below the surface are discourses of resistance always threatening to disturb this misleading serenity. From the 1880s on discourses were being constructed by Italian-American workers whose counter-construction always assumed a sky line of competing positions. In the struggle against that sky line the Italian-American working class exhibited a rich, diverse, and creative culture which exposed the limits of middle class hegemony.

My approach thus begins to illuminate the outposts, the margins, of Anglo-American middle class culture. It is far easier to isolate the key elements of that culture precisely because it is dominant. Dominance is inseparable from coherence. But as Gramsci argued in the *Prison Notebooks*, it is not as easy to outline the culture of the working class because of its position as a subordinate group:

> The history of subaltern social groups is necessarily frag-
> mented and episodic. There undoubtedly does exist a
> tendency…to unification in the historical activity of these
> groups, but this tendency is continually interrupted by
> the activity of the ruling groups….[3]

Accordingly, a history of working class culture cannot by definition be the product of a research strategy guided by precise sampling methods. This is a study in which I self-consciously drop a lead line into the depths beneath that seemingly serene Anglo-American surface. I am taking samples of counter-discursive production, cultural specimens through which I seek to convey the complexity of the counter-discursive forms which characterize the Italian-American working class. By its very nature, the counter-discursive yields an endless variety of forms, some overt and some more subtle. Therefore, my samplings were carefully chosen. Like Terdiman, I too have dropped my lead line where I suspect the most fruitful soundings could take place. I am not suggesting, however, that these are the only places to take a sounding.

Hence my focus upon funerals, adolescence, and Roman Catholicism. The cultural processes at work in these areas imply a host of values and meanings which, when compared with those same cultural constructions in the Anglo-American middle class, reveal a counter-discursive function transmitted across the generations. They are conveyed from one generation to the next because of the structural realities of capitalism in this region, along with the density of a social network described most accurately in Colleen L. Johnson's *Growing Up and Growing Old in Italian-American Families*:

> Where the social network is connected by relatives who
> share the same views and who are in frequent interaction
> with each other, it is proposed that the potential for
> change is minimized.[4]

Counter-discursive practice reveals how Italian-American workers confront power. In that confrontation they survey a social and cultural frontier upon which class conflict is played out. The discourses formulated and reformulated on both sides became embodied in behavioral patterns and institutionalized expressions operating to transmit, diffuse, and maintain beliefs. Forms of discourse suggest a class structure in which the reciprocal relations of power and powerlessness can never be fully understood unless viewed as a total system. There are deep emotional realities and psychological orders woven throughout the infrastructure of Italian-American working class life. Despite immersion in Anglo-American society—its schools, its workplaces, its churches, its mass culture—the history of the Italian-American worker is one of the reformulation of desires and needs initially constructed in rural Italy. The life conditions of the peasant had meant a different world view than that of the aristocracy in rural Italy. The life conditions of the worker subsequently meant a different world view than that of the middle class in New Jersey and New York.

As socioeconomic transformations occurred, the context within which the counter-discursive functioned also changed. Discourses on both sides became increasingly conscious efforts. The struggle was institutionalized in schools and churches. It meant confrontation over the notion of adolescence. The conflict over discourse also appeared in the mass media. In 1974, the "Uncle Floyd Vivino Show" first appeared on New Jersey Cable Television. In a presentation overtly appealing to Italian-American workers, Vivino interrupts the surface uniformity of mass culture, as described in *New Jersey History*:

> In the tradition of Eduardo Migliaccio, "Farfariello," the quintessential comedian of the Italian-American theater, "Uncle Floyd" attacks certain aspects of life in the United States. Among those to come under satiric fire are callous urban planners, pompous intellectuals, inflexible bosses, and those who are too taken with themselves. In the comedy world of "The Uncle Floyd Show," "Intellectual Digest" becomes "Intellectual Digress" where the moderator, Mr. Bianco, is regularly bored to sleep by his guests. Astronomer Dr. Carl Sagan becomes "Dr. Pagan," a wishy-washy professor who interprets "The Blasmos" for his viewers. Political analysts are ridiculed in "Liberal vs. Conservative," as the experts' debate rapidly loses sight of the issue and deteriorates into name calling and insult hurling.[5]

My emphasis upon the counter-discursive calls into question both the assumptions of assimilationist scholars working in Italian-American studies and the Marxism of Frankfurt School theorists.[6] In both approaches working class resistance to dominant forms of culture tends to be downplayed. Both approaches suggest a gradual yet certain embourgeoisement of the working class, Italian and otherwise. My exploration of counterdiscursive structures instead stresses the challenge to middle class hegemony posed by Italian-American workers, who in their opposition to the dominant discourse offer a variety of positions connected by their very resistance to the culture of Anglo-American domination.

Throughout the book I attempt to illustrate what the attack of the counter-discursive means for domination. Accordingly, I consider the reformulation of hegemony on the part of those holding power. The counter-discourse is a mode of opposition. That means that its internal consequences for the Italian-American working class is always mixed; this culture is a consistent mix of the personally liberating and the personally oppressive. Unlike some labor historians, I am not proposing a celebration of working class culture. I cannot offer community when it is not there.[7] Instead, as the counter-discursive works to affirm working class identity, it simultaneously has the effect of political debilitation. Italian-American culture resists Anglo-American hegemony—but that does not mean that working class culture is essentially fulfilling. As we shall see, young people were in fact denied Anglo-American middle class definitions of adolescence. But they were nonetheless exploited as workers by their own parents. My analysis therefore raises a question central to twentieth century labor history—how can we begin to explain a group which is conservative, rather than radical or liberal? How do we explain the importance of "place" in Bensonhurst in 1989 among fourth-generation Italian-Americans?[8] Why are Bensonhurst residents still suspicious of "outsiders," as their great-grandparents had once been in the Italian countryside?

Since this is a work of cultural history, my effort is directed towards the deep mental worlds of peasants and then workers as they manifest themselves in key areas of everyday life. I admittedly take certain liberties with rural Italian culture, understanding full well the demographic and social variations evident among southern Italian immigrants in the nineteenth century. My purpose has been to suggest, in the broadest possible fashion, the assertions of counter-discursive expressions which by definition are ambivalent, complex, and inconsistent. Accordingly, my interpretation of rituals focuses upon the connections between the subject of assertion and the complex acting out of that assertion; between the public production of the counter-discursive and its connection to the dominant discourse. The counter-discourse both expresses, and is an expression of, ritual. In other words, as scholars such as Jonathan Z. Smith have argued in works like *Imagining Religion*, rituals recreate the world of the producer—or at least the world desired by the producer.[9] The counter-discursive was often a desire to see the world in a way which placed one in opposition to domination. Rituals thus compete as much as they contemplate.

I also need to comment on my reading of popular sources. As with other subaltern groups, Italian-American workers, like the peasants before them, do not leave much in the way of primary sources. There is a problem with sources written by northern Italians and intellectuals when one's focus in southern peasants and urban laborers. Accordingly, I have tried to view such sources with a healthy skepticism. Wherever possible, I have attempted to reconstruct the counter-discursive from the perspective of the peasant and worker. I admit to a limited success in that regard. Because of this methodological problem, I was often compelled to rely upon fiction, again comprehending such issues as that of the novelist who is busily rearranging the world through symbolism. As a result, I understand that novelists never intended to write social history.

Nonetheless, many of the Italian and Italian-American novelists I utilize suggest to us key elements of the counter-discursive. Their bleak depictions of hopeless toil, their considerations of adolescence, and their treatments of Catholicism all reveal underlying cultural structures evident when laid at the frontier of the dominant. Removed from these outposts, it is harder to see the explicit nature of their resistance.

Finally, I stand guilty of reducing the internal complexity of the dominant and counter-discursive functions to a series of oppositions typically labeled "bourgeois" and "mezzogiorno," or southern Italian. It is my belief that the history of Italian-American working class culture in New Jersey and New York has been a story of resistance to ideological and cultural domination which has, at least in part, minimized the influence of generational differences.[10] Every discourse of the dominant class has been challenged by its opposite counter-discourse. This is a story of the subverting of consensus. It is an analysis of how resistance happens, of how it is possible to resist even in an age of mass culture. Thus in the end the cultural conflict becomes clear almost to the point of reductionism. After all, it was predicated upon an equally clear competition between social classes.

I wish to thank the Division of Graduate Studies and Research, University of California, Irvine, for generous support early on in this project. The New Jersey Historical Commission provided equally generous support at crucial junctures. The National Endowment for the Humanities funded me in a summer seminar at UCLA which provided the opportunity for fruitful exchanges with Robert Wohl, Ivan Strenski, and Mike Budd. Professor Strenski in particular provided editorial support in his capacity of editor for the journal *Religion*. Several portions of Part Three found their way into that journal with the help of his editorial patience. Needless to say, he is in no way responsible for my judgements there or in this book.

Jonathan Wiener, Michael Johnson, Mark Poster, David Pivar, and Jaime Vidal have all helped me at different points. My colleagues at El Camino College provided a warm and stimulating environment during the revision stage. I extend particular thanks to Nadine Hata, Maria Brown, Ellen Antoine, Janet Madden, Alfred Wrobel, Thom Armstrong, and Donald Haydu. John Diggins offered the possibility of new approaches, along with the example of his endlessly creative and questioning mind. My grandfather, the son of an Italian immigrant, reminded me of the realities not always revealed in archival sources. So too did Angela Stuehler, who has lovingly reminded me of those realities for many years. Finally, my parents need to be thanked. In their warm and humane way they always nudged me, reminding me to keep my feet on the ground.

Torrance, California
January 1992

PREFACE NOTES

1. See such seminal studies as Samuel L. Baily's "The Adjustment of Italian Immigrants in Buenos Aires and New York, 1870—1914," *American Historical Review*, April 1983, pp. 281-305; Dino Cinel, *From Italy to San Francisco: The Immigrant Experience* (Stanford, 1982); I. Rosenwaite, "Two Generations of Italians in America: Their Fertility Experience," *International Migration Review*, Fall 1973, especially page 275; John W. Briggs, "Fertility and Cultural Change among Families in Italy and America," *American Historical Review*, December 1986, pp. 1,129-1,145; Dennis J. Starr, *The Italians of New Jersey: A Historical Introduction and Bibliography* (Newark, 1985); G. Monticelli, "Italian Emigration: Basic Characteristics and Trends with Special Emphasis on the Post-War Years," *International Migration Review*, Summer 1967, pp. 10-24; J. McDonald and L. McDonald, "Chain Migration, Ethnic Neighborhood and Social Network," *Milbank Memorial Fund Quarterly*, 42, 1964, pp. 82-97; B. Cohler and H. Grunebaum, *Mothers, Grandmothers and Daughters: Personality and Care in Three-Generation Families* (New York, 1981); and Nampeo R. McKenney, Michael Levin and Alfred J. Tella, "A Sociodemographic Profile of Italian Americans," in *Italian Americans: New Perspectives in Italian Immigration and Ethnicity*, ed. Lydio F. Tomasi (New York, 1985), pp. 3-31.
2. See Anthony L. LaRuffa's fine study in which he refers to the "ongoing" process of ethnicity. LaRuffa thoughtfully argues that "these traditional communities" are constantly reproducing "cultural phenomena" whose immediate historical origins are discernible in the Italian countryside. See *Monte Carmelo: An Italian-American Community in the Bronx* (New York, 1988). Also see Marianna DeMarco Torgovnick's "On Being White, Female, and Born in Bensonhurst," in *The Best American Essays, 1991*, ed. Joyce C. Oates (New York, 1991), pp. 223-235.
3. *Selections from the Prison Notebooks of Antonio Gramsci*, eds. Quintin Hoare and Geoffrey Nowell Smith (New York, 1987), pp. 54-55. Also refer to C. Mouffe, ed., *Gramsci and Marxist Theory* (London, 1979); Christine Buci-Glucksman, *Gramsci and the State* (London, 1979); and my study, entitled "Gramsci's Views on Consent and its Basis as an Alternate Political Route, "*Differentia: Review of Italian Thought*, Autumn

1986, pp. 177-186. Richard Terdiman's *Discourse/Counter-Discourse: The Theory and Practice of Symbolic Resistance in Nineteenth-Century France* has been helpful here, as has Louis Althusser's "Ideology and Ideological State Apparatus (Notes toward an Investigation)," in *Lenin and Philosophy*, trans. Ben Breuster (New York, 1970). Also consult Michele Barrett, Philip Corrigan, Annette Kuhn, and Janet Wolff, eds., *Ideology and Cultural Production* (London, 1979); Michel Foucault, *Language, Counter-Memory, Practice*, trans. Donald Bouchard (Ithaca, 1977); Jürgen Habermas, *Legitimation Crisis*, trans. Thomas McCarthy (Boston, 1975); and Frederic Jameson, *The Political Unconscious: Narrative as a Socially Symbolic Act* (Ithaca, 1981). Donald M. Lowe's *History of Bourgeois Perception* (Chicago, 1982); Rainer Warning's "Irony and the 'Order of Discourse' in Flaubert," trans. Michael Morton, *New Literary History*, Winter 1982, pp. 253-286; and H.T. Wilson's *Marx's Critical/Dialectical Procedure* (London, 1991), were also useful.

4. Johnson, *Growing Up and Growing Old in Italian-American Families* (New Brunswick, New Jersey), p. 13.

5. Pamela R. Primeggia, Salvatore Primeggia, and Joseph A. Varacalli, "Uncle Floyd Vivino: A Modern Italian-American Comic," *New Jersey History* Fall/Winter 1989, pp. 6-7.

6. My analysis thus stands in some opposition to that of Richard Alba's *Italian Americans: Into the Twilight of Ethnicity* (Englewood Cliffs, New Jersey, 1985); and James A. Crispino, *The Assimilation of Ethnic Groups: The Italian Case* (Staten Island, New York, 1980). Also see Alba's "Comments on Papers by McKenney, Levin and Tella, and by Nelli and Vecoli," in *Italian Americans: New Perspectives in Italian Immigration and Ethinicity*, pp. 116-118. A relevant consideration is Rudolf J. Vecoli's "Change and/or Continuity in the Immigrant Experience," *Reviews in American History*, March 1984, pp. 109-114. For representative Frankfurt school theorists who stress a suffocating mass culture largely devoid of the possibility of the counter-discursive, see Theodore Adorno, *The Authoritarian Personality* (New York, 1950); and *Negative Dialectics* (New York, 1973). John Thompson's *Critical Hermeneutics* (New York, 1981), is an appropriate criticism of the Frankfurt school's general position on culture.

7. Although I do not go as far in some of my assumptions, I nonetheless agree with such criticisms of labor history as those expressed by John Diggins. See "Comrades and Citizens: New Mythologies in American Historiography," *American Historical Review*, June 1985, pp. 614-638. Italian-American workers mounted a sustained cultural resistance, but that is not the same as saying that they formed community and class-conscious solidarity.

8. See the insightful discussion of Murray Hausknecht, "Bensonhurst and Auschwitz," in *Dissent*, Winter 1990, pp. 100-102. Also consult Jonathan Rieder's *Canarsie: The Jews and Italians of Brooklyn Against Liberalism* (Cambridge, Massachusetts, 1985).

9. Also see Smith's "The Bare Facts of Ritual," *History of Religions*, 20, 1980, pp. 112-127. Further, see Kay F. Turner's "The Virgin of Sorrows Procession: Mothers, Movement, and Transformation," *Archè: Notes and Papers on Archaic Studies*, 6, 1981, pp. 71-92; Evon Z. Vogt, *Tortillas for the Gods: A Symbolic Analysis of Zinacanteco Rituals* (Cambridge, Massachusetts, 1976); Victor Turner, *Celebration: Studies in Festivity and Ritual* (Washington, D.C., 1982); Butler Waugh, "Structural Analysis in Literature and Folklore," *Western Folklore*, 25, 1966, pp. 153-164; Evan M. Zuesse, "Meditation on Ritual," *Journal of the American Academy of Religion*, 43, 1975, pp. 517-530; and William G. Doty, *Mythography: The Study of Myths and Rituals* (Alabama, 1986).

10. This is an area of Italian-American studies which remains to be studied in a systematic way. Such scholars as Valentine J. Belfiglio have begun to make headway, however. See "Cultural Traits of Italian Americans Which Transcend Generational Differences," in *The Italian Americans Through the Generations*, ed. Rocco Caporale (Staten Island, New York, 1986), pp. 126-142. Johnson, in *Growing Up and Growing Old in Italian-American Families*, points out that:

> In contrast to some ethnic groups like the Japanese Americans, it was somewhat surprising to find that Italian Americans rarely referred to their generation level (page 54).

She went on to add that:

Italian Americans rarely conceptualize generation level as a reference to explain behavior...Generation level meaning parents and grandparents, of course, is used within the family, but the eldest generation to Italians does not always refer to grandparents who never left Italy, or to the one of greatest genealogical distance that one can remember (page 54).

I.

RITUALS OF DEATH

1

THE PRECEDENT
IN ITALY

Nobody travels south of Rome . . .
  Norman Douglas, in *Old Calabria* (1915)

"La Miseria"

The pervasive feeling of misery felt by the peasantry was a favorite theme among social scientists and novelists in the Italian south of the nineteenth and early twentieth centuries.[1] Misery was not, these writers argued, a temporary state of mind. Instead, it was a constant feature of daily life. This world was not that highly romanticized community of rural folk spoken of in older accounts of immigration.[2] Hunger, earthquakes, economic exploitation, and malaria all served to foster a feeling of hopelessness.[3] The hard southern environment, with its lack of trees and unproductive soil (much of which was clay), only served to intensify the

perception of imminent death which the social structure then institutionalized. The novelist Ignazio Silone captured this sense of bleakness which
gave rise to a culture appropriately described in the following passage:

> At the head of everything is God, Lord of Heaven.
> After Him, comes Prince Torlonia, lord of the earth.
> Then come Prince Torlonia's armed guards.
> Then come Prince Torlonia's armed guards' dogs.
> Then, nothing at all. Then nothing at all. Then
>   nothing at all.
> Then come the peasants.
> And that's all.[4]

Hunger and malaria, the two most common features of daily life,
intensified the sense of life's tentativeness. Peasants lived an uncertain
existence. Time and again, the behavioral manifestations of malnutrition,
not to mention outright hunger, were observable among the peasants. The
lack of physical strength was reflected in gaunt bodies topped by shallow,
thin faces.[5] Indeed, the reality of physical debility was reflected in the high
number of military recruits from the south who were turned down at the
induction center because of stunted physical development.[6] It was also
evident in the statistics on pellagra and cholera, as well as the common
greeting, "*si mangado?*" ("did you eat?")[7] A general gloominess in their
social interactions was apparent. Two classic characteristics of the
peasantry associated with the effects of malnutrition were in evidence. On
the one hand, there was a notable apathy.[8] Along with this resignation was
the recognition of a kind of introverted behavior so often spoken of by
observers and folklorists.[9] Conversely, there were the traits of nastiness and
irritability spoken of by such writers as John Fante.[10]

The continuous outbreaks of malaria also served to construct the
peasant's world view. The resignation and fatalism embodied in "*la
miseria*" was exacerbated by this terrible scourge. The dreaded illness had
a direct relationship with the lack of food. A large number of fertile bottom
lands were infested with anopheles mosquitos. As a result, they could not
be worked with any degree of regularity—it at all. Accordingly, the
peasants were obliged to move upland into the hill country. There thus
arose a pattern of having to walk upwards of five miles per day to work in
the fields. Often underfed and malnourished, the agricultural laborer was

consequently compelled to use precious energy during this walk. Cultivation itself was also affected, as only those crops which were resilient could be safely planted. The farmer was unable to pay close attention to crops which required more care.[11]

Poor health conditions only served to render the body less capable of resisting malaria. In Basilicata, for example, deaths from malaria averaged 5,141 per year (which approached 20% of the population) between 1890 and 1894.[12] Outbreaks of disease, however, were not confined to malaria. Trachoma, an illness related to unclean living conditions, was the result of often atrocious housing arrangements. In Sicily, peasants lived in abandoned Greek tombs. Sarcophagi served as bedsteads in such instances.[13] Rural one-room huts housed livestock and family together. Writing in 1905, Luigi Villari commented that these hovels, which were typically constructed of straw or wattle-and-daub, were "squalid and miserable...cramped for space, ill-kept...and thoroughly unsanitary."[14] It was reported that peasants in Basilicata lived in caves and in the open, on hillsides.[15] For the peasant whose field was too far away to permit daily traveling, a shack in the field sufficed.[16] As historian Leonard Covello has written,

> ...sanitary conditions among the peasants were primitive indeed.... In most parts of Calabria, houses had a sordid look because of the smoke which blackened the house walls, inside and out, due to the fact that the Calabrians persisted in maintaining the...custom of cooking over an open fire on the floor.[17]

Coupled with the daily reality of hunger, disease, and unsanitary living conditions was the regularity of vicious earthquakes. Southern Italy rests upon one of the most active tectonic plates in the world.[18] As a result, the area has always suffered from frequent earthquakes and volcanic eruptions. A series of earthquakes shook the provinces of Calabria and Basilicata in 1905, killing untold thousands of people.[19] In 1906, an eruption of Mt. Vesuvius buried whole villages in Campania.[20] But probably the worst quake of the period took place in 1908. An earthquake and tidal wave hit the Strait of Messina. Most of Messina, Sicily, was leveled, along with the villages of the surrounding region.[21] Across the Strait, the city of Reggio di Calabria was destroyed. All told, on both sides of the Strait, approximately three hundred towns and villages disappeared.[22] It is estimated that at least 120,000 people died in this incident. This event was the culmination of a series of devastating earthquakes in Calabria, which suffered such destruction in 1854, 1870, 1894, 1905, and 1907. This pattern was evident in other regions as well.[23]

The disasters of nature, along with a lack of food and poor housing, all contributed to peasant feelings of *"preoccupazione"* and anxiety. This sense of despair was, more than anything else, the result of material deprivation over a long period of time. Contrary to the idealistic depictions of earlier historians, the peasant world was not a pretty one.[24]

The social distance between the various levels of peasantry and the *"gabelotto"* (overseer of the absentee landowner's estate), provided other sources of misery and oppression for the *"contadini"*. A government official, touring the south sometime in the late nineteenth century, captured the essence of this social relation when he wrote that

> ...the contadini were in every way slaves; they worked on their lord's farm for a stipulated number of days, they kissed his hand, suffered the gratuitous extractions which indeterminate clauses in contracts of service allowed him, and showed a grovelling deference...[25]

The material deprivation which accompanied daily displays of deference only served to heighten a perception of endless suffering. Pasquale Villari, writing in *L'Opinione* (1875), argued that the "social and economic conditions of millions of Italian peasants are incredibly poor..."[26] In an oral interview, a seventy-four-year-old immigrant from Abruzzi pointed out that the "conditions [were] very, very poor.... At that time, Abruzzi was the lowest country you could think of."[27] An emigrant from Apulia tells us that

> ...we was poor people and I was working day and night... a boy seven and a half, eight years old...go with a donkey...go around picking stones for the stonemason ...I would get up at four o'clock in the morning...to ten o'clock at night...sometimes with shoes on feet... sometimes with no shoes.[28]

Maybe the reformer Sidney Sonnino said it best when he pleaded for a realization that

> Our peasants there (in the south) are in worse conditions than the serfs of the Middle Ages...Peasants live like beasts...They have equally hard choices before them: submission and work until untimely death, or rebellion and violent death....[29]

Even a brief overview of the economic picture in Apulia, Abruzzi, Campania, Basilicata (Lucania), Calabria, and Sicily reveals the relentless destitution of the peasantry. The *contadini*, or tenant farmers, were small landholders who rented land from large landholders. There were at least two *contadini* groups. On the one hand, there were the *"messadri,"* or sharecroppers. This group worked small plots of land themselves, or they leased even smaller plots.[30] In this arrangement, owners supplied agricultural materials such as seed or vines, in return for an unspecified and legally unlimited amount of labor. The *"fittavali,"* on the other hand, paid an annual fee for land, which they then leased out in small plots. These two groups were the upper echelon of the peasantry. By far, the largest group of *contadini* were those who paid rent to the *fittavali* or the *mezzadri*. These were the *"giornatore"*—the agricultural laborers. This last group neither owned nor leased land. They simply traveled from one estate to another in a perpetual search for work. Approximately two-thirds of the rural folk in Calabria were in this category by 1890, along with one-half in Basilicanta. Theirs was a life of permanent underemployment—the average *giornatore* worked approximately 125 days per year. Between 1878 and 1906 the number of male and female day laborers above fifteen years old, per 10,000 emigrants, grew at a fairly steady rate, aside from a slight drop in female workers by 1906.[31]

PERIOD	MALE	FEMALE
1878–1880	2,133	1,287
1884–1886	2,284	1,417
1894–1896	2,564	1,482
1904–1906	3,221	1,376
TOTAL PERCENTAGE OF GROWTH	21.3% to 32.9%	13.0% to 13.8%

The level of wages were uniformly low in the *Mezzogiorno* peasant world. Sicilian *"broccianti"* (*giornatore*), earned an average of $.25 for twelve hours of work (1902).[32] While this figure had risen to $.31 by 1905, it was considerably lower than the average of $.45 per day received by male agricultural workers in Piedmont.[33] The differences between wage levels in the north and south are particularly dramatic in the category of summer earnings per month. I have shown these below, along with average wages per day in 1905:[34]

PROVENCE	AVERAGE DAY'S PAY (Men)	HIGHEST SUMMER EARNING (Monthly)
Piedmont	$.45	$17.41
Pomagna	.40	13.85
Latium	.40	17.50
Abruzzi	.40	9.35
Apulia	.33	8.04
Basilicata	.37	13.00
Calabria	.36	11.33
Campania	.34	8.50
Sicily	.31	8.35

Agricultural wages looked bleaker when the high cost of consumer goods is taken into account. The pre–1914 price of sugar, for example, was $.19 per pound.[35] Flour was $.04 per pound.[36] Of course, I am assuming the availability of such goods.

To compound their situation, *giornatore* were socially ostracized even among the peasantry at large. For example, sharecroppers would not generally allow their daughters to marry day laborers. As Alessandro Mastro-Valerio put it in a report delivered to the Industrial Commission On Immigration in 1901,

> In trying to ascertain the causes of this social Italian-American phenomenon, one should consider the conditions under which the Italian peasant leaves Italy...First, he leaves Italy poor, having been there for endless generations—perhaps since the Romans of old had their

> large estates in Apulia, Campania, Sannium, Luciana,
> Sicily, and Sardinia, of which Pliny says: *"Latifundia Italia*
> *perdire"* —only a servant of the glebe…This has been an
> ungrateful work, through which he has never been able
> to ameliorate his position….[37]

The last sentence of Mastro-Valerio's testimony is particularly suggestive, for it implies the reified quality of peasant poverty. Disease, political corruption, and economic exploitation, so often the products of man-made acts, eventually came to assume an "inherent" quality all their own. Such a perception intensified feeling of vulnerability and despair. Indeed, it is at this point that we begin to understand the consciousness of the peasantry, who came to believe in the legitimacy of rigidly hierarchical social order. Periodic peasant revolts, it should be remembered, seldom questioned the essential features of the social order. They were typically attempts to retain what little rights the peasants enjoyed.[38]

Death and Blackness

A profound sense of personal limitation thus was evident in these people. Nowhere was this clearer than in those aspects of their culture institutionalized in the peasant funeral. Death itself underscored, in a visual and ceremonial way, the desperate quality of daily life. The color black, which was used so often in various facets of peasant life, was of course pronounced in funeral rituals. Consequently, its use reflected larger life rhythms at work, all rooted in the perception of *"la miseria."* As in other cultures, funerals served as the public ritualization of this group's worldview. In effect, the funeral embodied a self-referentiality which emanated from the reality of each day. Death was not a transition to a happier existence, as the peasants did not adhere to Church doctrine regarding heaven.

In the *Mezzogiorno* conception of death, all of life's complexity is revealed. There is fear, anxiety, suffering, and even shrewdness. There is throughout an aching unification of desperation and vulnerability. The only solution is the survival of the living, not the redemption of the dead. That is why the soul of the deceased was both mocked and feared.

The Fear of the Soul

For the *contadini*, the departure of a relative's soul was not a happy event. More than anything else, this part of the funeral ritual embodied the peasant's perception of vulnerability. Both the body and the soul were susceptible to the attack of evil forces, which would try to occupy the body. In this state of limbo, the soul might attempt to return to the family of the living, it was only here that a comforting environment would be found.[40]

Accordingly, elaborate precautions were taken to ensure the soul's passing, or, as a Sicilian phrase put it, to "insure a good agony."[41] An initial reaction was to locate the most prized material possessions of the deceased. These objects were then placed next to the body.[42] Other items, such as coins, or food, were placed in the coffin in order to placate the soul.[43] The whole relation of the living to the dead was therefore one of fear and suspicion, and it culminated in the rituals of corpse removal.

Numerous accounts in both Italy and the New Jersey/New York region show that the deceased was carried out of the house feet first.[44] The point here was clear. The living hoped that the soul, tormented as it was by evil forces, would be confused. By not seeing the door at the time of departure, it would be harder for the soul to return to familiar surroundings. The procession to the cemetery, or to the catacombs of, say, the Capuchin Convent in Palermo, would take complex paths.[45] Again, the intent was to confound the soul's sense of direction. The wailing of the women which accompanied the procession from the house was accordingly forbidden on the way back from the burial place. Such noise, of course, would attract the attention of the tormented, seething soul of the departed.

But the fear of the soul did not end here. Peasants believed that the soul was able to observe what took place on earth in general, and in the village in particular.[46] As a result, the soul might not like what it sees—and attempt to return. This state of limbo could last indefinitely, or as long as the soul remained in purgatory. Prayers were thus intensified in order to move the soul into a tranquil space where it would leave the living alone. This area was, of course, heaven.[47] The fear attached to the looming presence of the soul cannot be stressed too much. Stories abound which indicate a belief in the soul's ability to take the form of potentially menacing animals. As one Neapolitan reveals, when he

...was a boy, there used to be a spot where a dog appeared at night...the people were afraid and asked the priest to help them. He went to the place at midnight, and when a dog appeared, sprinkled it with holy water and asked, "In the name of God, why do you appear?" He then said a prayer, making the sign of the cross, and the dog disappeared....[48]

But the priest was not always relied upon to act as an intermediary. The family of the deceased periodically took matters into their own hands. In such cases prayers were spoken in a sea of mourning clothes worn by the immediate family. Mourning rituals, full of prayers, dark clothing, and emotional lamentations, varied from region to region. For example, it was generally the custom in Sicily and Sardinia for the wife of the deceased to wear black for four years. Daughters retained the option of wearing gray clothing for the second year. Elizabeth Mathias points out that women were typically "dressed permanently in black...by...thirty." This was dramatically different from Anglo-American middle class customs of the period in which we find none other than Henry Ward Beecher proclaiming that people should "not borrow of the devil; choose some color that shall speak of hope, of release, of victory. Draw not over yourselves the black tokens of pollution. Do not blaspheme by naming that despair which is triumph and eternal life."[49]

The peasant idea of the soul knew nothing of Beecher's "hope" and "victory." Instead, the peasant conception of the soul functioned as a public language of accomodation with the reality of southern Italy. It was an effective and moving way of asserting oneself in an otherwise stagnant and exploitative social structure. The rituals of the soul regulated one's understanding of the social and natural environment. Not incidentally, the peasant was also afforded an opportunity to contest power through assertion in the supernatural world. The social function of the soul was thus one of providing peasants the possibility of overcoming typical constraints—thus allowing for the undermining of personal vulnerability, a key emotional component in a traditional society so focused upon power and reciprocity. In addition, the harnessing of the family's power—and even that of the village—in an effort to counteract the danger of the soul meant that a semblance of collective identity was momentarily reached.

Ironically, that solidarity was simultaneously undermined by the competitive nature of other aspects of the funeral ritual.

Striving for the Signori

The Sicilian novelist Giovanni Verga tells us that when Master 'Ntoni's son Bastianazzo died, no expense was spared, despite the family's precarious finances:

> ...Master 'Ntoni could see with his own eyes that everything had been done without pinching pennies, to honor the dead man; so much for the Mass, so much for the candles and so much for the burial—and Uncle Crocifisso counted it off on his thick fingers bulging in their cotton gloves, and the children gazed with open mouths at all those things that cost so much and were there for their papa: the coffin, the candles, the paper flowers;...that display of lights....[50]

Why would poverty-stricken laborers use up meager resources on a funeral? Certainly, some of the answer lies in the pacification of the soul. Some of it also lies in the competitiveness evident in these rituals. Peasants attempted, within the strict confines of meager budgets, to emulate the often elaborate funerals of the *"signori,"* or the *"galantuomo."* These landed nobles, or untitled large landowners, retained a feudal-like control over the *contadini* well into the twentieth century.[51]

The peasantry saw itself in an emotionally ambivalent way, both despising and yet emulating the values of social superiors. In such a rigidly hierarchical society, those at the bottom seem to have been ordained to be there. Those at the bottom could not help internalizing social images of peasant inferiority. This served as an important mechanism of social control for the *signori*. The *contadini* thus treated other members of their class as a sort of sub-species, seeing in others a mirror reflection of themselves.[52] As we shall see, this peasant consciousness was transported to New Jersey and New York—where it came to be simplistically perceived by some as a low level of self-esteem characteristic of the working class, Italian and otherwise.[53]

Funerals of the *signori* were hardly distinguishable from those of the peasantry. The difference was the amount of money spent on those same rituals. Revolving around the central concept of avoiding the return of the soul, the *signori* spent elaborate sums on food, processions, and professional mourners.[54] The *contadini*, within their means, emulated these often extravagant displays. In their efforts, we detect a rejection of their own kind. It was the politically powerful and the financially well-off who were respected.

A comparative examination of *signori* and peasant funerals in the mid-nineteenth century illustrates the lengths to which the *contadini* went to imitate their masters. The deceased of the upper class were laden with intricate floral wreaths. Surrounding the casket, these displays took a variety of forms: heavenly gates, half moons, stars, crosses, bleeding hearts, lyre, and even a clock with the hands positioned at the precise time of death.[55] While the typical peasant could hardly afford all of these displays, he could, nevertheless, select a cross of flowers or a clock.[56] The same is true of the processional band. The *signori* might have several bands eloquently attired. A peasant family, on the other hand, could afford one band simply dressed.[57] The rich might have a very extravagant hearse pulled by as many as eight horses.[58] *Contadini* were lucky if they could use even one horse. But the shoulders of friends would do—the point was to imitate the powerful as best as possible.

Wealthy landowning families buried their loved ones in expensive wooden caskets lines with zinc. On the top, we find the family's seal. Or possibly the professional emblem of the deceased. Maybe even military rank. The peasantry, unable to even come close to such displays, contented themselves with similarly shaped coffins made of pine. While the prosperous hired a bevy of professional mourners, the peasants relied upon old women in the village.[59] The gravesites, too, offer us a comparative display. Porcelain pictures enhanced the dignity of the site for the village elite. The dead peasant also had a picture on his or her tombstone—minus the porcelain inlay. While peasants were often obliged to tend the gravesite of their superiors, the poor too enjoyed such a practice. In the case of the latter, it was the family of the deceased who provided the service.

As I will stress throughout this book, the counter-discursive assumes complex and varied forms. Sometimes its assertion of difference lies in its ironic imitation of the dominant. In this instance, the reality of everyday life did not allow peasants to identify in any way with those whom they deeply envied and periodically hated. Further, it was generally difficult to compete with other members of their class because they were all so badly situated. Funerals, then, enabled the peasantry to momentarily blur the deep gulf between social classes. For a while at least, there was an emotional affinity with the elite, as well as the opportunity to look better than one's neighbor. This tradition was carried to America, as new types of *signori* made their appearances in the cities of New Jersey and New York. So too, did new forms of competition based on envy.

CHAPTER ONE NOTES

1. Examples include Luigi Villari, *Italian Life in Town and Country* (New York, 1905), p. 113; Antonio Mangano, "The Effects of Immigration on Italy," *Charities and the Commons*, XX, 1908, pp. 167-179; Elizabeth Gilman, "Italian Notes of Social Worker," *Charities*, XXI, 1908–09, pp. 1,264–1,267; Norman Douglas, *Old Calabria* (London, 1915)(see such pages as 240– "...such sights of suffering humanity..."); Sidney Sonnino, "Le Condizioni dei Contadini in Italia, 1875," *Scritti e Discorsi Parlamentari* (Bari, 1972), especially pp. 157-158; Giovanni B. Negri, *Sulle Condizioni delle Classi Agricole in Italia* (Como, 1878); Leopoldo Franchetti, *La Sicilia nel 1876. Condizioni Economiche de Amministrative* (Firenze, 1878); Franchetti, *Condizioni Economiche ed Amministrative delle Province Napoletane* (Firenze, 1875); and Giustino Fortunato, *Pagine e Ricardi Parlamentari* (Bari, 1920).

   For secondary analysis of "*la miseria*," consult Joseph A. Polizzi, "Southern Italian Peasantry: Socio-Historical Past and 'Natural Setting'", in "Southern Italian Society: Its Peasantry And Change" (Ph.D. dissertation, Cornell University, 1967), pp. 55-56; Leonard Covello, "Barriers Between Peasant and Other Classes," in *The Social Background of the Italo-American School Child* (Totowa, New Jersey, 1972), p. 86; and Richard Gambino, *Blood of My Blood: The Dilemma of the Italian-Americans* (Garden City, New York, 1974). Edwin Fenton and Booker T. Washington succinctly captured the degradation of the peasantry, in both the countryside and among those who had emigrated to the cities:

   > Accompanying this village mindedness was typical peasant fatalism. Endless toil and limited opportunities combined to make the peasant persistent, patient, subservient, and resigned to his fate. He worked doggedly year in and year out for the most meagre returns. He saved with the avarice which insecurity forced upon him. His obsequious behavior toward the nobility reflected the position in society in which he pictured himself. He had no real hope of improving his lot, only of staving off disaster. When a new adversity struck the hearthside, he was more likely to shrug his shoulders than to clench his fist. (Fenton)

> Booker T. Washington argued that the cities of South Italy
> had a larger class living in "dirt, degradation, and igno-
> rance at the bottom of society" than in any other cities he
> had visited. Negroes in the slums of New Orleans,
> Atlanta, Philadelphia, and New York were much better off
> than the "corresponding classes in Naples..." (Iorizzo and
> Mondello)

See Fenton, "The Emigrants," in "Immigrants And Unions, A Case
Study: Italians And American Labor, 1870–1920" (Ph.D. dissertation,
Harvard University, 1957), p. 24; and Luciano J. Iorizzo and Salvatore
Mondello, "The Coming of the South Italians," in *The Italian-Americans*
(New York, 1971), pp. 45-46.

2. A glaring example here is Oscar Handlin's *The Uprooted* (New York,
1951). In his first chapter, entitled "Peasant Origins," he assumes that
the *signori* protected the *contadini* (p. 15). But that was not always true.
In primary accounts, the evidence reveals that the large landowners,
whether titled or not, exercised a protofeudal ruthlessness relatively
untouched by the nineteenth century industrial revolution. Writing in
1916, Pasquale Villari wrote that the *signori*

> ...comprised a form of intolerable and destructive despo-
> tism. A few friends or relatives, sometimes even a single
> family, have made themselves masters...of this enormous
> power—there is no restraint....

Anton Blok, in his analysis of the ways in which landowners maintained
social order in Sicily, describes for us a turn of the century rural
harshness which completely undermines the presentation of Handlin.

> In agreement with the gabelloti, the overseer established
> the pattern of cultivation and was charged with direct and
> continual management of the whole enterprise...As a rule,
> strong men were recruited for this post, from those who
> were able to "make themselves respected"— inspire
> fear...He dealt with the peasants set to work on the
> estates...In this crucial task he was assisted by five armed
> campieri on horseback who watched over the fields. Like
> the overseer, these field guards had a reputation for

toughness, which they advertised by their arrogant airs and their carrying of arms.

See Villari, *L'Italia guidicata da un meridionale* (Milan, 1916), p. 86; and Blok, "The Latifondo," in *The Mafia Of A Sicilian Village, 1860–1960: A Study of Violent Peasant Entrepreneurs* (New York, 1975), p. 61.

3. Constantine Panunzio wrote of this despair in a most graphic fashion:

> For several centuries the worker had led a life which to all intents and purposes was narrow and cruel, degraded and degrading...His masters owned him...He was forced to work on the land of a given proprietor whether he wished to do so or not...If he committed an offense, it was to his seignior that he had to pay a fine; if he perpetuated a crime, the owner condemned him to death...He had no right to assemble with his fellows, even to consider his own affairs...The laborer's lot was even more difficult because his world was stagnant and limited...The pressure of population on the land and food supply was quite complete...Food was scarce and poor in quality. Chronic hunger hung upon the masses like a shadow. Devastating famines and plagues raged like flames...Under such conditions he [the *contadini*] could do nothing but resign himself to his fate. Energy, therefore, was lacking, lethargy and apathy hung like a pall upon men and a hopelessness of spirit seems to have been quite general and complete.

Refer to Panunzio's *Immigration Crossroads* (New York, 1927), pp. 1-2.

4. Ignazio Silone, *Fontamara* (Milano, 1953), pp. 28-29. Giovanni Verga, in his 1881 publication of *I Malavoglia* (The House by the Medlar Tree), wrote of life among the Sicilian poor. Like Silone, he too pointed out that "poor people are like sheep, and...always go one after the other...with eyes shut." Turn to the University of California Press edition, 1983, p. 249. Also useful in understanding the long Mezzogiorno reality of rigid class relations is Mario Puzo's *The Sicilian* (New York, 1985). For instance, he tells us on page 268 of "the traditional Sicilian peasant greeting to a man of higher rank—a priest, a landowner or a noble: "I kiss your hand."

5. Commenting on the Calabrian poor, Douglas remarked that "the food [is] monotonous and insufficient." Robert Foerster, writing at the turn of the century, pointed out that chronic hunger was responsible for the slight stature of *Mezzogiorno* men. He noted their under-developed chests and generally "inferior" physiques. Military conscripts called to serve from Sicily were generally rejected at rates which sometimes exceeded 90%; such rejections, Dennis Mack Smith tells us, were all based on physiological reasons. In summary, the fifth and sixth volumes of *Atti della Giunta per la Inchiesta e sulle Condizioni della Classe Agricola* (Roma, 1880-1885) contain scattered passages on the physiques of Mezzogiorno men.

   Refer to Douglas, "The Bandusian Fount," in *Old Calabria*, p. 41; and Foerster, "South Italy, People And Emigration," in *The Italian Emigration Of Our Times* (Cambridge, Massachusetts, 1919), especially p. 95.

   Two indispensable accounts of peasant nutrition are Antonio Marro, *La Razione Alimentare dell 'Alienato Povero* (Roma, 1888); and Angelo Celli, *Sull 'Alimentazione del Proletariato in Italia* (Roma, 1879). Marro's writings are particularly illuminating. Also look at the Sicilian folk tale about "Jesus and St. Peter in Sicily," in *Italian Folktales*, ed. Italo Calvino (New York, 1980), p. 594.

6. See the summaries of Luigi Villari, *Italian Life in Town and Country* (New York, 1905), p. 198; and Dennis M. Smith, *A Modern History of Italy* (Ann Arbor, Michigan, 1969), pp. 233-234. In 1913 Richard Bagot, in *The Italians of Today* (London, 1913), wrote that military service provided physiological enhancement to the "lower classes" (pp. 126-127).

7. Cesare Lombroso, *Sulla Pellagra e sulle Condizioni della Proprieta' Fondiaria e della Classe Agricola in Italia* (Roma, 1882). Mack Smith adds to Lombroso's grim account, and informs us that in 1881, there were approximately 100,000 reported cases of pellagra in that year alone. He also estimates that cholera epidemics killed about 55,000 people between 1884 and 1887.

   See Mack Smith, *Italy: A Modern History* (Ann Arbor, Michigan, 1959), p. 150; Foerster, "South Italy, People and Emigration," p. 95; Iorizzo and Mondello, "The Great Fear," p. 61; and "Review Of Evidence And Special Reports," in *Reports of the Industrial Commission*,

p. XI ("Contagious diseases"). Martin Clark's *Modern Italy, 1871–1982* (New York, 1984), is also helpful. In addition, see Guztav Schachter's description of Sicilian typhus and tuberculosis epidemics, not to mention malaria, in *The Italian South: Economic Development in Mediterranean Europe* (New York, 1965), especially p. 54.

8. About the only exception to peasant apathy was the trek to the village piazza to beg. Writing in 1844, Nicola de Luca revealed that

> ...he [the peasant] is covered with rags, he nourishes himself with acorns roasted on a fire, with roots and grasses, and in the dreariness of winter in swarms he presents himself in the public piazzas extending his honorable hand in order not to die of hunger....

Their resignation was reflected in a folk song from Abruzzi.

> *Ninuna canzone dei natali Abruzzi*
> *Le patetiche bande. Taciturni*
> *Falcian le messi di signori ignoti,*
> *E quando la sudota opra e compita,*
> *Riedono taciturni,...*

> No song of their native Abruzzi
> consoles the piteous bands
> Silent they reap the harvests
> of unknown lords; and when,
> by the sweat or their brows,
> their task is done, silent
> they go back...

de Luca, *Condizioni economiche ed industrioli della provincia di Molise net 1844* (Camposbasso, 1845), p. 29; and Anne MacDonell, *In The Abruzzi* (London, 1908), p. 19. Also see D.A. Roe, *A Plague of Corn—The Social History of Pellagra* (Ithaca, New York, 1973).

9. Carlo Levi, during his political banishment in Lucania, wrote of this indifference in a most dramatic way.

> The air was black with thousands of flies, and other thousands covered the walls; an old yellow dog was stretched out on the floor with an air of infinite boredom.

> The same boredom and a sort of disgust, born of the
> experience of injustice and horror, were reflected on the
> widow's pale face.

See Levi's *Christ Stopped At Eboli: The Story Of A Year* (New York, 1947),
p. 3.

10. Fante, *The Brotherhood of the Grape* (New York, 1977), p. 5.
11. A fine summary of agricultural work routines is found in George E.
    Pozzetta, "Backgrounds In Southern Italy," in "The Italians of New York
    City, 1890–1914" (Ph.D. dissertation, University of North Carolina at
    Chapel Hill, 1971), pp. 14-15.
12. Ibid., p. 15. Also consult G.A. Harrison's *Mosquitoes, Malaria and Man*
    (New York, 1978).
13. Ibid., p. 17. Also refer to Mack Smith, "The Political And Economic
    Scene," in *Italy: A Modern History*, p. 40; Giuseppe M. Galanti, *Descri-
    zione dello Stato Antico e Attuale, del Contado del Molise* (Napoli, 1791); and
    the description of *contadini* shacks which Douglas provides for us on
    page 234 of *Old Calabria*. I have provided an excerpt

> ...ill-contrived hovels, patched together with ropes, potato-
> sacks, petroleum cans and miscellaneous odds and
> ends...picturesque wigwams crowded with poor folk who
> have installed themselves within, apparently forever...
> There will be diseases, too; typhoids from the disturbed
> drainage and insufficient water-supply; eye troubles,
> caused by the swarms of flies and tones of accumulated
> dust...The ruins are overrun with hordes of mangy cats
> and dogs....

14. Villari, *Italian Life in Town and Country*, p. 113.
15. Herbert F. Sherwood, "Whence They Came?", *Outlook*, 88, 1908, pp. 407-
    415; Phyllis Williams, "Housing In Italy," in *South Italian Folkways in
    Europe And America: A Handbook For Social Workers, Visiting Nurses,
    School Teachers, And Physicians* (New York 1938), pp. 38-45; Foerster,
    "South Italy, People And Emigration," in *The Italian Emigration Of Our
    Times*, pp. 94-95; Schachter, "How Southern Italians Live: La Miseria E
    La Bella Figura," in *The Italian South*, pp. 70-71; and Sidney Sonnino, "Le

Condizioni dei Contadini in Italia, 1875," in *Scutti e Discorsi Parlamentari* (Bari, 1972), especially pp. 156-158.

The diaries of Anna B. Wilcox and William Henderson are also instructive. Wilcox, the wife of Paterson, New Jersey lawyer Asa A. Wilcox, kept a travel journal during a trip through the Mezzogiorno sometime between February 7 and May 3, 1905. On page 7, while in Campania, she noted that there was

> ...great poverty. Never saw such low types of humani-
> ty—Beggars everywhere—nearly take the clothes off one's
> back.

Henderson traveled through Italy during a much earlier period, between June 17, 1815 and March 12, 1817. He was an English wholesaler who dealt in the stockfish trade, operating out of Venice and Naples. His diary reveals diverse contact with a wide variety of Italians—*contadini* and otherwise. Like Wilcox, Henderson focused on the poverty he saw.

> ...the people of this Country are wretchedly poor, and
> debased by Ignorance, Superstition and Vice. Such are the
> Effects of a despotic Government and a Religion, consist-
> ing of Rites and Ceremonies without Morality. (p. 3,
> Monday, 6/1815)

Both of these diaries are in the Special Collections Room of Archibald Stevens Alexander Library, Rutgers University.

16. Williams, "Housing In Italy," p. 39.
17. "The Social Structure Of The Southern Italian Town," p. 72.
18. See the summaries of Mack Smith, "Giolitti And Liberal Reform," in *Italy: A Modern History*, pp. 234-235; Gambino, "Reasons For Leaving," in *Blood of My Blood*, pp. 65-66; and Pozetta, "Backgrounds In Southern Italy," p. 14.
19. Ibid.
20. Ibid.
21. Ibid.
22. Ibid.
23. Ibid. Also consult Foerster, "South Italy. Nature And Man," p. 63.

24. Thus Handlin assumed too much in *The Uprooted* when he wrote that "simple neighborliness, mutual assistance, were obligations inherent in the conditions of things..." (p. 12). So did Bagot in *The Italians of Today* (Chicago, 1913):

> A great deal of nonsense is talked and written by foreigners who have not lived in Italian country districts concerning the intense poverty which is supposed to exist among the Italian peasantry (p.32).

25. In Pozetta, "Backgrounds In Southern Italy," p. 8.
26. Consult the 1878 publication of *Lettere Meridionali* (Florence), p. 44. An often overlooked source is Gramsci's "The Southern Question" in which such observations as the "South can be described as an area of extreme social disintegration" are found. See *The Modern Prince and other writings* (New York, 1983), p. 42.
27. Richard N. Juliani, "American Voices, Italian Accents: The Perception of Social Conditions and Personal Motives by Immigrants," *Italian Americana*, 1, 1974/75, p. 9.
28. Ibid., p. 10.
29. Sonnino, "Le Condizioni dei Contadini in Italia, 1875," p. 158.
30. Good overviews of agricultural economic organization include Mack Smith, "The Political And Economic Scene," pp. 39-42; "Agriculture and Industry," pp. 44-46; and "Agricultural and Industry about 1880," pp. 148-150, all in *Italy: A Modern History*. Also consult Covello, "Social Classes," pp. 78-102; Pozetta, "Backgrounds In Southern Italy," pp. 10-11; Schacter, "The Economic Organization of Agriculture in Southern Italy," pp. 105-129; and Francis A. Ianni, "Economic Life," in "The Acculturation Of The Italian-Americans In Norristown, Pennsylvania; 1900–1950" (Ph.D. dissertation, Pennsylvania State College, 1952), pp. 90-92.
31. Computed from the summaries presented in the *Bollettino dell Emigrazione*, in the section entitled "Relazione sur servizi dell emigrazione per 1'anno 1909–1910," #18, 1910, pp. 504-511.
32. Andrew Rolle, "A Vision of The New Land," in *The Italian Americans: Troubled Roots*, (New York, 1980), p. 3.

33. In Charles W. Churchill, "The Italians Of Newark: A Community Study" (Ph.D. dissertation, New York University, 1942), p. 16.
34. Ibid. A good contemporary source on wages, though it is regionally narrow, is Agostino Caputo, *Inchiesta sulle Condizioni del Lavoro Agricolo e sugli Effetti dell' Emigrazione nella Provincia de Cosenza* (Roma, 1909).
35. Churchill, "The Italians Of Newark: A Community Study," p. 17.
36. Ibid.
37. Mastro-Valerio, "Italians," in *Reports of the Industrial Commission on Immigration, Including Testimony, with Review and Digest, and Special Reports. And on Education, Including Testimony, with Review and Digest.* Volume 15. (Washington, D.C., 1901), p. 495.
38. See the analysis of Mehmet Bequiraj, in *Peasantry in Revolution* (Ithaca, New York, 1966).
39. They thus institutionalized, for a moment, the pervasive sorts of feeling which Rose Grieco described:

> If we weren't meant to laugh and cry and tear our hair in anguish when we felt like it, then we wouldn't be human beings, but leaves or stones. Anyway, that's what I mean about wakes.

"Blessed And Comforted: They Who Mourn," *Commonweal*, March 27, 1953, p. 628.
40. Elizabeth Mathias, "The Peasant Funeral," in "The Italian-American Funeral: Persistence Through Change," *Western Folklore*, 33, 1974, pp. 36-39; Daniel Cowell, "Funerals, Family And Forefathers: A View of Italian-American Funeral Practices," paper given at the 1984 American Italian Historical Association Conference, Washington, D.C., pp. 8-10; Covello, "The Church and Popular Superstitions," pp. 113-116; and Gambino, "Religion, Magic, and the Church," who tells us that

> ...the most pathetic of the restless spirits were the souls of unbaptized infants, whom the contadini believed were doomed to a worldly limbo, condemned to walk the earth forever. These poor souls were mischievous rather than truly evil, and were regarded more with pity than with fright. The Holy Ghost was invoked more to console these shadows than to repress them (P. 226).

41. Giuseppe Pitre, *Biblioteca della tradizioni Popolari Siciliane*, Volume 15 (Palermo, 1889), p. 201.   Consult Donna R. Gabaccia's interesting discussion of Pitre's work in "Sicilian Social Ideals in the Nineteenth Century," in *From Sicily to Elizabeth Street: Housing and Social Change Among Italian Immigrants, 1880-1930* (Albany, New York, 1984), pp. 2-3.

42. Not only was the soul placated, but maybe even more profoundly, the defilement that is death was neutralized.   Defilement intensified the chaos of *la miseria* to an unacceptable degree.   Thus the placement of prized possessions near the deceased served the purpose of creating an acceptable duality.

43. See the photograph provided by Williams, "Death and Mortuary Practices," p. 209.   Also consult the references in note 53.

44. Ibid.

45. Ibid.

46. Ibid.

47. Ibid.   In some areas, a window was left open in the room of the deceased, so that the soul could visit its previous habitat.

48. In Williams, "Death and Mortuary Practices," pp. 199-200.

49. In James J. Farrell, "Religious Liberalism and the Dying of Death," in *Inventing the American Way of Death, 1830–1920*, (Philadelphia, 1980), p. 81.

50. Verga, *The House by the Medlar Tree*, p. 40.

51. Indeed, the *Mezzogiorno* peasants interviewed by Joseph A. Polizzi in 1963 and 1964 told of their perception of this time and again.   Polizzi tells us that typical peasant responses in the Sele region generally go like this:

   ...The last—we peasants,
   what do we count?

   ...The lowest—there is
   no respect for the peasants!

See Polizzi, "General Social Differentiation," in "Southern Italian Society: Its Peasantry And Change" (Ph.D. dissertation, Cornell University, 1967), p. 202.   Also consult Ann Cornelisen, *Strangers and Pilgrims: The Last Italian Migration* (New York, 1980); William A. Douglass' comment, among others, that the Kingdom of Naples "as a whole was one of the areas of Europe that was least receptive to liberal thought," in "Origins and the Feudal Order," *Emigration in a South Italian Town: An Anthropological History* (New Brunswick, New Jersey, 1984), p. 48; P. A. Allum, "Class Relations and Values," in *Politics and Society in Post-War Naples* (Cambridge, Great Britain, 1973), pp. 42-45; and Stephen C. Cappannari and Leonard W. Moss, "Estate and Class in a South Italian Hill Village," *American Anthropologist*, 64, 1962, pp. 287-300. Cappannari and Moss wrote that

> The traditional pattern of social stratification found in much of South Italy exhibited a high degree of linkage to the pre-existing feudal form…The disjunctive nature of the social systems represented in the schematic diagrams is indicative of the lack of social interaction between the various strata. In both the idealized conception of the feudal-estate pattern and the traditional South Italian form, the strata tended toward social closure (p. 287).

52. Scholars have commented on the pervasive harshness of *Mezzogiorno* peasant relations. Recent commentaries peaked with the "amoral familism" of Edward Banfield, though his critics urged modification of this concept. Two passages, shown below, capture the tempo of *contadini* life which often caught the eyes of historians and anthropologists.

> The jealous and vindictive temper of the people checks the approach of temptation. An injured husband takes the law into his own hands, and avenges the wrong done to his honor by a stab with a knife; and even mere imprudence and levity of conduct is often thus cruelly punished. Nor does the tone of public feeling severely reprobate this 'wild justice'….

And

> …The village is too small a world to live in. It is impossible to breathe freely in it. It is dirty; you must always hide something, or from someone; everyone lies about everything: money, food, friendship, love, God. You are

> always under the eyes of someone who scrutinizes you,
> judges you, envies you, spies on you, throws curses
> against you, but smiles, his ugly, toothless mouth out
> whenever he sees you.

And finally

> ...Italy is a stinking place. We are all like cats and dogs,
> constantly at each other's throats. I don't know why, but
> one can't trust even the Lord God himself. If you don't
> look after your own things twenty-four hours a day,
> people will spit on you, steal everything you have, and
> then will say that you did it to them.

Refer to George S. Hillard, "Begging," in *Six Months In Italy* (New York, 1853), p. 428; and Joseph Lopreato, "The Social Setting," in *Peasants No More: Social Class and Social Change in an Underdeveloped Society* (San Francisco, 1967), p. 66.

53. Richard Sennett and Jonathan Cobb, in *The Hidden Injuries of Class* (New York, 1973), do a fine job of capturing the emotional complexity of Italian-American working class life. Also see Anthony L. LaRuffa's *Monte Carmelo: An Italian-American Community in the Bronx* (New York, 1988); and Andrew Rolle, *The Italian Americans: Troubled Roots* (New York, 1980).

54. Mathias, "The Italian-American Funeral: Persistence Through Change," p. 49.

55. Mathias, "Italian Funeral Customs In Italy," page 49; and Cowell, "Funerals, Family And Forefathers."

56. Ibid.

57. Ibid. Williams tells us that

> The sight of a funeral procession was unlucky, especially
> to a married pair. When it was known that a funeral was
> to pass a house, the cautious housewife placed a broom at
> the entrance or on a window sill.

Williams, "Death and Mortuary Practices," p. 204.

58. Mathias, "Italian Funeral Customs In Italy," p. 49; and Williams, "Death and Mortuary Practices," p. 204. Years later, Carlo Levi described the

power enjoyed by those whose duty it was to announce an impending funeral procession through the village.

> These were his normal activities, but behind them lay another existence, filled with a dark, impenetrable power. The women teased him when he went by, because he had no beard, and rumor had it that he had never made love all his life long...They teased him, but at the same time he inspired them with respect and something like fear. The old man had a secret talent: he was in touch with forces below the earth, he could call up spirits, and he had a power over animals....

Levi, *Christ Stopped at Eboli*, p. 68.

59. The use of professional mourners became so disruptive that, as Williams tells us, Frederick III of Sicily condemned them. The funeral eulogies of these mourners helped to keep alive the feuds between families. Hence, they helped intensify local unrest. See Williams, "Death and Mortuary Practices," pp. 202-203; and Mathias, "Italian Funeral Customs In Italy," p. 49.

How different the grim nature of *Mezzogiorno* mourning, complete with the tearing of hair and loud wailing, from the serene beauty of an English rural burial described by William Tegg in 1876.

> ...the dead are carried to the grave with the singing of psalms and hymns: a kind of triumph, "to show," says Bourne, "that they have finished their course with joy, and have become conquerors"...it has a pleasing, though melancholy effect, to hear, of a still evening, in some lonely country scene, the mournful melody of a funeral dirge swelling from a distance....

Tegg, "Rural Funerals," in *The Last Act: Being The Funeral Rites Of Nations And Individuals* (London, 1876), p. 321. For broader socio-cultural perspectives, see Geoffrey Gorer's *Death, Grief, And Mourning* (Garden City, New York, 1967).

2

TRANSITION IN NEW JERSEY AND NEW YORK, 1880 THROUGH MID-CENTURY

Common labor, white $1.30 to $1.50
Common labor, colored $1.25 to $1.40
Common labor, Italian $1.15 to $1.25

> Public notice at New York's
> Croton Reservoir (1895)

Two central features of the peasant funeral—the anxiety over the soul and the quest for public status—were perpetuated in the practices of Italian-American workers through the middle of the twentieth century. These practices, when placed within the context of Anglo-American middle-class culture, are clearly different and, accordingly, could not have arisen from that milieu. Instead, what we witness is the perpetuation of a counter-discourse which stood in opposition to the dominant. To understand the rationale for that view, it must first be placed within the context of working class life in New Jersey and New York.

"a horde of steerage slime"

La miseria was not left behind in southern Italy. All of the characteristics which served to form that world view—hunger, a harsh physical terrain, economic exploitation, disease, and poor housing—were a daily reality for thousands of working and lower middle-class Italian-Americans in New Jersey and New York. This was as true for the rural communities of southern New Jersey as for the lower Manhattan of New York City.[1] Be it Elizabeth Street or Newark, Burlington County or Paterson, America, from the point of view of immigrants, did not always differ from Sicily or Calabria. As novelist Pietro Di Donato, writing from the vantage point of West Hoboken, New Jersey, put it,

> Our third-floor-right flat had four high-ceilinged, narrow rooms: the meagerly furnished front room...two bedrooms that received stale glimmers of day from an ever-dark light shaft...On the...wall...[was] an Italian calendar showing King Umberto and illustrated Saints' Days...On a shelf were the glass-encased painted statue of the Madonna and Child and votive lights...The labyrinthine hallway where the bogeyman hid was rank with the woolly smell of lamb-tail fat, onions, garlic, cabbage...-clean, well-dressed kids snarled at me: "Wop, guinea, dago, Tony-Macaroni, Hey!"[2]

Di Donato then went on, in the midst of this meanness, to describe his earliest conceptualization of death in northern New Jersey at the turn of the century, a description placed within the context of an industrial accident.

> Father and Mother took me to someone's flat. There were people crying: "The job killed him, on the job he was killed. The job!"
> There were flowers. A man was in a box...They closed the box and took it downstairs to a carriage. We rode in a carriage to church. Outside the church they put the box with the man in it down in a hole and covered it with dirt.

> Mother shouted to the women: "With our men building high walls for bread and wine we at home live in the shade of their death. Say we each day: 'Will my man come home this night alive?'"
> I then acquired the word Death.[3]

Di Donato "acquired" a concept of death in West Hoboken which underscored the key components of Italian immigrant life. Migration tampered with the peasants' notion of "destiny"—but did not remove it from the migrants' emotional framework. Accordingly, Di Donato's description was heavily laden with anxiety and foreboding—at the precise historical moment when the Anglo-American middle class was holding funerals exuding precisely the opposite symbolism. Just at in the case of Di Donato, another Italian-American worker, Rosario d'Agostino, described her feelings in a way which stood in stark contrast to the exhortations of such middle class spokesmen as the turn of the century funeral reformer C.W. Modie. d'Agostino wrote that

> My mother has begun to wail his goodness and his pain, how he sold his only shoes to feed his starving children.... Another one dead and still, she cries the pain of his life for the whole night.[4]

The perceptions of d'Agostino and Di Donato embodied the crossfire of the dominant and the counter-discursive. Italian funeral rites represented the world in ways profoundly different from what was in evidence in Anglo-American funerals. The struggle lay in the codes constructed on each side, codes which yielded public forums for an understanding of the social world.

We begin to see this crossfire in the observations of Di Donato's Newark laborers in the 1939 publication of *Christ in Concrete*. It is also evident in Giuseppe Cautela's description of a Brooklyn funeral in 1928.[5] Products of a harsh life in the *Mezzogiorno*, the worst suspicions of the immigrants concerning their view of human nature were confirmed upon arrival in an especially hard New Jersey and New York—and, as novelists and the reports of school officials indicate, a combination of public and parental influences served to inculcate similar perspectives in Italian-American working class children. As a result, death was not sentimentalized in the way that it was among the Anglo-American middle class of the period. Nor was it radically separated from the perception of self. For Di Donato's mother, death only served to reinforce the vulnerability of the nonperson; of a person which society obviously viewed as unimportant. Vulnerability was accepted as immutable. This was quite different from the perceptions of a C. W. Modie, or even of an earlier bourgeois commentator on "proper" funeral arrangements such as Henry Ward Beecher. Writing on such figures, Jackson Lears has commented that despite "premodern examples, the impulse to 'let go' was rarely more than fleeting." It was far easier for such elite bourgeois groups to feel constrained by death; to fail to see the process of dying as logical culmination. Given the American version of *la miseria*, it was hard for Italian-American workers to see it as little else.

Hunger and Disease

The continuance of *la miseria* began aboard the ships which took the peasants from ports in Naples and Genoa to New York harbor.[6] Indeed, *la miseria* began on the trip to the port itself, where the grim view of human nature was confirmed. It was not uncommon for emigrant recruiters to lie to their charges on matters of fares and destinations. A Genoese travel agent told peasants of a palace where a benign queen ruled. This palace was even filled with a dazzling array of delicacies.[7] Steamship agents regularly went through southern villages, and eagerly related stories designed to induce the emigration of cheap and pliable labor to the industries and cranberry fields of New Jersey and New York. These agents were employed by passenger lines, private concerns, and state govern-ments.[8] It is estimated that by 1896, 7,169 travel agents roamed the rural areas in search of prospective clients.[9]

Arrival in lower Manhattan did not bring relief from these agents. In a 1909 New York *Report of the Commission of Immigration*, we are told that there were "porters, hackmen, runners, and sharpers who besieged the alien on every hand, persuading, directing or advising him...and trying to get possession of his baggage."[10] Stories abound about emigrants misled past New York, and into the copper refineries of Butte, Montana, the coal industry of Colorado, or the mines of West Virginia.[11] The fact that these labor agents were typically Italian only served to reinforce peasant suspicions of one another.

Ironically, the voyage presented by these agents as a passage away from hunger and disease turned out to be instead the continuation of those two seemingly intractable qualities of life. Once aboard the "English Anchor Line" or the "Giuseppe Verdi," the hunger and disease of the village became exaggerated to a point not previously experienced by the *contadini*. Their very placement in the hull of the ship, or the steerage section, physically epitomized their position in the world. Once there, as in the *Mezzogiorno*, there was little to do but get along. Short story author Daniel A. Sarago wrote of the passage over.

> ...the stench from the steerage became intolerable. Due
> to the lack of sanitary conditions, the smell of urine and
> the vomit of the seasick prevailed. Tony felt the tight-
> ness of filth and disease in his throat....[12]

While Tony, along with his mother and sister, shivered together in the damp and cold steerage area, others aboard ship were warm and well-fed. Later managing to reach the upper deck, he

> heard music coming from the large hall in front of
> him...Peering through a porthole he saw an elaborate
> ballroom with highly polished mahogany floors that
> reflected the images of the magnificently dressed milion-
> ari dancing back and forth...with face pressed to the
> glass in a mesmerized state, he didn't hear the chuckling
> sailor suddenly pick him up from behind and threaten to
> feed him to the sharks if he didn't get back down below
> where he belonged.[13]

Tony had originally gone to the upper deck for relief from the rigors of steerage. On a previous occasion, he had found a kindly gentleman who had given him food. When the sailor threw him below decks, the point became clear for Tony—that his America was to be a mere glance at those who live above the level of physical self-preservation. Dancing and fine food were part of someone else's life. For Tony, only hunger and disease remained—or at least the threat of it.

Once settled in New Jersey and New York, the first two generations of working and lower middle-class Italian-Americans were typically destined to live the life of a Tony. The gnawing pangs of hunger always felt by the *contadini* did not always subside in the New World. Like Tony, most attempts to lead a life outside of steerage proved to be futile. One simply managed as best as possible below decks.

And that was not always good enough. They "live on a deficient, if not actually insufficient, diet," wrote activist Antonio Stella in 1904.[14] One elderly Italian-American told me during an interview that "as a boy, our father cut up a pizza bread three ways—that was it for supper.[15] Historian Andrew Rolle writes of watery soup dishes.[16] *Pasta e fagioli*, or "pasta fazool" in that unique Italian-American dialect, was another common dish, consisting only of beans and macaroni.[17] During the last years of his life, Uncle Luigi, the Rochester, New York relative of novelist Jerre Mangione, asked

> ...what kind of system is this when an old man is given
> [in welfare] only sixteen dollars a month to live on—
> about fifty cents a day, mind you, to feed and clothe
> himself? If it were not for my children, I'd starve to
> death.[18]

Robert F. Foerster provided what was probably the most stark portrayal of all. Writing in 1919, he pointed out that Italian workers

> ...often have but one warm meal a day. Of meat they
> eat little.... When all is said, however, the Italian diet,
> [is] insufficient in quantity, ill constituted as to the cost
> of its elements, and defective in variety.[19]

The "lightness of the Italian's physique," commented on by Foerster and such medical doctors as Antonio Stella, only served to compound the problem of tenement life. Living in close quarters was unsanitary enough, doing it with bodies weakened through poor nutrition could prove to be fatal.[20]

As in southern Italy, the housing of Italian-American workers through mid-century was, more times than not, crowded, unsanitary, and poorly ventilated. It is no wonder that diseases such as tuberculosis thrived under such conditions.[21]

By 1910 this disease, along with anemia, had reached alarming proportions in the New York metropolitan area.[22] In New York City, for example, Stella reported that on Elizabeth and Mulberry Streets, his

> ...personal experience with some of the houses...is that the average has not been less than thirty or forty cases of infection for each tenement yearly, the element of house-infection being so great. I remember some rear houses in Elizabeth Street, and one in Mott Street,...that yielded as many as twenty-five cases in the course of a year to my personal knowledge alone.[23]

It is thus more than a mere coincidence that in Albert Pecorini's *La Grammatica—Enciclopedia italiana—inglese per gli Italiani degli Stati Uniti*, a guide book written for Italian-Americans in New York City in 1911, we discover four full pages taken up with hospital locations and diseases.[24]

In addition to the prevalence of consumption and anemia, another health problem dogged the steps of Italian-Americans during these years, consequently serving to help in the creation of funerals with something very different to say. As in the Italian south, the former peasants and their descendants in northern New Jersey lived in close proximity to malarial plains. Such heavily settled towns as Lyndhurst, Bogota, and Lodi lay close to the great Meadowlands swamp.[25] So too did four northern counties with the densest Italian-American populations in the State by 1930—Essex, Hudson, Passaic, and Union.[26] Fred E. Crossland, in his study of Bergen County, might as well have been describing Calabria when he wrote that "moving on down into Lodi Township [there were] marshes [and] swamps...."[27] Even as early as 1754 we find written references to the inhospitable swamps of northern New Jersey. In Governor Belcher's report of that year to the Lords of Trade, the northern area of the state was referred to as the "Drowned Lands."[28]

By 1912, the New Jersey Legislature had created mosquito extermination commissions in the affected counties.[29] In 1914, attempts were made to drain the salt marshes of Bergen County, an endeavor which did not yield much success in the war on the mosquito. In 1938 the *Bergen Evening Record* tells us that

...Bergen County has approximately 8,000 acres of salt marsh...This entire area was potential breeding ground, and swarms of mosquitoes rose in broods from these meadows and forced their humming way into the surrounding communities.[30]

One of these affected towns was West Hoboken, in Hudson county. In "*La Smorfia,*" Di Donato tells of a land where the dreaded "Jersey mosquito" reigned. His descriptions are so graphic that one of them merits an extended presentation.

...the night air was not breathable; it was a turgid mass carrying the...stinging insects and mosquitoes from the Jersey swamps; with this followed a rash of itch measles...which made us scratch and bawl...We made trips to the Jersey meadows and brought back bundles of cattails to light the night to war off the insects.[31]

But the mosquito was not always fought off with success.   With the mosquito came fever.

...Doctors Florio and Cicione were in conference. Dr. Ciccione was distraught. They were talking about his patient, Teodoro, the grown son of La Regina..."He came home ailing from work yesterday—today he is being consumed as with fire!" I raced on my bicycle with the medicine to the house of La Regina. My mother and other paesanos were grouped around Teodoro's bed. I stayed by Mother and watched Teodoro die. Within a week there were many more cases throughout West Hoboken with the identical symptoms: sudden, raging fever and rapid death. It was named pulmonia espagnol—The Spanish flu. La Virgine's "La Morte" had arrived. There was a ditty among the street kids that ended with: opened the window and in-flew-Enza. The sad melodies of keenings and the sight of bouquets on doorjambs and caskets became commonplace....[32]

The experiences of Di Donato's neighbors only served to reinforce the perception of futility. One was abe to exert personal control only within strict confines delineated by impersonal forces, be they nature or people.

Thus the scourge of the Meadowlands mosquito, along with hunger and poor housing, both served to reinforce the perception of life based upon exclusion.[33] In other words, the lives of Italian-American workers were not founded upon a notion of individual desire, a state of mind which some scholars have too often assumed was there.[34] It was hard, if not impossible, to have much optimism when the harshness of life kept repeating itself on either side of the Atlantic. One woman therefore asked too much when, in 1911, she urged for a realization that "grief is self-pity...perhaps if we were less centered upon our own happiness grief over the loss of our beloved ones would not be the terrible thing it is."[35] In the Italian-American funeral ritual, grief was not self-pity. Rather, it was a realistic appraisal of daily existence.

Fear of the Soul Persists

The anxiety over death was visible, at least in part, in the old apprehension of the soul. As in the *Mezzogiorno*, there was a pervasive fear among the family of the deceased that the dead would, in some way, return to haunt the living. As one Trenton, New Jersey resident reminded us in a 1981 interview, "There was a fear—a superstition some would say—that unless care was taken Death would follow the mourners back from the cemetery to claim other victims."[36]

In scenes reminiscent of the old country, complex routes were followed from the cemetery back to the home of the dead person's immediate family.[37] This was designed to confuse the soul of the deceased, and make it harder to invade the dwelling places of the living. Social worker Phyllis Williams observed that the "modern Italian funeral in America has little in common with its counterpart in South Italy, but the people still hold their old notions about the return of the ghost to its former home."[38] Accordingly, such writers as Magione tell us that one family imagined that "unless they were hospitable to the dead, the corpses of their relatives would rise from their graves and attack them."[39]

So the placation of the soul complemented the intricate return routes from the cemetery. Food and other prized items were typically used in this regard. Placed in or near the coffin, their purpose was to calm and reassure the spirit. A Trentonian remarked that "jewelry, rosary beads and rings were always left in the coffin...."[40] One middle-aged man in Lyndhurst, New Jersey, who asked to remain anonymous, told me that coins were sometimes put in the pockets of the deceased.[41] The death of small children merited the placement of food, as Williams illustrates in the 1938 publication of *South Italian Folkways in Europe and America*.[42] Fear, said one dissenting Italian-American in Rochester, New York, "is as the bottom of all this sacrificial nonsense committed in the name of religion."[43] He then described the Sacca family.

> They were most afraid of the dead...Once every year they would lay out an enormous banquet table with place cards bearing the names of close relatives who had died. The table would be loaded with food—a complete dinner with all courses, including a glass of fine brandy and my favorite dessert, cannoli. There were chairs placed around the table but no one ever sat in them... The food would stand on the table for three days. By that time everyone in the family pretended that the dead had eaten all they wanted.[44]

Mangione recalled that as a child, he and his playmates "were convinced that one night a year [the Feast of the Dead, celebrated in late October] some of the same corpses we had seen so carefully buried would push their way up through six feet of earth...."[45]

Ironically, even death rituals embodied the continual, unceasing act of often arduous labor. The often large quantities of food put by the corpse required long hours in the kitchen. So too did the meals staged for relatives and friends during the wake. This point did not escape the attention of novelist Mario Puzo. In *The Fortunate Pilgrim*, he explored the psychological tensions of Italian-American workers living in the New York tenements of the 1930s. Discussing such women as Tenth Avenue's Lucia Santa Angeluzzi-Corbo, he reminds us that

> Even death brings labor and toil: coffee to be made for
> intimate mourners, wine served, gratitude and affection
> shown for the dutifully presented sorrow of relatives and
> friends.[46]

A final soothing of the soul took place subsequent to the burial. Prayers were said with the intent of easing the soul out of the space occupied by the living—in order to avoid the dangers of a spiteful spirit.[47] Mourning clothes were also sometimes worn by women.[48] The most systematic appeasement took place late in October or early in November of each year. Typically held on the second of November, "The Day of the Dead" was a time in which families went to mass and held vigils at the gravesite.[49] Food was again left on the kitchen table to placate the soul. Some observers speculated about the effects of such ceremonies on the young. One writer remembered that children "were never very happy about it [the Feast of the Dead] because the idea of paying homage to the dead always seemed unnatural, especially since none of our American playmates had such strange holidays in their homes."[50]

The myth of the soul found its functional equivalent in the rituals surrounding death. The rituals had a hesitant but clearly repetitive, obsessive quality. The rituals dramatized the basic anxieties of the Italian-American worker, fears rooted in real economic and social dislocations. The basis of anxiety was no less rooted in the swamplands of northern New Jersey. There was a mutual and intricate relationship between the myths and rituals of death on the one hand, and the realities of life on the other. Thus the laborer De Angelo was able to speak of death as "terrible, a hopeless abyss...."[51] It was not "terrible" because it meant the end of life. Accordingly, De Angelo's sign that "there was no hope, no consolation."[52] Ironically, other aspects of those death rituals also offered the possibility of hope. We are able to see this in the funeral procession itself.[53]

The Struggle for Status

A new type of elite developed over time, particularly in such ethnic, working-class enclaves as those found in the New York metropolitan area, or the "Burg" further south, in Trenton. For the urban peasant, the *"prominenti"* became the elite of the New World. An occupationally heterogeneous group consisting of professionals, wealthy businessmen, and *"padrone"* (labor sponsors), they tended to be classically conservative in the most narrow of terms. Provincial and often arrogant, they exercised an enormous amount of power in places like New York City.[54] Their social control was typically maintained through their ability to offer employment, loans, and other assorted services.[55] Outside of mainstream American centers of power through both choice and prejudice, they helped to form a parallel social structure within the Italian-American community which replicated the lord-peasant social relations of the Italian south while, simultaneously, serving as a mirror reflection of the class rigidity seen in America at large.[56] It seems safe to say that they were not structurally assimilated outside of the ethnic enclaves until well after the end of World War II.[57]

These *"promenenti"* were, in other words, the American manifestation of *Mezzogiorno* aristocracy. The historian George Pozzetta has gone so far as to argue that a "true middle class was lacking in the New York colonies."[58] For all intents and purposes, he was right. The *promenenti* often behaved in a fashion which was decidedly non-bourgeois. For example, Giovanni Morosini, in 1901, dedicated $100,000 to aid in the restoration of the Campanile in Venice.[59] In such displays of disposable wealth, the *promenenti* became legitimized, from the workers' point of view, as society's true standard bearer; as people worthy of their lofty social position. The ability to provide services intensified this image. Rather than be rebelled against, they were to be emulated. Writing in 1904, Boughton Brandenburg noted that "the lower class Italians in this country continue to pay respect and homage...without regard to the changed and democratic conditions under which both gentlemen and peasant are now living."[60] One way that workers paid homage was to imitate the rituals of their leaders. It is the emulation evident in funeral rites that interests us here.

In their quest to copy the behavior of the *promenenti*, Trentonians such as those depicted by the anthropologist Peter Peroni, along with the people discussed in Trenton's *Daily True American* and in Williams' account, constructed patterns of public ritual which were also designed to compete with equally status-conscious neighbors. In speaking of the trend toward extravagant tombstones, Peroni noted a long-term trend remarking that these "symbols of affluence (within the boundaries of working and lower middle class life) are particularly evident in the newest section of the cemetery."[61]

We thus detect a funeral designed to produce status. The lengths to which workers went in this regard is indeed astounding—especially when one considers their low household budgets. Williams provides us with a noteworthy passage.

> Two families who were living in modest circumstances even for Italians spent large sums—$900 and $600—for each of two funerals. In the first instance, $1200 had been realized from the deceased's insurance policy. The family continued to live in much the same manner and paid off a few back debts with the balance of the sum received. In the second case, the $600 represented the full amount of the policy. This family had its funeral and applied for relief at a local agency.[62]

She went on.

> …A man on relief was carrying an insurance policy on his mother-in-law's life as well as on his own. A social worker from the city charity department suggested that he reduce his mother-in-law's policy to one for $200. This would pay for a modest funeral. "And what a funeral!" he asserted. "I should be the laugh of the neighbors."[63]

In both passages we see a concern for the funeral as a status-producing event. Even with low incomes, the quest for momentary dignity proved too strong to resist. And it was evident in more than just the proliferation of fancy tombstones.[64]

The funeral procession itself tells a similar story. In December of 1942, the death of Louis Stefanelli was reported in the *Italian Tribune* of Newark.[65] Stefanelli is a classic representative of the *promenenti*. An engineer and building contractor, he was also a member of numerous organizations which carried great local prestige. Among these were the State Board of Professional Engineers of New Jersey and several building and loan associations.[66]

The account of his funeral reveals a pattern typical among the Italian-American elite. Just like the aristocracy of the Italian south, Stefanelli's family celebrated a high mass with special sacraments, or a "high mass of requiem."[67] Just as in the old country, the procession to Holy Sepulcher Cemetery was elaborate; as a consideration of the pallbearers reveals.

> Honorary pallbearers were City Commissioner Villani, Freeholders Giffoniello and Rawson, Juvenile Court Judge Forlenza, District Court Judge Masucci, Anthony F. Minisi, Peter A. Cavicchia, Nicholas Albano, Richard V. Bonomo, Frank Cozzoline, Joseph De Deo,....[68]

This huge throng of dignitaries finally reached their destination at Holy Sepulcher. Stefanelli was then placed in the family vault, in a scene reminiscent of the imposing monuments of marble found in such regions of the Italian south as Calabria.[69]

The funeral of one Leonardo Covello of Trenton, who was not a member of the *promenenti* class, is a good example of how the humble emulated the rich and influential. In doing so, such laborers ritualized the philosophical outlook of the conservative Italian countryside on the streets of New Jersey and New York. They practiced rituals which suggested the same restrictive and binding qualities apparent in the villages of southern Italy. They still had something to express in New Jersey and New York, something which had little in common with the dominant liberalism of wider America. The rituals of death expressed values which seemingly defied questioning, for the reality of working class life appeared to make those values self-evident. Italian-American workers, in their persistent concern with the fate of the soul, along with the drive to compete with neighbors through an emulation of the powerful, rejected the new and instead endorsed tradition:

> The funeral was a large and orderly affair...the two story house was jammed full of mourners at the meeting hour and the whole Italian quarter was sitting out on the doorsteps watching the gathering. The Christopher Columbus Society turned out one hundred seventy strong with white gloves and badges with black over them. Undertaker Crawford was in charge and his

> black-plummed hearse was drawn by four jet black
> horses. The funeral cortege did not pass directly to the
> church but up Hudson, back to Clinton and then the full
> length of Mott so that its splendor could be fully appreci-
> ated by the quarter. This is said to be the custom
> whenever anyone dies there.[70]

Such historians of the funeral as James J. Farrell and Daniel Cowell
have argued that the gradual shift from home wakes to funeral homes,
evident by the 1920s, was largely the result of a larger "professionalization"
of American society which, not incidently in this case, had the effect of
denying death's stark reality.[71] For example, the advent of embalming,
Farrell asserts, gave the body a "born-again appearance."[72] Such lofty
spiritual aims did not induce the Italian-American shift to the use of funeral
homes, however. Instead, the main purpose was to have as impressive a
public display as possible. By the end of World War II, as the second
generation of Italian-Americans fully matured, the wake had emerged as a
major social occasion which had, as its purpose, the emulation of the
promenenti through competition with other workers. Just as the elite in Italy
had distributed elaborate announcement cards at their funerals, so too did
the urban villagers grasp for status through the use of a name register.[73] It
became important to scrutinize the names on that register in order to see
what people of importance had attended.[74] While middle class Americans
had argued that "the garniture, parade, and sequel of death is painful and
shocking," Italian-American funeral directors like Newark's Charles J.
Rotondo eventually capitalized on his community's quest for prestige
through the public spectacle of the funeral.

> The services of the modern director include much more
> than the care of the body and the directing of the rites.
> He is also a professional man trained and experienced in
> all the legal and social questions which come up when
> death visits....[75]

For his clients in the middle of the twentieth-century, the important social
question was how to best impress one's fellow workers.

CHAPTER TWO NOTES

1. See the scrapbook of Charles K. Landis, which holds pamphlets and newspaper clippings concerning the Italians of Vineland, New Jersey between 1884 and 1901. This is located at the Vineland Historical And Antiquarian Society. Also consult Dimitry T. Pitt's "Migratory Child Labor on New Jersey Farms" (M.A. Thesis, Columbia University, 1933).
2. In *Three Circles of Light* (New York, 1960), pp. 5–6.
3. Ibid., p. 7
4. "Wake," in Betty B. Caroli et al., *The Italian Immigrant Woman in North America* (Toronto, 1978), p. 376.
5. "Italian Funeral," *American Mercury*, October 1928, pp. 200–206.
6. "Lavoci della Commissioni federale per l'immigrazione negli Stati Uniti," in the *Bollettino Dell 'Emigrazione*, number 7, 1910, pp. 10–41; Daniel A. Sarago, "Journey to the New Land: An Immigrant's Story," *Italian Americana*, 4, 1978, pp. 177–183; Grazia Dore, "Some Social And Historical Aspects Of Italian Emigration To American," *Journal of Social History*, Winter 1968, pp. 95–122; G.E. Di Palma Castiglione, "Italian Immigration Into The United States, 1901–1904," *American Journal of Sociology*, September 1905, pp. 183–206; Richard Gambino, "Receptions in the New Land," in *Blood of My Blood: The Dilemma of the Italian-Americans* (Garden City, New York, 1974), pp. 95–97; and Vittorio Di Revel, "Delle condizioni dell 'emigrazione negli Stati Uniti nell 'anno 1882," *Bollettino Consolare*, 1884, n.p. Alberto Giovannetti, in *The Italians of American* (New York, 1979), painted a typically grim picture.

   > ...there were ships with artificial decks which enabled them to take on more human cargo. There were sections with three types of bunks and the most narrow of corridors. The ventilation was so inadequate that people had to make the containers of nauseating fumes suffice for the 2.25 mc. of air below deck that was prescribed by the regulations. The bulkheads were tight indeed but not heated even though they stood close by the boilers. One had to stand in a long line to use the few toilets that were available. In third class the filth abounded (pp. 86–87).

7. Dore, "Some Social And Historical Aspects Of Italian Emigration To America," p. 101.

8. See George Pozzetta's summary, "The Process Of Leaving," in "The Italians Of New York City, 1890–1914" (Ph.D. dissertation, University of North Carolina at Chapel Hill, 1971), pp. 48–50.

9. Ibid., p. 50.

10. New York, *Report of the Commission of Immigration* (Albany, 1909), pp. 71–72.

11. Introductions to the abuses encountered in these places include Gino C. Speranza, *"Inchiesta sugli abusi contro gli Italiani nel West Virginia,"* *Bollettino dell' Emigrazione*, 1903, pp. 10–23; Luciano J. Iorizzo and Salvatore Mondello, *The Italian-Americans* (New York, 1971); and Richard Gambino, "Receptions in the New Land," in *Blood of My Blood*, pp. 116–118. In fact, Thomas Sowell argues that many "settled in places they first saw as contract laborers, establishing Italian-American communities that still exist in such places as Omaha, Syracuse, Newark, and Detroit." See "The Italians," in *Ethnic America: A History* (New York, 1981), pp. 114–115.

12. Sarago, "Journey to the New Land: An Immigrant's Story," p. 178.

13. Ibid., pp. 178–179.

14. See Stella's whole article which captures, in a few pages, the poor diet and unhealthy living conditions of Italians in New York City—"Tuberculosis And The Italians In The United States," *Charities*, 12, 1904, pp. 486–489.

15. Oral interview with Eguidio Iula, a sheet-metal worker from Lyndhurst, New Jersey, December 28, 1981. I also suggest that the reader consult A. Richard Rizzo's "Interviewing Italian-Americans About Their Life Histories," *Italian Americana*, 3, 1976–1977, pp. 99–109. Conducting interviews can be risky if cultural boundaries are not recognized. Rizzo provides the interviewer with a fine model for working in the Italian-American community. Also refer to Gary Y. Okihiro's "Oral History and the Writing of Ethnic History: A Reconnaissance into Method and Theory," *Oral History Review*, 9, 1981, pp. 27–46; and Corinne A. Krause's "Oral History in Pittsburgh—Women, Ethnicity, and Mental Health: Rationale, Procedure and Methodology," in *The Italian Immigrant Woman In North America*, eds. Betty B. Caroli; Robert Harney; and Lydio F. Tomasi (Toronto, 1978), pp. 260–268.

16. In "Dispersal," *The Italian Americans: Troubled Roots* (New York, 1980), p. 23. Gertrude G. Mudge provides a far happier view of the level of nutrition in her "Italian Dietary Adjustments," *Journal of Home Economics*, April 1923, pp. 181–185. Her statistical analysis of the types of food eaten by New York Italian-Americans, based upon surveys compiled by Reba Reed of the New York Association for Improving the Condition of the Poor, illustrates a solid variety of foodstuff drawn from all basic food groups. It is interesting, nevertheless, that this is the only primary reference of the period, which I have located, that yields such a joyful appraisal.

17. Rolle, "Dispersal," p. 23; and an oral interview with Marie Pulsinelle, an 80 year-old retired seamstress and floor lady from Newark, New Jersey, July 12, 1985.

18. Mangione, "New Bread, Old Wine," in *Mount Allegio: A Memoir of Italian American Life* (New York, 1981), p. 233.

19. Foerster, *The Italian Emigration of Our Times* (Cambridge, Massachusetts, 1919), p. 386.

20. Indeed, Stella, in "Tuberculosis And The Italians In The United States," provides chilling statistics on the mortality rates of Italian-American children under fifteen years of age on such streets as Elizabeth, Mulberry, and Mott.

21. Ibid. Also consult R. L. Breed, "Italians Fight Tuberculosis," *Survey*, 23, 1910, pp. 702–703; Stella, "Tuberculosis among the Italians," *Charities*, 21, 1908, p. 48; Stella, *La lotta contro la tubercolisi fra gli Italiani nella citta di New York ed effetti dell' urbanesimo* (Roma, 1912); and John C. Gebhart, *Growth and Development of Italian Children in New York* (New York, 1924).

The growing concentration of first and second generation Italian-Americans in northern New Jersey also brought with it, because of poor housing and bad nutrition, a dramatic increase in tuberculosis cases. By 1918, the State Legislature had enacted Chapter 147, a piece of legislation which reflects the concern of the elite over "rates for maintenance of indigent patients..." By the time that Chapter 113 was written in 1921, it seems clear that the main worry of legislators was the financing of public sanitariums for tubercular patients.

> The State House Commission shall fix the rate or rates
> per capita payment for state patients in each state

institution or group of institutions, including the allow-
ance for clothing of state patients, upon recommendation
by the commissioner, and shall likewise fix the per capita
rate or rates to be paid such institutions for the maintenance and clothing of indigent patients in such institutions chargeable to the counties.

Also refer to the "Public Health Week" section of the *Bergen Evening Record*, 7 May 1938, for such articles as Joseph R. Morrow's "5 Schools Battle to Halt Spread Of Tuberculosis" (p. 10A). Morrow, a medical doctor, referred to tuberculosis as a "serious menace" which required the maintenance of "control measures...actively extended."

22. In the *Report on the Condition of Woman and Child Wage-Earners in the United States*, Volume II (Washington, D.C., 1910–11), an investigator working among laborers at home wrote that

As a class the home workers visited in New York are
anemic, poorly nourished individuals...The most apparent disease symptoms common to women doing this
work are badly nourished bodies, pallor, anemia, ca-
tarrh...(p. 295).

In Jerry Della Femina's often fierce polemical autobiography, *An Italian Grows in Brooklyn* (Boston, 1978), the fear of another dreaded disease is discussed—polio. This passage is particularly illuminating:

The big fear among diseases was polio. The rest of the
world was avoiding close contact in the summertime,
staying out of swimming pools, avoiding overexertion.
Avenue V in Brooklyn took another course: every kid in
the neighborhood wore a small packet of raw camphor
around his or her neck. Hundreds of packets of camphor
mysteriously appeared during the polio epidemics and
every child wore one.
    This wasn't the turn of the century. This was the
United States in 1949...But the old ladies of Brooklyn
were sticking to their camphor bags. Forget that they
hadn't been in Sicily for forty years. Sicily still clung to
them like olive oil (p. 75).

According to the records of the new Jersey Tuberculosis League, housed at Rutgers University, the number of cases actually rose throughout the first half of the twentieth century. Between 1945 and 1950, for example, the number of patients in New Jersey sanitariums increased by 117%. Unfortunately, the League's records did not specify how many of these patients were Italian-Americans, though much of their work was carried out in areas with large Italian-American populations, such as Jersey City and Newark.

23. In "Tuberculosis and the Italians in the United States," n.p.

24. Consult Pecorini's *La Grammatica-Enciclopedia italiana-inglese per gli Italiani degli Stati Uniti* (New York, 1911). Other studies focusing upon matters of health include Antonio Mangano's fascinating monograph, entitled "The Italian Colonies of New York City" (M.A. thesis, Columbia University, 1903); Genoeffa Nizzardini's "Health Among the Italians in New York City," *Atlantica*, 16, 1934, pp. 406–408, 411; and her "Infant Mortality for Manhattan, Brooklyn, and the Bronx, 1916–1931," *Italy America Monthly*, 2, 1935, pp. 12–17.

25. Jesse B. Leslie and John P. Peterson, "Bergen County Mosquito Commission Wages War," *Bergen Evening Record*, 7 May, 1938, n.p.; "Swamp Skating Arena," *Bergen Evening Record*, 10 November 1944, n.p.; C.J. Heusser, "History of an Estuarine Boy at Secaucus, New Jersey," *Bulletin of the Torrey Botanical Club*, LXXVI, 1949, pp. 385–406; and Henry B. Kummel, *The Geology of New Jersey* (Trenton, New Jersey, 1940).

    Just as in southern Italy, this part of New Jersey has suffered from a lack of fresh water. Throughout northern New Jersey's history, droughts have loomed as a menacing threat. For instance, see "Bergen County To Get No Part Of Water Supply," an undated article in the Bergen County archives, Hackensack County Library, Hackensack, New Jersey. Refer in particular to the analysis offered by Clyde Potts, an engineer.

26. See the maps provided in Dennis J. Starr's *The Italians of New Jersey: A Historical Introduction and Bibliography* (Newark, New Jersey, 1985), pp. 9 and 10.

27. Crossland, "Population Growth In Bergen County 1840–1890," in "Bergen County, New Jersey: A Study In Population Growth" (Ph.D. dissertation, New York University, 1953), p. 40.

28. In William A. Whitehead et al., eds., *Archives of the State of New Jersey: Documents Relating to the Colonial, Revolutionary, and Post Revolutionary History of the State of New Jersey,* VIII, part 2, pp. 79–80.
29. Leslie and Peterson, "Bergen County Mosquito Commission Wages War," n.p. Also consult C. F. Bennett's letter to Wendell J. Wright concerning the "endeavor to rid the county of the mosquito" (4 January 1915), in the minutes of the meeting of the Bergen County Board of Chosen Freeholders, 1 February 1915, p. 42.
30. Ibid.
31. *Naked Author* (New York, 1970), p. 8. It is important to note that there are towns in northern New Jersey which, because of their elevation and distance from the meadows, are spared the influx of mosquitoes which harassed the residents of towns such as West Hoboken. It is consequently more than a mere coincidence that Rutherford, a town north of Lyndhurst and west of the meadows, has generally been the residence of the area's manufacturing and commercial elite. From their geographic perspective, the swamps have been more the focus of scientific curiosity than anything else. This is evident as early as 1898. In contrast to the reaction of someone like Di Donato, T. N. Glover wrote that

> The Hackensack meadows are interesting in many ways. They form a famous tramping ground for botanists and have furnished specimens for all the great herbaria of the world. Very rich are they in sphagna and ferns that grow in moist places.

See "The Hackensack Meadows," in *Things Old and New from Rutherford,* ed. Mrs. M. G. Riggs (New York, 1898), p. 28.
32. Di Donato, *"La Smorfia,"* pp. 8–9.
33. Rudolph J. Vecoli has summarized this form of alienation which was both chosen, and forced upon, the Italian-American working and lower-middle classes. His comments merit an extended quotation.

> ...Young adults, their personalities had been molded by the traditional cultures of the paesi where everyone was known and named according to his family's reputation and status. Even the wrenching transplantation to

> America could not alter this basic identity.   Chain
> migrations of relatives and paesani maintained the
> peasant culture and network of social relationships.
> Whether in the work gang or the neighborhood, the
> immigrant tended to remain with his own people...Sep-
> arated as they were by dialects, customs, and prejudices,
> the immigrants from different regions of even paesi shied
> away from each other. They had little sense of a com-
> mon nationality, of being Italian. Italy for them was a
> matrigna (stepmother) who had driven them from home
> in search of bread and work. Wary of stranieri, suspi-
> cious of institutions, they trusted only la famiglia or at
> most the cirle of paesani.

See "The Search for an Italian American Identity: Continuity and
Change," in *Italian Americans: New Perspectives in italian Immigration and
Ethnicity*, ed. Lydio F. Tomasi (New York 1985), pp. 91–92.

A good example of the greeting extended to Italian immigrants in
northern New Jersey is found in the pages of the *Paterson Morning Call*.
From about 1886, and easily through the 1930's, Italian-Americans were
openly mocked and ridiculed. Such a stance was typically rooted in
racist biological theory, as this passage illustrates.

> Italy is sometimes spoken of as the home par excellence
> of personal beauty. This is a mistake, for though among
> certain classes beauty is common, the average is not
> high. There are beautiful women at Rome and Naples,
> but they are not often seen. At Rome one may stand
> sometimes on the Corso and see 100 carriages drive past
> without observing one that can even be called good
> looking...It is unusual to see among them a handsome
> man or woman....

Most articles of this type made a continuous reference to the "dark or
swarthy" Italians who are allegedly inferior to the northern Europeans
in general, and the English in particular.

> There are many beautiful women in England, and many
> more whose color and general appearance of health
> would entitle them to the same distinction....

Refer to "Personal Beauty. Differences As To What Constitutes The Highest Type," *Paterson Morning Call*, 11 May 1886, p. 7; "Did Not Understand English," *Paterson Morning Call*, 27 May 1886, p. 1; and "A Slippery Italian," *Paterson Morning Call*, 26 July 1886, p. 1.

34. Even such vehement supporters of the notion of "upward mobility" as Richard D. Alba have been forced to admit that "a comparison of all Italian Americans in 1940 with all Italian Americans in 1950 or 1960 muffles the changes that have taken place in the interval, because so many in the group will have been stable in their position." See his "Social Mobility," in *Italian Americans: Into the Twilight of Ethnicity* (Englewood Cliffs, New Jersey, 1985), p. 83.

35. In James J. Farrell, "Modernization of Funeral Service," *Inventing the American Way of Death, 1830–1920* (Philadelphia, 1980), p. 180.

36. In Daniel Cowell's "Funerals, Family And Forefathers: A View Of Italian-American Funeral Practices," paper given at the 1984 American Italian Historical Association Conference, Washington, D.C., p. 23.

37. Indeed, Phyllis H. Williams asked who "has not seen the long, dreary procession of rented cars rolling slowly through the streets?" See "Death And Mortuary Practices," in *South Italian Folkways in Europe and America* (New York, 1969), p. 208.

38. Ibid., p. 205.

39. Mangione, "God And The Sicilians," in *Mount Allegro*, p. 94.

40. Quoted in Cowell's "Funerals, Family And Forefathers: A View Of Italian-American Funeral Practices," p. 23.

41. Interview held on July 31, 1985, in Lyndhurst, New Jersey, at the respondent's home.

42. In Williams' "Death and Mortuary Practices," p. 209.

43. Mangione, "God And The Sicilians," p. 93.

44. Ibid, pp. 93–95.

45. Ibid., p. 98.

46. Puzo, *The Fortunate Pilgrim* (New York, 1985), p. 229.

47. An elderly priest in Hoboken, New Jersey, showed me numerous prayer cards, in both Italian and English, which he personally knows to have been in use since the early 1940s. Because they were, and are, designed for what the Bishop has termed a "pagan" belief in the evil nature of haunting souls, this priest asked to remain anonymous. In other words,

they are distributed without the bishop's knowledge. "It is," he told me
in the summer of 1984, "the only way to keep the Italians in church."
One card, for example, portrayed the blessed virgin and baby Jesus on
a glowing cloud. On the reverse side, "A Prayer to the Blessed Virgin
(Never Found to Fail)," is found:

> O Most Beautiful Flower of Mount Carmel, Fruitful Vine,
> Splendour of Heaven, Blessed Mother of the Son of God,
> Immaculate Virgin, assist me in this my necessity. O Star
> of the Sea, help me and show me herein you are my
> Mother.
>
> O Holy Mary, Mother of God, Queen of Heaven and Earth, I
> humbley beseech you from the bottom of my heart, to succour me
> in this necessity; there are none that can withstand your power.
>
> O, show me herein you are my Mother, O Mary, conceived
> without sin, pray for us who have recourse to thee. (3 times)
>
> Sweet Mother, I place this cause in your hands. (3 times)

Williams, in "Death and Mortuary Practices," also pointed out that
"families send to their friends and relatives cards that bear a special
prayer for the deceased. Repetition of this prayer gains indulgence for
those who cooperate and mercy in Purgatory and at the Judgment Seat
for the departed soul (p. 210)." The use of the Virgin and baby Jesus as
intermediaries between the agonizing soul and God's kingdom was
evident not just on the prayer cards, but further, on some tombstones
as well.

48. On Morris Street in Garfield, New Jersey, people whom I interviewed
    in the winter of 1981 told me that one elderly Italian-American woman
    that I had seen had been wearing a black dress for at least "twenty
    years." Jerry Della Femina, in *An Italian Grows in Brooklyn*, writes that

> ...the women put on black for the funeral—but every-
> thing, from stockings to dresses to sweaters, is black—
> and in many cases the black dresses stay with them for
> the rest of their lives. If the widow is over thirty-five,
> she puts on black and never removes it again. Ever. I

must have been seventeen years old before I realized that
the black dress and the slightly sagging black stockings
were a uniform of the neighborhood. Now, the woman
wearing that black dress started life out wearing a
flowered print dress, but at the first funeral she switched
to black and that was it....

"When my Joey died...," a lady in black might say.
"My Joey" might have been dead for three months, three
years, or thirty years. Mourning was a way of life, and
when a woman talked about an incident that occurred in
1923, she discussed it as if it took place the day before
yesterday (pp. 171–172).

49. For instance, see Mangione's "God And The Sicilians," pp. 97–98;
Williams, "Health and Hospitals," pp. 172–173; and Richard Gambino,
"Religion, Magic, and the Church," pp. 226–227.
50. Mangione, "God And The Sicilians," p. 97.
51. In Cowell, "Funerals, Family And Forefathers: A View Of Italian-
American Funeral Practices," p. 23.
52. Ibid.
53. Accordingly, Cowell tells us that

I recall that when grandfather died in 1955 at the age of
88, his wake was held in the home and the funeral was
begun there. He looked dignified in the [his] vested
suit.... Small change was placed in his pocket, as well as
other momentos of the Knights of Columbus, Fourth
Degree, the Sons of Italy and other fraternal societies of
which he had been a member.

In "Funerals, Family And Forefathers: A View Of Italian-American
Funeral Practices," p. 9.
54. Gino Speranza's "America Arraigned: Villari's Gli Stati Uniti d'America
e l'emigrazione italiana," *Survey*, 33, 1914, pp. 84–86, is an interesting
account of this group. So is Joseph W. Carlevale's *Americans of Italian
Descent in New Jersey* (Clifton, New Jersey, 1950). Carlevale compiled a
fascinating volume containing thousands of short biographical sketches.
While some *promenenti* were college-trained lawyers, physicians, and

teachers, the majority were listed as "industrialists" (800) or "business-men" (8,000) struggling to be accepted as legitimate heirs to the *Mezzogiorno's galantuomini* class. For instance, there is the life of Anthony S. Cupo:

> ...General Insurance Agent in Clifton. Born Garfield Nov. 1, 1911. Son of Joseph and Mary (Mastrolia) Cupo. Educated in the public schools. In the insurance business since 1940. Formerly laundry supervisor...Mr. Cupo is member of several civic, social, political, and charitable organizations. Pres. of Parker-Dayton Ave. Businessmen Ass'n. (p. 170).

55. Look at John Russo, who was the owner of the Russo Trucking Company on 725–23rd Street, Union City, New Jersey. Moving into the business with his father Joseph in 1920, the outfit grew to be one of the largest employers of truckers and attendant workers in Hudson County. By 1950, they had at least twenty-six pieces of equipment. Accordingly, Pozzetta has argued that as the *prominenti* "supplied a great range of economic, social, and intellectual services that clannish, suspicious immigrants were either unwilling or unable to acquire elsewhere, the *prominenti* wielded tremendous influence over colony affairs."

    See Carlevale, *Americans of Italian Descent in New Jersey,* page 594; and Pozzetta, "The Italian Community," in "The Italians of New York City, 1890–1914," p. 232.

56. Silvano Tomasi has argued that the mutual-aid societies which they often led only served as vehicles to advance *prominenti* interests. Advert to his *Piety and Power: The Role of Italian Parishes in the New York Metropolitan Area, 1880–1930* (New York, 1975).

57. Even Alba has been forced to admit that

> ...most Italian-American adults have been reared under the immediate influence of the Old World or immigrant cultures...concentration implies the existence of substan-tial-sized ethnic communities, zones of more vivid ethnicity, which are highly visible because they are located in the largest metropolitan areas. Their presence is likely to affect more assimilated Italians, for whom they serve as tangible reminders of their own recent

> ethnic pasts, perhaps keeping some ethnic memories
> alive and making ethnicity itself a more salient social and
> person characteristic.   As long as Italians remain so
> compacted in the urban Northeast, these communities are
> never far away.

See "The Demography of Italian Americans," in *Italian Americans: Into
the Twilight of Ethnicity*, p. 129.

58. Pozzetta, "The Italian Community," p. 233.
59. Ibid.
60. Brandenburg, *Imported Americans* (New York, 1904), p. 16.
61. Peter A. Peroni, II, "Family, Social Relations, and Religion," in "Chambersburg—Its Enculturative Process" (Ed.D. dissertation, Rutgers University, 1977), p. 114. I have also seen this trend in other New Jersey cemeteries which cater to working and lower middle class Italian-American communities, such as St. Joseph's in Lyndhurst, and Calvary in Clifton.
62. Williams, "Death and Mortuary Practices," p. 208.
63. Ibid., p. 209. In 1943, Marie Concistré wrote that the "poorer families often go into debt in order to have everything as beautiful and as elaborate as possible." See "Funerals," in "Adult Education in a Local Area; A Study of a Decade in the Life and Education of the Adult Italian Immigrant in East Harlem, New York City" (Ph.D. dissertation, New York University, 1943), p. 27.
64. The New York metropolitan area is full of cemeteries replete with elaborate tombstones and grave markers. My visit to St. Joseph's Cemetery in Lyndhurst, New Jersey revealed an almost complete Italian-American site. An employee of the grounds in 1985, Serri Kleint, told me that most of those buried there were laborers and small business owners.
65. "Louis Stefanelli, 51, Succumbs at Home," *Italian Tribune*, 11 December 1942, p. 1.
66. Ibid.
67. Ibid.
68. Ibid.
69. Ibid. Thus Norman Douglas wrote in 1915 that "the Taranto cemetery, beyond the railway quarter [is] somewhat overloaded with pretentious

ornaments...." Consult "Memories of Gissing," in *Old Calabria* (London; reprint of this 1915 edition, 1983), p. 300.

70. *Daily True American*, 20 October 1899, n.p.
71. Cowell, "Funerals, Family and Forefathers: A View of Italian-American Funeral Practices," p. 32; and Farrell, "Modernization of Funeral Service," in *Inventing the American Way of Death, 1830–1920*, pp. 146–183. Farrell argues that American funeral directors, by 1920, generally agreed that the

> ...old funeral rites impeded the progress of civilization. As religion centered on love, as science spread rationali- ty, and as psychology stressed boosterism, the continua- tion of funeral services which elicited fear and loathing seemed anachronistic. People rejected "the false idea of death" and substituted instead a "proper" idea of death (p. 183).

But the sanitized version of a wake which Farrell discusses does not apply to the people under study. Charles W. Churchill, in 1942, gives us an idea of the somber environment at an Italian-American wake in Newark:

> An Italian "wake" usually lasted three or four days. Palms, floral wreaths and giant crucifixes hung over the coffin, which lay in the principal room of the flat, preferably near an open window. Relatives, neighbors, friends—even mere curiosity seekers—dropped in to remain for a few minutes or many hours. Mourners were expected just to express their formal condolences to the bereaved after which they proceeded to the rail at the foot of the coffin and offered prayer for the dead. They would sit silently watching the dead or talking in whispers in the dim candle-light...

> In the kitchen...the men gathered, garbed in rude work- clothes, smoking gnarled pipes or stogies and drinking the wine which was occasionally served. A safe distance from the lamentations of the women, they discussed the eternal problems of life and death, or reminisced about

the departed and his numerous predecessors to the grave
here or in Italy.

Churchill, "Early Life in Newark," in "The Italians of Newark: A Community Study" (Ph.D. dissertation, New York University, 1942), pp. 36–37.

72. Modernization of Funeral Service," p. 163.

73. Looking back on his life in the Italian section of Brooklyn, della Femina wrote that attendance "was taken at wakes by asking visitors to sign the book as they entered the house.... A mourner could miss signing the attendance book, but if he gave a mass card his attendance was noted by the family." See *An Italian Grows in Brooklyn*, p. 176. Also see Elizabeth Mathias, "The Italian-American Funeral: Persistence Through Change," *Western Folklore*, 33, 1974, p. 49.

74. Registers eventually yielded, at least in some wakes, to the practice of giving mass cards. See Colleen L. Johnson's "Funerale," in *Growing Up and Growing Old in Italian-American Families* (New Brunswick, New Jersey, 1985), p. 99; and Peroni, "Chambersburg—Its Enculturative Process," p. 113.

75. Advertisement in the *Italian Tribune*, 19 July 1949, n.p.

3

THE MODERNIZATION OF FAMILIAR FORMS THROUGH 1980

"Holy Mother, pierce me through;
In my heart each wound renew."

>   Excerpt from a prayer card for sale
>   in the late 1970s at the Ippolito-Stellato
>   Funeral Home, Lyndhurst, New Jersey

A Guiding Force Remains

The mass cards, or the "prayer cards" as some workers called them, were counter-discursive incursions into the terrain of the dominant. From the perspective of the dominant they were an interruption not easily contained, they were an unpleasant questioning of dominant assumptions about the "prosperity" of postwar America. They were also the expression of how Italian-American workers perceived social relations in New Jersey and New York. For example, in one card, the language of subordination is quite clear—the word "servant" appears three times, "merciful" or "mercy" twice, and "hope," "comforted," and "faith" once.[1] All of this in only one paragraph. Deeply rooted emotions were reconstructed in language. In the context of wider postwar America, such a world view was smuggled in through the funeral service.[2]

The guiding force behind the funeral, its continued emphasis on a grimness not apparent in the funerals of the Anglo-American middle class, lay in the most recent American version of *la miseria*. The new forms which old fears took all had their starting point in a poverty which continued to plague this group in New Jersey and New York. Just as their parents and grandparents before them, the younger generation looked upon Anglo-American mainstream death practices as irrelevant. Indeed, we should not assume that they were even thought of much, or that their views were received in the way that the sender intended.[3] When Dorothy Rowe, a clinical psychologist specializing in grief therapy, agreed with colleague James Carse that sorrow is characterized by a "lack of effective speech, [and] no interest in the future," she assumed that these traits are not features of daily life for some people.[4] In short, she failed to see that such behavioral patterns are not necessarily unique to mourning, that grief itself can be an exaggerated expression of what is felt the year round. For Italian-American workers, it was an emotional nucleus; this is what Richard Gambino meant when, in describing funeral home lamentations, he spoke of "the vicarious catharsis...."[5] We are consequently obliged, as we did in the previous two chapters, to contextualize death rituals. The persistence of poor housing conditions is an appropriate place to start. Organizations like the Congress of Italian-American Organizations (1965), the Council of Belmont Organizations (1973), and Services Through Organized People (1970), along with the Neighborhood Council to Combat Poverty (1967) all had, as one of their primary goals, the struggle for better housing in the New York metropolitan area.[6] As we learn in one Council of Belmont Organizations pamphlet, its

> ...major objective is to enhance the living, working, economic and social level of the section and its residents. It hopes to maintain the vitality and future viability of Belmont as an ethnic working class center in a crises plagued city.

> The organization is involved in many activities
> including job referral, landlord and housing problems,
> food stamps, Medicaid, Medicare, S.S.I., improving
> quality neighborhood education, psychiatric referrals,
> senior citizen problems, group organizing, half fare
> cards, visits to the home bound, housing improvement....

Organizations like those mentioned above had plenty of work to keep them busy. Patrick Gallo, in his discussion of housing among the Italian-Americans in Greenwich Village during the 1970s, described one widow's apartment.[8] The building was in almost total disrepair—for example, this tenant, one Mrs. Ferraro, was without running water because of broken pipes.[9] Her plight was repeated many times over by other Italian-American workers of this region during the postwar period. Writing in 1972, David K. Shipler pointed out that this group continuously confronted neighborhoods "ravaged by poverty and decay."[10] People such as a forty-six year old Pabst Blue Ribbon factory worker interviewed by Shipler, lived in "shabby brick row houses on a narrow street in the North Ward...."[11] This man, whose parents immigrated from Italy, had managed to get through the second year of high school.[12] Unskilled, he depended upon the Pabst factory for his livelihood. In short, there was no place to go. He thus stated that "if you run from Wakeman Avenue today, you're going to run from Mt. Prospect Avenue tomorrow, and if it's from Mt. Prospect Avenue tomorrow...."[13]

But compared to some, the factory operative interviewed by Shipler was lucky. Consider the housing situation of Manhattan residents in the Chelsea area, between 14th and 34th Streets. Unlike the Pabst worker in Newark, Italian-American stevedores and their families were not able to make decisions about where they wanted to live. During the 1960s, real estate developers moved into Chelsea to rebuild the neighborhood into an upper middle-class residential area. As John Lewis wrote in a 1977 article entitled "Brownstone Boom Routing Chelsea's Poor,"

> Dilapidated brownstones are being fixed up, tenements
> are being rehabilitated, chic restaurants and elegant
> antique shops are springing up everywhere.

> Rents are soaring and so are real estate values...real
> estate speculators interested in a quick buck are driving
> out a lot of "low-rent" people.[14]

One resident, a member of the Chelsea Coalition on Housing, pointed out that rents "are just unbelievable. People have to double up or cut down on food."[15]

Other speculators "interested in a quick buck" took more direct routes to financial solvency. The work of arsonists, like real estate investors, had the effect of displacing Italian-American workers. Developments in the Bushwick section of Brooklyn are a case in point. In the summer of 1977, the "La Marca's block...had three fires destroy 11 buildings and rout almost 50 families...."[16] On just one street alone—Harmon Street—fires set during that summer claimed six buildings.[17] In their description of Bushwick's Italian-American community, Martin Gottlieb and George James told their readers that

> The Casuso family, which goes back three generations on
> the block [have for the time being refused to move.]
> Octavio Casuso, a strapping professional wrestler won-
> dered how long he could stay. "I can't sleep here any
> more," he said. "Three, four times I wake up every
> night afraid. The smallest noise, I'm afraid is a fire."[18]

The anxiety displayed by Casuso was suggestive of an environment which seemed to trap and threaten him at every turn. For some, such perceptions were carried even further through a life lived in "stuffy one-room" apartments with no guarantee of "proper nutrition."[19] Richard Lombardo, a social worker at Manhattan's Mott St. Senior Citizen Center in the 1970s, confronted such people and their homes daily.[20] He told of at least seventy Italian-American workers who were in need of regular meals in a 10-block area of "Little Italy" alone.[21] In his description of the poverty which plagued this group, he also struck out against the image of Italian-American familial solidarity.

> You know, they say that the Italians are always taken are
> of. But it's just not true. It's hard to find the poor, old,
> frightened people because they're shut in and they don't

> want to call attention to themselves. But I hear about
> them from their neighbors and I've visited them in
> apartments with roach nests three-feet wide, rats crawl-
> ing on the bed and toilets that don't work.[22]

Toilets were not the only things that did not work. The seemingly pervasive corruption of local government only served to confirm the generally negative view of human nature. What made matters worse was that even on this level, the regional bureaucracy seemed unable to orchestrate purposeful social action. In areas such as Newark, Jersey City, Lodi, and Paterson, the political machinery moved to the tune of "*trasformismo.*" This southern Italian term, which suggests the presence of charismatic authority and intricate networks of patronage, has its origins in the parliamentary battles of the *Risorgimento.*[23] Just as dissenting deputies in the nineteenth century shifted votes in exchange for personal favors, so too did the local politicians of the New York metropolitan area often make their decisions within the framework of alliance systems and links with organized crime. An excellent illustration of this during the postwar period is Elizabeth's Mayor Thomas G. Dunn, who refused federal aid from the Model Cities program because he did not want Washington investigators to scrutinize his city's government.[24]

Political power in this area has historically been maintained through a combination of two very broad routes—zoning and physical threats. Writing in the *Hackensack Record* in 1970, Edward Flynn and Sharon Rosenhause argued that zoning laws served chiefly as a means of protecting elite interests.[25] Michael Barone and Neal R. Peirce point out that "Bergen County provides one of the most dramatic illustrations in the U.S.A. of how local governments use their zoning powers to bolster their own fiscal positions in a way that fosters racial and economic ghettos."[26] Numerous studies revealed that low-wage workers typically traveled several hours daily to suburban jobs because they were unable to secure affordable housing in more affluent towns like Bedminster, Old Tappan, Alpine, Bernardsville, or Far Hills where, by the 1970s, the minimum size residential lot was ten acres.[27] Italian-American workers thus remained in congested and decaying urban cities such as Elizabeth, West Orange, New York, Jersey City, Hoboken, Garfield, and Union City. The concentration of poor people who generally lacked the intellectual or financial resources for sustained political action only served to help consolidate the power of a Dunn or Newark's Hugh J. Addonizio. While scholars such as Michael N. Danielson and Jameson W. Doig assert that "in recent years...blacks, Hispanics, Italian-Americans, and other low-income residents of the older cities have mobilized the political influence latent in a concentration of people with shared problems," the historical fact remains that initial organizing is not the same as sustained and purposeful political activity.[28]

When zoning failed to achieve the desired level of local political control, a combination of bribery and intimidation was utilized. It typically occurred at election time. Persuasion took a variety of forms—the withholding of liquor and taxi licenses, allocation of jobs, or just plain physical coercion.[29] The objective was always to move the electorate and the candidates in the proper direction. The son of immigrants who owned a small grocery store in Jersey City remembered that:

> If my parents hadn't gotten down to the polls, say, by four o'clock on election day, a black limousine with two men inside pulled up to the store. One man would get out and say to my father "All right...time to vote." So my father would get in the car with him while the other one waited with my mother. Then, when he got back, it would be my mother's turn. The men were always very polite. But, of course, you voted like you were supposed to.[30]

The point is that in emotional terms, the world of the postwar Italian-American worker had much in common with that of the *contadini* in the *Mezzogiorno*. Limited political and historical knowledge combined with a persistent material poverty to produce a people who were capable of being active social agents only within the strictest of confines. Politics, the dominance of those who controlled resources, and even disease, seemed to be the work of mysterious forces outside human control. Reification was thus not simply the result of advanced capitalist production, for these same emotional qualities were evident in the behavior of peasants in southern Italy under the nineteenth century feudal mode of production and its non-economic array of coercive social relations.[31] Jonathan Rieder, in his analysis of working and lower middle class Italian-Americans in Canarsie (a section of southeast Brooklyn), was accordingly moved to observe that

> ...Canarsie Italians were relatively casual about remote
> political events and affected indifference to public affairs.
> Family, neighborhood, and jobs defined the horizons of
> their attention land knowledge.... Suspicion was more
> than a symptom of a paranoid personality: it reflected
> the alienation of provincial Italians from the political
> system. Many of them felt that they were the objects
> rather than the initiators of influence.[32]

Mysterious forces were not only at work in city halls, corporate board-
rooms, and hospitals. They were also quite alive in the realm of the dead.

"Happy 2nd Birthday in Heaven"

So ran the "In Memoriam" refrain of Marie Marotta to her husband Peter
in the fall of 1977.[33] On that same day, the family of Samuel Demelio
publicly declared that this was Samuel's "first anniversary in heaven."[34]
The parents of Theresa Lagenestra wished her a "happy birthday in
heaven."[35] The wife and children of Joseph S. Magula did not mince any
words in their yearly message. Subsequent to the customary greetings of
goodwill, they transcended the boundaries of propriety with a stern
warning to Joseph's soul: "Always in!"[36]

In the admonition of the Magula family there is the old peasant dread
of the returning soul reformulated in the pages of a popular working class
newspaper, the *New York Daily News*. But in all of the other "In Memoriam" entries without this unashamed openness, we also see the fear that the
soul of the deceased yearns to return to earth. As a result, the family never
forgets a special occasion. The purchase of newspaper space to remember
the deceased was ostensibly designed to prevent the soul from returning
home. Community familiarity and family warmth was instead delivered to
the soul through public notice.

The rational perspectives of the dominant deny the possibility that
families renting newspaper space could literally believe in *Mezzogiorno*
conceptions of the soul. But the perspective of the counter-discursive in this
instance is understandable when one acknowledges that Italian-American
workers in this region display little interest in change. That emotional

reality, coupled with the constraints of the social structure and the demographic density of neighborhood and family, combined to produce a perpetuation of myths and rituals whose immediate historical roots lay in southern Italy. Thus the counter-discursive continued to rear its head at key cultural junctures. Accordingly, Elizabeth Mathias, in her 1974 publication of "The Present Day Italian Funeral," is able to propose that "folk religious practice went underground."[37] As she suggests, going underground is not to disappear. She stresses the continued sense of suffering and anxiety ritualized in funeral ceremonies. While often modifying old forms in order to appear "American," families like the Marotta's were, more profoundly, displacing anxieties produced by socio-economic pressures. Unable to control mounting taxes, under-employment and unemployment, a lack of housing, or the squalor of the inner cities, they turned to mastering the supernatural instead.

Throughout an examination of anniversary greetings to the soul, fear and a longing for stability continuously surface. On other occasions, outright suffering was depicted. In Newark's *Italian Tribune*, there was a poignant example of this in the "Death Notices" section. To cite just one instance, look at the "In Memorium [to] Angelo Del Russo" in June of 1974.[38] Submitted by wife Angela and children Angelo and Diane, this half-page section was a virtual embodiment of the long-standing habits of obedience and deference practiced, both willingly and unwillingly, by Italian-American workers. Gone were the *signori* whose hand had to be kissed, but still present was the local leadership, both in and out of the workplace, who required "respect." Ironically, the pecking order was seldom questioned, for it provided a sense of local stability and unity. Besides, why question what is "natural?" The Del Russo family thus paid tribute to Angelo.

> Yes Dad, it is very true there were those who slighted you. Yet I cannot recall you retaliating in a violent manner. Your touch was always gentle, your criticism was cautious and constructive. There were many times when you turned the other cheek. At times your actions would disturb us because you would allow people to hurt you without any due reason. We were always able to sense when you were offended. Nevertheless, you were always prone to keep those offenses inward.[39]

Fittingly, the appeasement of the soul and the quiet sadness of the urban workers ritualized in the process of bereavement took place at a moment when currents were running the other way in mainstream American funeral practices. In 1975, David Dempsey was moved to write that "the American funeral is being challenged on the ground that it frequently does not symbolize what the deceased stood for in life and thus no longer serves the needs of his survivors."[40] I am suggesting that Italian-American working class death rituals did exactly what Dempsey argues Anglo-American funerals did not. This point is crucial to a consideration of the soul's function, not to mention the display of sorrow. It thus requires elaboration.

The ritual of pleasing the soul through public notice enabled the living to exercise some control in their lives. Ironically perhaps, a strange sort of freedom was attained by the survivors. To shout "Always in!" was to reach an ontological plane otherwise denied. The social constraints of working class life remained as mere nature, an unconquered territory seemingly controlled by a select few. But in the control of the soul individual initiative emerged, and the routes selected to attain that end remained within the realm of personal prerogative.[41] By refusing to go along with the mainstream American practice of shielding "ourselves from the dying [or the dead]," the families taking out notices like those cited carved out for themselves a realm of freedom.[42] From their perspective, human potentialities could only be reached within realms that negated common existence.

The Funeral as Holiday

Italian-American workers rejected, indeed often ignored, the dominant's construction of death practices. They continued to build upon, and maintain, death myths and rituals whose explanatory powers were shaped and transmitted within the framework of working class life. When Brooklyn writer Jerry Della Femina remembered that in the "1940's and 1950's funerals were the Knicks and the Rangers all rolled into one," he was saying that such occasions enabled workers to temporarily transform the character of life through the ceremonialization of death.[43] Just like the Slavic workers studied by Herbert Gutman who had engaged in "prolonged merriment," the Italian-American workers of Brooklyn viewed death "as a legal holiday" which merited at least three to four days off from work.[44] Della Femina thus tells us of a typical community reaction in the postwar period.

> ...it was a four-day holiday, and it knocked off an entire work week. Let's say that the person died on a Monday afternoon. The funeral home would come and take the body away, then return it—probably on Tuesday morning. Then three days of wake would follow, and the funeral itself would be on a Friday.[45]

It is at this juncture that an important break is evident with Anglo-American bourgeois practices. First of all, the postwar period is replete with evidence that, for the most part, Americans dashed away from a recognition of death's finality and took refuge instead in a fantastic array of escapist devices.[46] Not surprisingly, these practices usually fell within the province of "professionalism." While the professionalization of funerals was also emerging in Italian-American working class areas, the difference lay in the portrayal of death via the funeral director. In the funeral advertisements of Italian-American newspapers, the funeral director was depicted as someone who helped the family to mourn—not to escape from mourning.[47]

This was quite visible in the linguistic constructions of the death-related advertisements. In an age of "floral tributes," Pennella Florist of Newark spoke of "flowers."[48] At a time when the Commission on Mortuary Education proposed the uniform use of the title "funeral director," undertakers such as Newark's John A. Paolercio insisted on presenting themselves as "morticians."[49] While "slumber rooms" were becoming increasingly popular in many suburban areas, Brooklyn morticians embalmed bodies and then brought them to the home of the family.[50] In the dominant's name changes, we see a sterilization of death. In the refusal of Italian-American workers to generally go along with that, we can see the continued emphasis upon ignoring elements of bourgeois culture which did not appear to be important within the matrix of working class realities. While the "holiday" aspect of the funeral lay in the excuse to socialize and

not work, that purpose always remained secondary to the overriding importance of sorrow.[51]

Colleen L. Johnson has argued that "Italian funerals remain more
elaborate than are generally found today."[52] She is correct in two respects.
On the one hand, there is little evidence to suggest that the wider sterilization of death took root in Italian-American working class wakes. Personal
testimonies contained in novels, along with sociological and anthropological
studies, all point to a continued emphasis on open grief.[53] So too do the
mass cards and funeral advertisements of the period.[54] Appropriately,
Johnson observed that

> Family and friends still acknowledge the need for the
> mourning process in the company of loved ones in order
> to accommodate to the loss. Abundant tears and moan-
> ing are still recognized as the proper expression of grief.
> To give up these customs would mean to many any
> improper expression of respect for the deceased. In fact,
> where the loss is great, such as in the death of a child,
> expressions of grief continue for years. Frequently,
> classified ads in the obituary sections of the paper carry
> a picture of the deceased and a word to the beloved on
> the anniversary of the death.[55]

On the other hand, there emerged in the post-1945 period a profound
continuation of the use of the funeral as a status-producing event. The
"elaboration" which Johnson speaks of was especially apparent in this
regard, and it began with the wake itself. An examination of the evidence
suggests that during the 1950s, wakes were generally moved out of the
home and into funeral centers, though as late as 1964 Newark's De Capua
Funeral Home advertised that it offered its services "at your home or in the
quiet dignity of our air conditioned chapels...."[56] While most workers
continued to refer to these occasions as "wakes," there are instances in
which they were called "laying outs" or "viewings."[57] Floral arrangements
became more extensive than ever. Set around the open casket, they took a
variety of fascinating shapes. We thus find pillows, blankets, and crosses.[58]

There is evidence that by the mid-1940s, it was quite acceptable to have
the body embalmed before a home wake.[59] The advent of embalming was
accompanied by the increasing attention paid to the clothes worn by the

deceased. While peasants in the *Mezzogiorno* were satisfied with simple clean clothes, their descendants went far beyond that by the 1950s. Still, in both cases, the emphasis remained on status. For the working class in America, it was an accomplishment to be able to purchase a new suit or evening dress for someone to be buried in. For the family, a sense of dignity unattainable in life was achieved in death, as the passage below implies.

> ...here was a man who never wore a tie in his life. Suddenly he's about to wear his first tie, except he's dead. There also were a lot of dead guys in Brooklyn who wore their first suits and white shirts at their own wakes.[60]

The number of people attending the wake was an indication of the dead person's standing in the community. When the community activist father of Mary Sansone died in South Brooklyn, "he had so many people visit him that the funeral parlor was mobbed for three days."[61] She went on to add that such an outpouring of interest indicated that "an awful lot of people...respected what he did."[62] Della Femina spoke candidly when he asserted that if the deceased "filled the seats [they] had a good life."[63] Johnson observed that "relatives and associates also attend, out of respect for the family even if they are not personally close to the deceased."[64] Rose Grieco described the resentment that would start if guests failed to come to the wake.

> ...no matter how numb and dazed with grief the bereaved were, hardly eating or sleeping for three days and nights, so lost in their world of despair that the goings-on in this world no longer existed for them, somehow they managed to remember if a fifth cousin's brother-in-law from Weehawkin didn't show up. I guess the reason is that Italians are in dead earnest about their wakes. When somebody dies, they drop everything, and even if they don't have a car, no matter how old or sick they are, they take trains and ferries and subways and always show up.[65]

Through 1980, register books were used to record the signatures of those present.[66] Other sources reveal that this was not always the case, as more informal greetings were in evidence among other families.[67]

Within the funeral home itself, the open casket bearing the body of the deceased was displayed at the front of the room. As in the wakes previously held at home, people would file by for a final look. Some stopped to kneel in front of the coffin in order to gaze at the deceased and engage in prayer. Other families encouraged the survivors to touch the corpse as well. It was during this process that death was confronted in a way not encouraged by the funeral practices which such observers as David Dempsey and Jessica Mitford uncovered.[68]

Familial hierarchies were delineated during the wake. Those closest to the deceased, in terms of blood relation, sat closest to the coffin. As one proceeded towards the rear of the room, the blood lineage became less direct, and culminated in non-blood acquaintances located in the rear.[69] This ordering was kept intact during the funeral at the church, and in the subsequent procession to the cemetery.

Funeral masses were the next step in the cultivation of social recognition. For people of importance, it was absolutely imperative to have a "high Requiem Mass." Thus the death of *Italian Tribune* publisher Fred J. Matullo in 1968 merited a "solemn High Mass of Requiem...in St. Lucy's Church."[70] So too did the death of Carmine Savino, owner of the Lyndhurst *Commercial Leader* and the *North Arlington Leader*. For the more obscure workers of the region, a simple Mass was sufficient.[71] Sometimes, however, even this relatively plain ceremony was not mentioned, as in the death of one Patrick Lo Presti of Lyndhurst, a retired employee of Kearney's United Cork Company.[72] Dying from a heart attach after engaging in "landscaping work around the house" of Peter Mancuso, Lo Presti's funeral was not spoken of in the *Commercial Leader*.

The class stratification present in the distinction between High Mass and Mass was not evident among the Protestant churches of the area.[73] When Hackensack teacher Jennie Berry died in 1958, she received the customary services offered by the Second Reformed Church, despite the fact that she was a member of an elite Bergen County family which traced its roots back to John Berry, the seventeenth century deputy governor of New Jersey Colony.[74] Reverend W. Carman Tremboth of Teanick, New Jersey's

Community Church, an institution which prided itself on "transcending denominational lines," also paid no attention to social class when conducting the funeral of young Audrey Hoch in 1956.[75] But the priests at Sacred Heart Church in Lyndhurst certainly noticed the influential standing of John E. Guidetti and Carmine B. Savino when they conducted High Requiem Masses for those two.[76] Guidetti, who had been a detective in the Bergen County Prosecutor's office, was credited by Joseph Carlevale with being "the leader of Lyndhurst Italians for 15 years."[77] Carlevale then went on to say that

> ...since his being in Lyndhurst [he] has taken [an] active part in civic, social and charitable affairs, especially among aliens. Has been the means in helping over 500 Italians to become useful American citizens.[78]

In the allocation of High Requiem Masses death assumed the force of the Church itself, which institutionalized a social hierarchy that appeared to be immutable. "The code was rigid and we didn't break the code," Della Femina wrote, "the code broke us."[79]

Della Femina was only partially correct, however, For while there is no evidence suggesting a questioning of the allocation of High Requiem Masses, workers did continue, nevertheless, to demand a dignity in death which they did not, and often could not, in life. This was the dynamic that propelled the quest for status most noticeable in the selection of funeral homes and gravesite markers. The emergence of the Zarro Funeral Home in Bloomfield, New Jersey is a good illustration.

Bloomfield was, like nearby towns Nutley and Belleville, an Italian-American working class center populated by factory operatives, retail clerks, and some small shopkeepers.[80] In 1945 the Zarro Funeral Home opened its doors for business on 145 Harrison Street. Catering to the desires of its local clientele, the Zarro family sought to create an environment dedicated to the "comfort of relatives and friends of the deceased." To accomplish this goal, the "Zarro firm...spared no expense for the convenience of... mourners."[81]

Upon entering the Home, visitors were ushered into one of several "chapels" all eloquently decorated in a fashion quite distinct from that of a crowded apartment or a tiny "Cape Cod" style house. In rooms with a seating capacity of two hundred, guests were dazzled by "mahogany century furniture and Wilton broadloom rugs." The walls of the vestibule were "covered with white Italian marble," which, it was pointed out, were "a distinct deviation from the stained glass of the usual funeral home."[82] Foyer and basement floors were covered with black and white terrazzo. On the lower floor, there was a "smoking room" with comfortably arranged "leather furniture" for the use of those mourners who wished a break from the grim viewing upstairs.[83]

This aura of respectability was continued via the construction of elaborate monuments in the many cemeteries which abound throughout the New York metropolitan area. The importance of these monuments cannot be exaggerated. In his 1973 comment on St. Joseph's cemetery in Lyndhurst, *New York Times* writer Martin Gansberg discovered that

> To most residents of Lyndhurst, things would be perfect
> if they remained as they are. Few appear disturbed by
> the fact that a cemetery—St. Joseph's—is situated in the
> heart of the Ridge Road business district.[84]

Within the confines of St. Joseph's, the "ostentatious display" noted by Peroni in Chambersburg was evident in the Bergen County as well. There we find, for example, the elaborate tombstones of laborers.[85]

In such public ritualizations there was the attempt to acquire in death what was not always attainable in life—prosperity and self-respect. By the late 1970s, this emotional reality became more acute, as the postwar drop in real wages, along with inflation, diminished even further the material resources of the area's Italian-American working class.[86] The complicating factors of a 16% increase in Italian-American welfare cases (between 1969 and 1971), the highest white drug addiction rate in New York City by the early 1970s, and, next to Puerto Rican youth, the lowest high school completion rate by the end of the 1970s, all pointed to an intensification of impoverishment in areas such as Bensonhurst, Coney Island, Sheepshead Bay, the North Ward of Newark, East Harlem, Garfield, Lodi, and Westchester.[87] Newark community activist Steve Adubato summarized many a worker's feeling when he said that "we are the working-class people who haven't made it in America."[88]

Working class funerals, like the peasant ones preceding them, were a subtle yearning for something new, something which the dominant either could not or would not offer. The working class critique is discoverable in the apparent differences with Anglo-American practices. For to compare those differences is to reveal how irrelevant the dominant conception of the world is when viewed from the working class perspective. The subordinate class was on display in these death practices, albeit in politically innocent trappings. Nonetheless, there was a rich array of symbols which made social and political values clear. Paramount was the insistence on the status of the extended family within the context of the local community. The rule was always to maximize the reputation of the family, to deny the relevance of acting for the common good. Just as important was the preoccupation with the looming presence of the soul. Attempts to placate the soul normalized the perception of individual powerlessness through a continuous effort to satisfy a world perceived as demanding, unpredictable, and capricious.

We are thus forced to confront what appeared to be a major and long-standing difference with the dominant American view, held for the last century, that death should be an event which is given as little attention as possible. Phillippe Aries has even gone so far as to argue that westerners have denied the existence of death, through "sanitized" funeral rituals, because it violates the postwar emphasis on happiness.[89] Such a perspective is far too generalized to be of much heuristic use. Certainly, it does not apply to the Italian-American workers presented here. The continued emphasis on mourning, the preoccupation with the soul, and elaborate displays does not indicate a turning away from death. Instead, such practices reveal the ways in which working people have responded to a historic process of pervasive exploitation and deprivation, be it at the hands of the *signori* or the factory owners, field guards, or ward bosses. Ironically, they have usually done so in ways that tend to perpetuate habits of political debilitation.

CHAPTER THREE NOTES

1. Unnamed prayer card for sale at the Ippolito-Stellato Funeral Home, Lyndhurst, New Jersey, 1979.

2. Jessica Mitford has pointed out in *The American Way of Death* (New York, 1963) that Americans generally, throughout the postwar period, tend to ritualize death in one of two ways. On the one hand, there was simply a denial of death's finality, emptiness, and mystery. What emerged instead was an emphasis "on the same desirable qualities that we have all been schooled to look for in our daily search for excellence: comfort, durability, beauty..." (p. 16). Mitford also detects a reassuring "quasi-scientific" language used by funeral industry leaders.

   On the other hand, death was used to celebrate a distinctly Anglo-American vision of the past. In her discussion of the "Valley Forge" casket advertised in the October, 1961 issue of *Casket and Sunnyside*, we are told of a "patriotic theme [which] comes through very strong..." (p. 57). Quoting from the advertisement, Mitford tells us that the casket was

   > ...designed to reflect the rugged, strong, soldierlike qualities associated with historic Valley Forge.... Its charm lies in the warm beauty of the natural grain and finish of finest maple hardwoods. A casket designed indeed for a soldier—one that symbolizes the solid, dependable, courageous American ideals so bravely tested at Valley Forge. (p. 57)

3. Thus Rose Grieco pointed out in 1953 that mourning went on years after the death of a loved one, even in the midst of an American mainstream culture which was quickly turning away from prolonged periods of grief. She wrote that

   > Even today, after all these years, when my father or my aunts are seated at the head of their table, with children and grandchildren who have become quite thoroughly assimilated waiting eagerly for the turkey to be carved, at some moment during the long dinner we know that we will be reminded of our Aunt Rose's tragic death. Our

parents were never trained to steer their thoughts into pleasant channels, but rather to remember forever their loved ones, regardless of what unhappy thoughts come with those memories.

Although writing about death practices among different ethnic groups in Connecticut, Sarah Langley has argued that ethnicity must "be considered a major factor in the formation of individual death-related behaviors." While her study of such groups as Italian-Americans, Hispanics, and Slavic-Americans overlooks class differences, her general point applies to New Jersey and New York. It was through the prism of the ethniclass that Italian-Americans modified, but did not drastically change, their death practices.

See Grieco, "Blessed and Comforted: Those Who Mourn," *Commonweal*, March 27, 1953, p. 629; and Langley, "An Exploratory Study of the Effects of Age, Ethnicity, Religion, Education, Sex and Health on the Formation of Death-Related Behaviors" (Ph.D. dissertation, New York University, 1979), p. 82.

4. Rowe, "Constructing Life and Death," in *Personal Meanings of Death: Applications of Personal Construct Theory to Clinical Practice* (New York, 1984), p. 15.

5. Gambino, "La Serieta—The Ideal of Womanliness," in *Blood of My Blood: The Dilemma of the Italian-Americans* (Garden City, New York, 1974), p.161.

6. These and other such groups are listed by Andrew Brizzolara in *A Directory of Italian and Italian-American Organizations and Community Services in the Metropolitan Area of Greater New York* (Staten Island, New York, 1976).

7. Located in the files of the Council of Belmont Organizations in the Bronx, at 2405 South Boulevard.

8. Gallo, "Italian-Americans and the Urban Crisis," in *Old Bread, New Wine: A Portrait of the Italian-Americans* (Chicago, 1981), pp. 277–278.

9. Ibid. Also refer to the study of Italian-American workers living below the federally established poverty level, in a 1975 publication released by the Congress of Italian American Organizations. Written by Josephine Casalena, it was entitled "A Portrait of the Italian-American Community

in New York City," and it can be found at the Federation of Italian-American Organizations, 6419 11th Avenue, Brooklyn.

10. Shipler, "The White Niggers of Newark," *Harpers*, August 1972, p. 82.
11. Ibid.
12. Ibid.
13. Ibid.
14. Files located at the Federation of Italian-American Organizations office; Lewis, "Brownstone Boom Routing Chelsea's Poor," *Daily News*, 16 October 1977, n.p.
15. In Lewis, "Brownstone Boom Routing Chelsea's Poor," n.p.
16. Martin Gottlieb and George James, "Family With Roots Flees Hell of a Burning Bushwick," *Daily News*, 12 October 1977, p. 4.
17. Ibid.
18. Ibid.
19. Claire Spiegel, "Shut-Ins An Age Old Problem," *Daily News*, 16 October 1977, n.p. Also refer to the papers of the Neighborhood Council to Combat Poverty, located at the office of the Little Italy Restoration Association, 180 Mott Street.
20. Spiegel, "Shut-Ins An Age Old Problem," n.p.
21. Ibid.
22. Ibid.
23. A good introduction to this topic is Judith Chubb's "Politics in the South, 1860–1943," in *Patronage, Power, and Poverty in Southern Italy: A Tale of Two Cities* (London, 1982), especially pp. 19-24.
24. Michael Barone and Neal R. Peirce, "The Inner Ring," in *The Mid-Atlantic States of America: People, Politics and Power in the Five Mid-Atlantic States and the Nation's Capital* (New York, 1977), p. 252. These authors write extensively of the client networks established in the New York metropolitan area:

> Gradually the tentacles of organized crime spread across New Jersey. A police chief was bought here, a mayor there. Selectmen, sheriffs, and county political leaders were also cajoled, threatened, or greased. The money rolled in, from gambling, narcotics, loan-sharking, and labor racketeering. By the late 1960s, organized crime was

estimated to gross up to $1 billion annually in northern
New Jersey. (p. 241)

Representative articles include Martin Arnold's "Where the Ward
Politicians Still Call the Shots," *New York Times*, 22 November 1970, n.p.;
Ronald Sullivan's "Jersey Mayor Indicted with 3 Alleged Mafiosi," *New
York Times*, 7 May 1970, n.p.; and Charles Crutzner, "New Tapes by
F.B.I. Link Politicians to Jersey Mafia," *New York Times*, 7 January 1970,
pp. 1 and 26.

25. In Barone and Peirce, "The Inner Ring," p. 250. Also refer to Ronald
Sullivan's "Jersey Town's Zoning is Voided: Court Orders Housing for
Poor," *New York Times*, 3 May 1972, p. 42; commenting on this instance
of exclusionary housing practices, Judge Martino argued that the
"patterns and practices clearly indicate that the defendant municipality
(Mount Laurel), through its zoning ordinances, has exhibited economic
discrimination in that [the] poor have been deprived of adequate
housing and the opportunity to secure the construction of [subsidized]
housing."

26. "The Inner Ring," p. 250. One report issued by the New York metropolitan area's *Regional Plan News*, entitled "Housing Opportunities"
(September, 1969), revealed that 80% of the region's total population
was unable to purchase even a "low-priced" home in the area. Also
refer to the Tri-State Regional Planning Commission, "Jobs and Housing
in the Tri-State Region," *Interim Technical Report* #42402223 (New York,
1971); and the Regional Plan Association's *Westchester County Supplement
to the Second Regional Plan* (New York, 1971). In their study of the area,
Michael N. Danielson and Jameson W. Doig point out that in

> ...Franklin Lakes, which welcomed a large IBM installation
> but not garden apartments, the local beneficiaries of the
> taxes generated by nonresidential development are equally
> unwilling to provide housing for workers: "There is lots of
> empty land and cheap housing further out—there's no
> reason why people should feel that they have to live in
> Franklin Lakes just because they work here."

In "Excluding the Less Affluent," in *New York: The Politics of Urban
Regional Development* (Berkeley, 1982), p. 102.

27. Further south, in Princeton Township, two candidates for a local office in 1966 successfully defeated an open challenge by civil rights groups and the working-class Italian-American Federation for an end to restrictive zoning practices. With the backing of that town's residents, both Republican office seekers argued against the intrusion of Italian-American workers. One candidate, John D. Wallace, was quoted as saying that he did "not see the point of providing housing for anybody and everybody." The other politician, David Thomson, pointed out that residents did not "want this Statue of Liberty in Princeton." See Jacqueline Pellaton's "Issue of Low-Cost Housing Divides Princeton Candidates," *Trenton Times*, 27 October 1966, n.p.
28. Danielson and Doig, "Concentrating Resources in the Older Cities," in *New York*, p. 274.
29. In one F.B.I. report released in 1972, we find a common scenario. Mickey Bontempo of Newark, a former president of the Newark City Council, was a mayoral candidate in that city during the early 1960s. He accepted $5,000 and the offer of a State Water Commission job in return for a withdrawal from the race. Bontempo was then ignored as Newark Mayor Hugh Addonizio found himself unable to appoint Bontempo because of obligations elsewhere in the complex network of patronage. Angelo (Gyp) DeCarlo, a capo in Gerardo Catena's mob, became angry at Anthony (Tony Boy) Boiardo, the leader of Monmouth County operations, because of Boiardo's links with Addonizio. DeCarlo consequently feared that Boiardo was attempting to usurp the former's image from Addonizio's point of view.

Accordingly, DeCarlo remarked on April 20, 1962 that "it was apparent that [Boiardo and others] were anxious to get something going in the county [probably Hudson] and when it gets going good they can 'sell it to the others'." This network of favors and alliances could be written about for pages, as it extended through the Democratic leader of Hudson County, John V. Kenny, through Kenny's obligations at the Martland Medical Center, and back through Thomas Finn's interests at the Jersey City Medical Center in the wake of his dispute with Jersey City mayor Thomas Gangemi (who was forced to resign in 1963 when it was discovered that he was not a U.S. citizen).

See "Excerpts From F.B.I. Transcripts of Tapes Released at the DeCarlo Trial," *New York Times*, 7 January 1970, p. 28. Also refer to Christopher Norwood's *About Paterson: The Making and Unmaking of an American City* (New York, 1974).

30. In Norwood, *About Paterson*, p. 62. Norwood also discussed the environment surrounding the 1966 mayoral election (p. 95):

> In the poor sections of the city, [the 1970 New Jersey census suggests that Italian-Americans comprised about 41% of the Paterson population]...people were convinced that there were cameras in the voting booths and feared retaliation for making an independent choice. The Honest Election League of Paterson reported threats of the loss of jobs, public housing, and welfare. Some union members charged that they could not obtain their paychecks without making a contribution to the Democratic campaign.

31. Thus in his discussion of "reification and the consciousness of the proletariat" Georg Lukacs argued that "we must be quite clear in our minds that commodity fetishism is a specific problem of our age, the age of modern capitalism." *History and Class Consciousness: Studies in Marxist Dialectics* (Cambridge, Massachusetts, 1971), p. 84.

32. Rieder, *Canarsie: The Jews and Italians of Brooklyn Against Liberalism* (Cambridge, Massachusetts, 1985), p. 38. Norwood argues that "most people in Paterson did not have direct knowledge of the inner workings of government..." (p. 157), while Mina, a secretary in the New York metropolitan area, complained that "the problem is, who is or what is the government?" See the interview in Patrick Gallo, "Political Power-lessness," in *Ethnic Alienation: The Italian-Americans* (Rutherford, New Jersey, 1974), p. 147. The beat poet Allen Ginsberg remarked that

> In a city the size of Paterson, there are maybe 150 people who really know what's going on. They're the ones who are involved in it or who have access to the gossip. As for everyone else, their basic civic relations are cut off.... The result is a complete mythification of public consciousness. In the end, people are walking around in the midst of a clearly defined hell. But they can't put their fingers on its

causes or structure. Finally, they just decide that life is hell.

In Norwood, *About Paterson*, p. 149.

33. *New York Daily News*, 9 October 1977, p. 169.

34. Ibid.

35. Ibid.

36. Ibid.

37. 'The Present Day Italian Funeral,' in "The Italian-American Funeral: Persistence through Change," *Western Folklore*, 33, 1974, p. 43. She also points out on page 47 "that many meanings of symbols are now understood only in terms of stock explanations which no longer have a basis in the majority of the Italians' active belief system."

38. *Italian Tribune*, 14 June 1974, p. 28.

39. Ibid.

40. "Bury the Dead?", in *The Way We Die: An Investigation of Death and Dying in America Today* (New York, 1975), p. 169.

41. In a 1985 interview of Serri Kleint, an employee of St. Joseph's Cemetery in Lyndhurst, I was informed that statues of the Blessed Virgin, Jesus, and St. Francis of Assisi, along with floral arrangements and perpetual lights, were all utilized by mourners to "sooth the nerves." When I asked for elaboration, she replied that these people "did not question what was not understood." It therefore seems that just like the *Mezzogiorno contadini*, Italian-American workers were still placing objects near the soul in order to calm it.

42. Dempsey, "The God from the Machine," in *The Way We Die*, p. 15. Diane di Prima, the Italian-American poet who has written of working class life in the Bronx of her "Italian Grandpa," actually suggested the freedom of death in her poem "In Praise of Dying." See her *Selected Poems, 1956–1975* (Plainfield, Vermont, 1975), p.50; and "April Fool Birthday Poem For Grandpa," in *Revolutionary Letters Etc.* (London, 1971), pp. 3–4.

43. Della Femina, *An Italian Grows in Brooklyn* (Boston, 1978), p. 175.

44. Herbert Gutman, *Work, Culture & Society in Industrializing America: Essays in American Working-Class and Social History* (New York, 1977), p. 24; and Della Femina, *An Italian Grows in Brooklyn*, p. 175. George Cuomo, a third generation Italian-American from the Bronx, tells us in

Family Honor of a wake held at a farm which enabled people to come for days; people who had "probably been working too hard anyway; a little break would do wonders." In Cuomo, *Family Honor: An American Life* (Garden City, New York, 1983), p. 479.

45. Della Femina, *An Italian Grows in Brooklyn*, p. 172.   In 1950, the sociologist William M. Kephart made an interesting observation.

> ...viewing [of the body] in all classes has become restricted to one day or one night, customarily the night before the funeral...exceptions to the foregoing statement occur in the case of nationality groups such as the Poles and Italians, where the viewing lasts for three days.

See his "Status After Death," *American Sociological Review*, October 1950, pp. 640-641.

46. Paul Jacobs described Forest Lawn cemetery in Los Angeles as a "pleasant innovation...[in which] no tombstones are permitted, only markers, set flush with the ground so that there is in fact the pleasant appearance of a park with sweeping green lawns."   In "The Most Cheerful Graveyard in the World," *The Reporter*, September 18, 1958, p. 28. also refer to Cedric Belfrage's discussion of Long Island's Pinelawn cemetery, which was described in one advertisement as a "Cheerful L. I. Cemetery [which] appeals To Young Couples," in "Be Happy! Go Cemetery!", *American Mercury*, July 1951, especially p. 104.

47. For instance, the Raymond Funeral Center of Vailsburg, New Jersey, in the business of "Serving the Italian Community of E. Orange and Vailsburg Since 1941," stressed the following motto: *"Ottimo Stabilmento Di Pompe Funebri."* This "excellent establishment for funerals" focused on a word—*funebre*—which literally translates not only as "funeral," but further, as "gloomy," "dismal," or "mournful." See this advertisement in Newark's *Italian Tribune*, 14 June 1974, p. 28.

48. Ibid.

49. Ibid., 9 February 1968, n.p.   In the advertisement above Paolercio's, Carmine J. Bernardinelli, a mortician on Mt. Prospect Avenue in Newark, spoke of his customer's "Time of Heartfelt Sorrow...."

50. Della Femina, *An Italian Grows in Brooklyn*, p. 169.   George Cuomo reminds us that this also went on in the mid-1920s.

...the body was taken in a morgue wagon to the Della Peccio Funeral Home on Tremont Avenue, where it was laid out and brought to the apartment, the casket carried up the single flight of narrow stairs and placed on a low stand in the living room.

In *Family Honor*, p. 43.

51. Della Femina, *An Italian Grows in Brooklyn*, pp. 184–186; and Johnson, "Funerale," in *Growing Up and Growing Old in Italian-American Families*, p. 100. Johnson remarks that mourning as a "ritual recognition far exceeds current American practices of deemphasizing death." This was certainly true in a number of Italian-American working class newspapers, such as The Garfield *Messenger* (which became the *Bergen Gazette* on January 7, 1954) or the *Passaic Citizen*. In Newark's *Italian Tribune* on March 15, 1974, Albert Gatto submitted a photograph of himself and his dead father (p. 26). Underneath the photograph, Gatto proclaimed that "Our lives have been said this year." Kephart noted that "emotionality is apparently a function of class position within these [ethnic] groups. Italian funeral directors stated that upper class Italians were much more restrained in their mourning, and the same situation was reported for the Jews and Poles." See his "Status After Death," p. 641.

52. "Funerale," p. 98.

53. I have cited evidence which pertains to New Jersey and New York. Italian-American workers elsewhere also exhibited this tendency. Langley's sample surveys of three Connecticut towns in 1979 illustrates this. So too do the novels of Denver's John Fante, a free lance writer who has worked as a hotel clerk, a stevedore, and a factory laborer. In *Dago Red* (New York, 1940), Fante described the mourning at "Aunt Carlotta and Uncle Frank's house" (pp. 155–156).

As soon as she sat down in the street car, my mother started to cry, so that her eyes were red-rimmed when we got off at Aunt Carlotta's street...the two sisters fell upon each other and wept helplessly. Aunt Carlotta had wept so much that her face was raw as a wound. Her arms were around my mother's neck, the hands handing loosely, the fingernails gnawed until there were tiny blood tints at the quick.

Also refer to Langley, "Part IV: Attitudes Toward Mourning," in "An Exploratory Study of the Effects of Age, Ethnicity, Religion, Education, Sex and Health on the Formation of Death-Related Behaviors," pp. 78–79.

54. Files at the Ippolito-Stellato Funeral Home, Lyndhurst, New Jersey; files at the Zarro Funeral Home, Bloomfield, New Jersey; and the papers of the Del Russo Printing Company of Newark.

55. "Funerale," p. 100.

56. Advertisement in the *Italian Tribune*, 11 September 1964, n.p.

57. Interview with Lena Zarro, March 1986; interview with Louis Stellato, March 1986. These people are connected with the Zarro Funeral Home and the Ippolito-Stellato Funeral Home, respectively.

58. Cowell, "Funerals, Family and Forefathers: A View of Italian-American Funeral Practices," paper delivered at the 17th annual American Italian Historical Association Conference, November 1984, Washington, D.C., p. 30.

59. Della Femina, *An Italian Grows in Brooklyn*, p. 169; and Johnson, in "Funerale," who points out the "earliest undertaking establishments in Easton had both men and women as embalmers" (p. 98).

60. Della Femina, *An Italian Grows in Brooklyn*, p. 177.

61. In "Taking Care of the Neighborhood," in *Nobody Speaks For Me! Self-Portraits of American Working Class Women*, ed. Nancy Seifer (New York, 1976), p. 52.

62. Ibid. Sansone's father was a community organizer in South Brooklyn.

63. *An Italian Grows in Brooklyn*, p. 175. Johnson notes that, during the funeral procession to the cemetery, there "is great pride in the 'bigness' of the event which is usually stated by the number of cars in the procession" ("Funerale," p. 100). Peter Peroni noted that in Trenton, the "number of people who attend the wake is important, because it indicates the popularity of the deceased." Kephart argued that "Italians...customarily have large funerals and large funeral processions; in fact, within this group, size of funeral and length of procession seems to vary directly with social class." See Peroni's "Religious Life, Church and Death," in "Chambersburg—Its Enculturative Process" (Ed.D. dissertation, Rutgers University, 1977), p. 113; and Kephart's "Status After Death," p. 642.

64. "Funerale," p. 100.
65. "Blessed And Comforted: They Who Mourn" *Commonweal*, March 27, 1953, p. 630.
66. Peroni, "Religious Life, Church and Death," pp. 113–114.
67. Ms. Zarro spoke of the "intense emotional community" created "spontaneously" at the wake, while Della Femina tells us that if a mourner missed "signing the attendance book...he gave a mass card [so that] his attention was noted by the family" (*An Italian Grows in Brooklyn*, p. 176).
68. Nor by the research of Belfrage, who in his discussion of such cemeteries as Long Island's Whispering Willows Memorial Park, noted people

> ...who continue to seek routes of escape from the inevitable. They see the morrow of the old man's death as a time for his widow and orphans to be economizing rather than plunging on fancy hardware and the songs of canned nightingales as piped from concealed microphones in Perpetual Care cemeteries. They pale at the thought of being rouged, powdered, and arrayed in weird costumes for display purposes....

"Be Happy! Go Cemetery!", p. 106.
69. Interviews with Stellato and Zarro; and Johnson, "Funerale," p. 100.
70. "Solemn Rites Held For Our Publisher Fred J. Matullo, Who Succumbed at 64," *Italian Tribune*, 8 March 1968, p. 1. Also consult "Lorenzo Romanelli, Founder Of Italian Nat'l. Circle, Dies," *Paterson Morning Call*, 10 July 1954, p. 17.
71. I have conducted a content analysis of the Death Notices in the *New York Daily News* for a fifteen year period between 1957 and 1972. These years were chosen because of the availability of evidence; in this instance, the *Daily News*. Taking into account my inescapable dependence on Italian surnames, I conducted a cluster sampling guided by a simple random sampling of subclusters down to the month of October for the years 1957, 1962, 1967, and 1972. For each of these years, the percentage of workers and lower middle class people receiving a simple Mass remained consistently high, as shown below:

NUMBER OF ITALIAN-AMERICANS
RECEIVING A HIGH REQUIEM
FUNERAL MASS BETWEEN 1957 AND 1972
FOR FOUR SELECTED PERIODS

	TOTAL DEATHS	NUMBER OF SIMPLE MASSES	NUMBER OF HIGH REQUIEM MASSES
1957	404	378 (93.5%)	26 (6.5%)
1962	336	317 (94.3%)	19 (5.7%)
1967	792	748 (94.4%)	44 (5.6%)
1972	859	852 (99.2%)	7 (0.8%)

It should also be noted that out of all the surnames I examined, only those of Italian origin received the High Requiem Mass. Further, the only other area of life beside that of the professions or wealthy businessmen which merited a High Requiem Mass was the increasing number of Vietnam War dead by the late 1960s. See, for example, the death of Vincent and Iluminada Cubero's son listed on October 22, 1967, p. 104.

72. "Dies Cutting Grass," *Commercial Leader*, 7 September 1950, p. 7. The same was true for Newark newsstand worker John P. Sierchio. See "John P. Sierchio Dies Suddenly," *Italian Tribune*, 8 March 1968, p. 1.

73. The Protestant churches tended to have class divisions along denominational lines, i.e., Methodist and Episcopalian. Because of this, class divisions were not as paramount within the churches themselves. It is thus appropriate that the Reverend John R. Hawkins of Bogota, New Jersey's Bogart Memorial Church said in 1954 that "there is no division in heaven." This church is a particularly good example of this trend, as its records from even the prewar period attest. As church historians Matthew H. Loughridge and Joseph M. Morgan wrote in 1936, "the community idea is not merely a name with this church but is a reality, carried to a very practical conclusion." There consequently was a concerted effort by church leaders to break down class divisions within the church through an incorporation of widely divergent denominations.

Parishioners were encouraged to maintain their ethnic and denominational traditions in ways that Italian-American workers were told not to
by Catholic authorities. At Bogart Memorial, "denominational differences [were] forgotten...the Christian purpose in life is the only condition
for membership." As the partial list below of active parishioners
indicates, church leaders were serious about what they preached:

> Baptists, Northern 30
> Baptists, Southern 2
> Presbyterian Church in the U.S.A. 177
> Protestant Episcopal Church 60
> Methodist Episcopal Church (North) 164
> Lutheran Church 36
> Moravian Church 6

See Wilma Supik's "Our Church is a Family," *Bergen Evening Record*, 25
September 1954, p. 5; and "Bogart Memorial Reformed Church: Thirty-
Fifth Anniversary," February 27, 1936, Special Collections Room,
Hackensack Public Library, pp. 12–14.

74. "Jennie Berry is Dead at 87," *Bergen Evening Record*, 18 April 1958, n.p.
75. "Mrs. Audrey Hoch Dies at Hospital," *Bergen Evening Record*, 10 May
    1956, n.p. Also refer to a pamphlet published by The Community
    Church of Teaneck, dated September 11, 1955. Located at the Hacken-
    sack Public Library, I especially call attention to a description of the
    church's purpose on the first page.
76. Consult the undated entry in the Register of Deaths book at the Sacred
    Heart rectory, Lyndhurst, New Jersey, n.p.
77. Carlevale, *Americans of Italian Descent in New Jersey* (Clifton, New Jersey,
    1950), p. 327.
78. Ibid. That was quite an accomplishment from the point of view of the
    Irish Catholic hierarchy, which was determined to liquidate any vestiges
    of Italian-American cultural identity. I will expand upon this point at
    length in Section Three. Suffice it to say for now that at the time of the
    incorporation of the Italian-American working class church Our Lady
    of Mount Carmel, located on the south side of Lyndhurst, not a single
    Italian priest or lay person leader was to be found in a congregation

which, by 1980, was still bilingual. The certificate of incorporation, granted through the Newark diocese office of Bishop Thomas J. Walsh on March 3, 1931, listed Father Thomas J. McDermott as pastor. He was to be assisted by "lay members" Thomas F. Dougherty and Joseph M. Kearney. This certificate is located at Our Lady of Mount Carmel's rectory, Lyndhurst, New Jersey.

79. Della Femina, *An Italian Grows in Brooklyn*, p. 122.
80. See the introductory comments about this area by Barone and Peirce, "The Inner Ring," p. 251.
81. "New Zarro Funeral Home Typifies Firm's Tradition," *Italian Tribune*, 28 September 1945, p. 1.
82. Ibid.
83. Ibid. Such ostentatious display was the natural continuation of the older peasant desire to be as extravagantly fancy as possible during the funeral. On the other hand, one can argue that the "fear of death" written about by Christopher Lasch is, at least on one level, the culmination of an Anglo-American process with immediate historical roots in the eighteenth century. In a New Jersey manuscript entitled "Church Days," Frances A. Westervelt described the simplicity of a northern New Jersey funeral around 1730. Such simple grace, with the possible exception of the mid to late nineteenth century, could have easily become transformed into a complete turning away by the mid-twentieth century.

> ...When there was a death among their members...the church district [notified] the people of [the] time of the funeral and [invited] those [people] to be the pallbearers— At each funeral the Pastor and Doctor side by side pre-ceeded the corpse to the grave—each wearing a homespun white linen sash 3 yards long across the body back and front from the right shoulder to the left hip—the ends hanging loose....

Once at the cemetery, the gravesites subsequently erected tended to be plain. In Little Ferry, New Jersey, on Liberty Street, there is an old burial ground dating back to the nineteenth century. The tombstones are striking precisely because they are so unpretentious. Most of them merely record the name and the longevity of the deceased: "Richard R.

Mattison, died November 27, 1892 aged 29 years 10 mos 29 days," or "Cornelia J. Smith, died Aug 15, 1866, aged 1 yr 11 mo 6 ds."

    See the Westervelt family file at the Hackensack Public Library, Special Collections Room; and Lasch, "Narcissism and Old Age," in *The Culture of Narcissism: American Life in An Age of Diminishing Expectations* (New York, 1978), p. 209.

84. "Change is Slow and Taxes Low in Lyndhurst," *New York Times*, 8 April 1973, n.p. Also see a relevant piece by James V. Costanzo, entitled *New Neighbors, Old Friends: Morristown's Italian Community, 1880–1980* (Morristown, New Jersey, 1982).

85. Peroni, "Religious Life, Church and Death," p. 114; interview with Kleint, summer, 1985.

86. In Casalena's "A Portrait of the Italian-American Community in New York City," we find a demographic survey revealing that 1 out of every 5 Italian-American families in the city lived below the federally-established poverty level. Official federal or city census reports tell us nothing about the level of Italian-American working class income because "poverty," as a statistical category, is broken down only by "white," "Black," and "Spanish-speaking." Therefore, a reliance on studies such as Casalena's is imperative. Another useful source is the National Opinion Research Center surveys. As Gallo summarized in 1981, NORC data revealed that 20% of Italian-American families earned under $4,000.00 annually. 50.9% earned annual wages amounting to a high of $9,999.00 in the early 1970s. The high range of working class income is misleading, however, because it represents the statistically small craftsmen and foremen whose wages were not typical of the ethniclass as a whole. For instance, even a cursory examination of the Consumer Income section of the Department of Commerce reports in 1970 reveals the sharp drop from the "labor aristocracy" of crafts-men/foremen ($9,253.00) down through operatives ($7,644.00) and into the laborer category ($6,462.00). See Casalena's discussion of working class income, along with Gallo, "The Urban Crisis," p. 281; Phyllis C. Martinelli, "Italian-American Experience," in *America's Ethnic Politics*, eds. Bernard Eisenberg and Joseph S. Rovcek (Westport, Connecticut, 1982), especially pp. 224–227; Nicholas Pileggi, "Risogimento: The Red, White and Greening of New York," in *America and the New Ethnicity*, eds. David R. Colburn and George E. Pozzetta (Port Washington, N.Y., 1979), pp. 119–120; and U.S. Department of Commerce, *Current Population Reports*, Series P-60, #78 (Washington, D.C., 1970), p. 6.

87. Consult Pileggi's summary, pp. 119–120.

88. In Martinelli, pp. 225–226.   Also advert to Shipler's interview of Adubato in "The White Niggers of Newark," pp. 78–79.
89. *The Hour of Our Death* (New York, 1981).

II.

THE CRUCIBLE
OF ADOLESCENCE

4

THE ABSENCE
OF ADOLESCENCE,
1880–1920

Everything, in short, suggests
the culmination of one stage of life...
>   G. Stanley Hall, in *Adolescence* (1904)

The children were inculcated with the
idea that, with the advance of puberty,
they were quite mature persons.
>   Leonard Covello, in *The Social Background*
>   *of the Italo-American School Child* (1972)

An Absence of "Distinctive Dangers"

Bourgeois psychologists and reformers of the late nineteenth and early twentieth centuries were especially sensitive "to the distinctive dangers of early adolescence."[1] Such writers as G. Stanley Hall, Orison S. Marden, George F. Browne, and Roy M. Jacobus all sought to modify the "normal psychic changes" said to affect those in their early to late teens.[2] Through the use of such carefully arranged institutions as the high school, the Boy Scouts, or the playground, middle class activists worked for an internalization of individual restraint designed to meet the daily realities of an emerging corporate order.[3] Embedded in this effort was the assumption that the stage of adolescence is a clearly recognizable period of life, like infancy and old age. In the Italian-American families of this region, however, such a concept was typically absent. Accordingly, the "distinctive dangers" of youth were viewed by Italian-American workers as the dangers of "human nature" itself.

Understanding the inner workings of the Italian-American nuclear family begins with a consideration of the *Mezzogiorno*. Observers in the provinces of late nineteenth century Italy pointed out that adulthood for both boys and girls began roughly between the ages of ten and twelve. One Sicilian proverb expressed this reality in the clearest of terms: "When hair begins to grow between the legs, one is fit to marry and work."[4] While marriage could certainly be seriously considered by puberty, work had actually begun a few years before that. It was not uncommon to see boys at the age of seven working in the fields of the *signori*.[5] If they were more fortunate, an apprenticeship might be arranged with a village artisan.[6]

The emergence of a boy into a man was recognized publicly through a series of linguistic devices and changes in apparel. The advent of maturity ceased to be questioned when the boy began working for wages or learning a trade. Seen at that point as a full-fledged adult, the boy was, at least in some provinces, referred to as a *"compare."* Depending on the provincial dialect, this can be translated into "equal," "crony," "accomplice," or "partner."[7] Before reaching adulthood, village boys are reported to have run barefoot, wearing shoes only during public celebrations. Once they started to work for wages, however, the right to wear a sort of moccasin, or *"scarponi,"* became customary.[8] *Scarponi* were the footwear of the *contadini* laboring in the fields. To allow the youngster to wear such clothing signified the beginning of maturity.

Peasant girls also went through public acknowledgments that childhood had ended. Once girls ceased to spend their day helping only intermittently with chores and playing with ragdolls, they began to work for wages in the fields. Other girls engaged in household chores which necessarily took her out of the house. Such duties might consist of hauling water from distant creeks or fountains. Other young women could be found at open streams doing laundry. Still others might be found doing domestic labor in the more prosperous homes of the *galantuomo*, or the land owners. Once engaged in these adult activities, the girl was not called a "*picciridda*" any longer. Instead, villagers addressed her as a "*cummaredda*," or "little godmother." The suggestion of a maternal role at such a young age was not a mere phrase. For many young women, agricultural labor in fields miles away from the village meant the absence of parents from early morning until very late in the evening. In some areas, fields were so far away that parents and older brothers and sisters only returned to the village once per week, simply sleeping on the land at night. As a result, the *cummaredda* were responsible for the care of young children and the preparation of meals.[9]

Whether one reads the literature pertaining to boys or girls, the common thread remains the abrupt transition from childhood to adulthood without an intervening space for introspection or involvement in institutions not directly related to family or work needs. It was inconceivable to peasant parents that the onset of puberty brought with it a special stage of intellectual, physical, and moral development.[10] Pressing financial burdens precluded the sort of view which was being expressed across the Atlantic by such liberal theorists as Orson S. Folwer, the architect and phrenologist whose teachings on "premature labor" never reached immigrant peasant parents or their working class offspring for more than reasons of illiteracy or difficulty with English.

> If you want to wear your children out at 30...send them to work at 8 or 9, but if you would have them live to be a hundred, give them the reins till they are twenty or upwards, and allow them to be boys and girls....[11]

The sanctity of human life was another relevant perspective brought to bear on the conception of adolescence. Anglo-American bourgeois writers concerned with adolescence argued that the family should, at least ideally, use the adolescent period to develop a sense of familial warmth and intimacy. The young person was thus the focus of the family's love and attention. In the late nineteenth century *mezzogiorno* peasant family, this kind of concern was not a cherished goal. Family members of all ages were simply bound together by financial and social constraints which did not even acknowledge the possibility of intimacy as a desirable objective.

This sometimes had a devastating impact on young people who were viewed as nothing more than objects of manipulation by their own families. While Marden at the turn of the century alluded to the benefits of a "bright, alert, intelligent, harmonious atmosphere" for young people, Robert Foerster in 1919 directs our attention to the reality of Sicilian sulphur mines. In *The Italian Emigration of Our Times*, he pointed out that only

> ...recently, in Sicily, has it ceased to be common for them [agricultural laborers] to sell their sons into a kind of slavery in the sulphur mines, receiving from the piccioniere, at no interest, a sum of 100–200 lire, while their half-naked boys spent their days carrying heavy loads from the mine's depths to the surface, doomed to baneful toil until the loan should be repaid.[12]

Foerster was not the only observer to comment on such practices. In 1926 Umberto Zanotti-Bianco published *La Basilicata*, in which we find out that many

> ...Italian children left their native towns forever, being traded in to traffickers in human flesh who... after paying for the boys, put them to strenuous labor in strange places, often to death-causing work.... Or they were made itinerant harp or violin players, organ grinders, street singers or plain mendicants who worked for entrepreneurs. Often with a purpose of preserving the boys' soprano voice, a nasty operation was performed on them.... So extended was this traffic in children that in 1873 a special law had to be enacted to curtail the vicious practice.[13]

Commentators studying the *Mezzogiorno* peasantry constantly spoke of the mean quality of familial relations. In a document issued by the *Associazione Nazionale per gli Interessi del Mezzogiorno*, readers were informed that "peasant families take better care of domestic animals from which they derived direct benefits.... A pig would be washed with soap and even combed, while a child would be left neglected."[14]

The perception of children was that they generally served only to drain public or private resources. Accordingly, their right to be full members of society became, at best, questionable. This view was reiterated in the popular proverbs catalogued by the noted folklorist Giuseppe Pitre.[15] Such expressions as the "door [of a house] is open to him who contributes—otherwise, you stay outside" expressed a pervasive view of the household which stood in stark contrast to the popularized bourgeois views of a Hall or Marden in America. Young people in the Italian south were viewed as economic tools by their parents—not as harbingers of a vague "national future" in need of thoughtful guidance and care. Financial constraints negated the possibility of peasant parents providing the luxury of a prolonged period of searching, while peasant ideals did not justify it even if it could be afforded.[16]

In New Jersey and New York, the reluctance of immigrant parents to accept the American idea of an adolescent period beginning in puberty quickly became apparent. And just as in Italy, working class parents rejected the notion of elementary education.[17] Just as *contadino* children had been sent into the fields to labor, so too were they now made into "little adults" in the factories and fields of the east for the benefit of the family. "It was common for Italian boys and girls to leave school to help out the family income," lamented one elementary school teacher.[18] "Parents," the teacher went on, "were openly opposed to the long educational period of the elementary school...."[19] Another teacher, Grace Irwin, wrote of her experiences at Newark's Seventh Street school.[20] Despite the $50.00 bonus she had received to teach at the Italian school in 1920, she found it hard to continue in the midst of community resentment. "Who is to blame?" Irwin asked.[21] She replied that "the question should be, 'What is to blame?' Perhaps it is just one generation piling their hard knocks and ignorance upon the next."[22]

Teachers such as Irwin failed to comprehend that the school's stated purpose of perfecting human character, a position echoed repeatedly in the Newark Board of Education records, was a goal viewed by Newark Italians as dangerously unrealistic. It is thus not surprising to find in the 1895

Newark Board of Education records a report that the grammar school with the city's highest Italian population had merely one graduate in a nine year period.[23] While it had been relatively easy for the Newark administration earlier on to propose that such dropout rates were the result of financial necessity, it would have proven far tougher to admit that a decisive repudiation of a central socializing institution for the young was taking place.[24]

The Futility of Moral Perfection

While the dominant culture's adolescent theorists had insisted that the "psychic changes" evident in the young were the result of a stage of life, Italian-American workers instead saw the changes attendant to puberty as the life-long characteristics of adulthood. From their point of view, efforts directed at character formation were inappropriate. The school, with its emphasis on moral teachings, was, quite naturally, a prime target.

As early as 1858 Horace Bushnell had begun to lay the foundation for the school's purpose. A theorist of adolescence, he argued that the family should be a setting of character formation. In *Nature and the Supernatural* he proposed moral guidelines which were later institutionalized in the schools of the New York metropolitan area. Foremost among his arguments was a belief in the essential goodness of the child.[25] In order to induce this change, he proposed that families and schools "let the child have his way and act himself out freely, without restraint...."[26] This could be done, Bushnell thought, because of the goodness of youngsters which only needed a lack of repression to be fully exhibited. He consequently asked

> If development can do all that is promised, why not give it a hearty god-speed everywhere, and let every human creature, old and young, act out what is in him, in the speediest, most unrestricted manner possible?[27]

In other words, individuals have unique capacities to be rational and good. Schools simply had to be designed to unleash the young person, rather than prove restrictive—at least for schools with middle class students.

This was evident at the opening of a new school in district thirty-seven of Carlstadt, New Jersey, in February of 1874.[28] Behind the speaker's podium there was a huge banner which read "Education, Moral and Intellectual, the Safety of a Nation."[29] Before it paraded a host of educators including County Superintendent E. E. Vreeland and State Superintendent Apgar, who all extolled the possibility of the school and the family as breeders of a "perfect man."[30] Nearby, the "new school house" in Leonia had walls "adorned with mottoes" designed to perfect the spirit of youth.[31] William Barringer, the Newark Superintendent of Schools in 1891, argued that in the school's quest for human perfectibility, a healing of the city's "clashing interests" would take place.[32] Barringer, like Apgar and Vreeland before him, believed that adolescence was an opportunity to carry out what writers such as Bushnell had asserted was possible—the uplifting of humanity to a new moral plane. "Man can raise himself," Bushnell had concluded, "by his own will, that is, by this humanly supernatural force...."[33] The school was to play a major role in the endeavor. "If we have a vicious and ignorant citizenship," Barringer warned, "it will only be fair and just to conclude that the Public School System is a failure."[34]

This liberal ideology seeped into every facet of the public school. Even lessons in penmanship were utilized in an effort to "perfect" the student's character. The 1888 notebook of Louis Wygarst is a good illustration.[35] A "common school" student in Hackensack, New Jersey, Wygarst practiced his handwriting through a study of the views of such propagandists as England's Samuel Smiles.[36] The fifth page of the Wygarst notebook is where the young student commenced his handwriting. Some of what he copied from that point on is shown in the following passage.

> Integrity
> ...Young man, base all your actions on a principle of
> right; preserve your integrity of character, and in
> doing this never reckon the cost.[37]

The idea of absolute moral principles attainable through a perfection of character was echoed in an 1883 speech in Englewood, New Jersey. In June of that year, the commencement exercise of Bergen county's public schools was held.[38] Lillie F. Hover of Hackensack was a keynote speaker. The very title of her speech, "What We Should Be," embodied her view that "a high standard of social excellence" was not only possible, but further, was desirable. Along with her argument that education was a life-long process, she maintained that

> It is profitable to all to search out truth in this
> beautiful world...those doing the most good are best
> loved by their fellow-men. Uprightness in all things
> is the best guarantee of success.... High and noble
> thoughts should inspire us and be life shining
> stars.[39]

It did not take long for the children of immigrant parents to reject such high-mindedness as unrealistic. One man, recalling his elementary school experience in New York City, said that the

> ...longer I went to school, the more I became con-
> vinced, as I long suspected, that the teacher spoke of
> conditions which were ideal, rather than real. The
> virtues of honesty and American courtesy which he
> recited so dutifully were forgotten by me as soon as
> I realized that my existence depended on my own
> ability to get things by hook or by crook.[40]

To be able to "get things by hook or by crook" was more than a mere reaction to the harsh living conditions of New York City's working class slums. It spoke to the underlying continuity between the life of the young person in the fields of the *signori* and that of the young person on the streets of New York. The youngster was still crushed by circumstances which the school could not, or would not, acknowledge. These influences continued to distort and deform human growth. The social identity of mere "existence"—induced by the determining variable of a capitalist market-place, was, however, not confined just to city streets. In a *Monthly Labor Review* report entitled "Work of Children on New Jersey Truck Farms," we are told that "the children were practically all white, and to a large extent of foreign parentage, Italians being the most numerously represented."[41] "The objectionable conditions hound here were similar to those in Maryland and Virginia...children...[were] put to work unduly early, set to tasks too heavy for their years, and kept at work for overlong hours...."[42]

Scholars who have written about Italian-American history have acknowledged the fact that the child's family did not, indeed could not, oppose such exploitation. The key to understanding this is the persistent refusal over the generations to recognize the adolescent stage as one with special needs which set it apart from other times of life. A crucial point in this regard was parental unwillingness to accept the possibility of character perfection. This was the strongest ideological basis for a recognition of adolescence, and it was this very belief that parents rejected because of their own view that human nature could never be perfected. Instead of wasting time in school or the Boy Scouts, children, who as humans could not be redeemed anyway, best served the family when they labored for wages in the marketplace or use values in the home.

In their repudiation of the school's primary mission, parents preached the creed summarized by Angelo Masso in *Vita moderna degli Italiani*: "rely on no one for direction or advice."[43] This was especially applicable to strange *Americani* who professed to know the best direction the future should take. Such popular proverbs as "whoever forsakes the old way for the new knows what he is losing but not what he will find" revealed the reluctance of parents to accept the idea that a pursuit of individual self-interest could yield a common social good.[44] This is what Pietro Di Donato was saying in *Three Circles of Light*.

> ...man, beast by nature, in your twilight, with
> dulled fangs, will subdue to your side, and then you
> shall fold your hands and welcome your grave....[45]

Seldom did this conservative view fail to permeate family relations as well. "You give your family an inch of confidence," Di Donato wrote, "and they take a mile."[46] Besides, as workers argued, school officials failed to recognize just how limited one's intellectual capacity was. Accordingly, Jerre Mangione's mother in Rochester warned that "too much reading would drive a person insane."[47] Ironically, formal education was viewed by some as culminating in moral retrogression. Evil was the result of putting so many inherently bad people in a schoolhouse. Hence, the view of Public School 22 in the Bunker Hill section of Paterson, known by area residents as "Bunker's College of Criminal Knowledge."[48]

These views of human nature quickly translated into the refusal of parents to allow their young people to attend school. A Newark Board of

Education report issued in 1904 focused on the persistent problem of Italian truancy.[49] Fred Miles, in "The Italians of Newark," discussed the frustration of truant officers over the failure of Italian-American families to cooperate with teachers and administrators.[50] In 1911, Olindo Marzulli published *Gl'italiani di Essex*. A study of Italian-Americans in New Jersey's Essex county, Marzulli tells us that most Italian-American youth in such Newark elementary schools as 13th Avenue, Franklin, Bergen, and North 7th Street never graduated.[51] William Melivitzky, the supervisor of foreign languages in Newark's public schools, told Charles W. Churchill in 1910 that all of Newark's high schools contained approximately forty Italian-American students.[52] Other areas of the region showed similar trends during this period.[53]

If one accepts the proposition that immigrant parents rejected the goal of what the medical doctor Luther Gulick in 1899 called "the righteousness of later life," then we must ask what they replaced it with.[54] The answer is conformity. It was a sense that an individual's submission to the community hierarchy should be the product of continuous external devices rather than individual self-restraint learned through formalized programs of character formation. The nuclear family had the responsibility for carrying this out.

Among the peasants of southern Italy we find the prevalence of popular sayings such as *"i figli si devono domare"* ("children must be tamed"). Leonard Covello has noted that this particular proverb was also "used in connection with the taming of animals."[55] In Italy, this taming was done through a combination of three methods. The most obvious of these was physical punishment. *"Bisogna inculcare nei figli timore e rispetto"* ("it is necessary to inculcate fear and respect in our children"), and *"mazza e panella, fanno i figli belli"* ("a stout stick and bread turn out good children") were two peasant expressions of this point of view.[56] The severity with which parents or older siblings undertook this endeavor was profound, as the story of young Pasquale reveals.

> ...Pasquale, eager for a good time, got up early, went through his brother's pockets and stole a half lira...and went off to the fair. His brother got up, missed the money and also missed Pasquale. The family suspected his whereabouts and set out to

bring him home....

When they got him home, his brother in the presence of the whole family, stripped him, tied him to a bedpost, and with a heavy rope soaked in water, gave him a terrible beating. No one dared or even offered to interfere when this was going on. The brother then ordered that a plate of macaroni be placed before Pasquale and then called in the dog who ate the entire dish. Pasquale was kept tied to the bedpost until nightfall.

Pasquale, years later, related this story with a great deal of admiration and respect for his brother, who thus probably saved him from becoming a thief....[57]

The second method of insuring conformity was instilling fear, especially with tales of evil spirits. Such fables as "Nick Fish" drove home the point that young people who refused to work and obey parental authority were doomed to ostracism and death.[58] The third and possibly most effective method for controlling youth was the curse.

"Chi non ubbidisce mamma e tana, fa la morte di un cane," or "those who disobey their mother and father, will die like a dog" was a popular expression in Basilicata.[59] Other curses directed at young people by their peasant parents included *"che lo possono mangione i cani"* (may you be eaten up by dogs) and *"possa gettare il sangue in mezzo alla strada"* ("may your blood flow in the streets").[60] In the story "Stinkpot," the protagonist eventually finds himself in jail after failing to heed his mother's warning not to marry Venera.[61] "Those who don't respect their parents," the narrator said, "cause their own ruin and come to a bad end."[62] Another young man married a woman against his father's wishes. In this instance, the father's curse was made explicit: *"si possa perdere il nome mio in casa tua"* ("may my name be lost in your home").[63] The person interviewed in this case recalled that Americans failed to realize that the

...words of a father or mother, particularly their benediction or their curse, are powerful things.

The young people tried hard to break this curse. When their first male child was born, they gave him the name of Giambattista, the name of the

> grandfather. The child lived a few months and
> died. The second male child was again given the
> grandfather's name, and he also lived a few months
> and died. They had four male children and they all
> lived just a few months and died.
>
> You scoff, you unbelievers, but be assured that
> a mother's curse is even more powerful than that of
> a father, and once it is pronounced, nothing can be
> done about it.
>
> You have no idea how every one in the village
> felt about this occurrence. It made you pause before
> doing anything contrary to the wishes of your
> parents....[64]

What actually killed the children is not of importance here. What is important can be best captured in a single phrase: might makes right. The point of such stories was clear on several emotional levels. Foremost among these was the denial of an individual choice guided by what the theorist of adolescence Luther Gulick called "subjective righteousness." Inherent in Gulick's view was a drive to create a new, perfected world which encouraged, at least ideally, the autonomous development of human potentialities. A belief in curses, and the knowledge that physical punishment always loomed as a possibility, precluded young Italian-Americans from having such a vision. Because punitive measures seemed to work, youngsters such as Pasquale grew up to be the new dispensers of "reality."

This was readily attested to by immigrant parents early in the twentieth century. Unable to comprehend the moral objectives of someone such as Hackensack's Lillie F. Hover, parents argued that teaching "is to make things remembered. And memory requires a scar or two on your body."[65] An Italian-American driver of a delivery wagon in New York City recalled that pulling some of his younger brother's "hair, he [remembered] all streets and all addresses. The bald spot on his head is better than having studied a map of the city."[66] Another parent lamented the softness of American teachers, and recalled that the teacher in Italy "used his fists good and often. In our estimation he had the right to do it and there was nobody who would object."[67] Frank, a shoemaker, did not hesitate to reveal his disgust with American educators who "do not even scold a child much less give him a good beating."[68] Finally, an immigrant from Calabria told an interviewer that it was shocking to discover that teachers "don't believe in corporal punishment."[69] Or at least the *Mezzogiorno* version of corporal punishment.

It thus seems safe to conclude that the available evidence points to a view of young people as little more than beasts of burden which, as human beings, possessed a bad nature.[70] The immigrant generation was particularly open in its opinion that it is an illusion to seek human virtue. Human behavior, incapable of perfectibility, was therefore thought of as subject to the same causal laws of nature as animals. Any quest for dignity lie not in the realm of character formation, but instead, in constant character suppression through surveillance. Any appeal to rationality or moral principles only served to invite trouble. This was clearest when dealing with a youngster's emerging sexuality.

Strafolaria and the Code of Sexual Etiquette

"*Strafolaria*" was a Sicilian term which described a female "who either flaunted her sex brazenly or was suspected of misbehavior with men."[71] In Rochester, New York, the term was applied to women whose mannerisms were "considered too free and easy."[72] Such women tended to flirt with both married and unmarried men. By Sicilian standards they were scantily dressed. They also smoked too much.[73] It was thought that all of this resulted from a parental failure to control a natural sexual drive which could not lend itself to internal restraints based upon moral appeals.

In *Mezzogiorno* villages, young women were particularly subject to parental and community surveillance from the time of puberty onward. Young women and men of all ages were kept strictly apart. Whether working in the fields or attending school, there was a constant vigil over the virgin. The sexual drive was seen as too powerful to be held back with mere moral warnings and the perfection of internal restrains. Donna Gabaccia has written of the anxiety which resulted among those peasant men whose work in distant fields precluded the steady control of the sexuality of female family members.[74] Nevertheless, the elaborate system of courtships, chaperonage, and outright seclusion seemed to serve its purpose reasonably well. The primary goal, of course, was the prevention of illegitimate births. Look, for example, at a statistical comparison of seven *Mezzogiorno* provinces and five northern ones between 1906 and 1909, as recorded in the *Annuario Statistico Italiano.*[75]

AVERAGE RATE OF ILLEGITIMACY
AND ABANDONMENT IN SOUTHERN ITALY
PER 100 LIVE BIRTHS, 1906–1909

NORTHERN ITALY		MEZZOGIORNO	
Emilia	10.3	Abruzzi	2.7
Lazio	15.7	Apulia	3.1
Marches	7.9	Basilicata	2.3
Tuscany	6.3	Calabria	5.4
Umbria	9.6	Campania	3.2
		Sardinia	5.0
		Sicily	4.3

Young peasant men were, at least upon initial examination, allowed a degree of sexual freedom totally denied to the young women. State-supported bordellos allowed young men to learn the mechanics of sex before their wedding. While premarital chastity was the ideal for young-sters of both sexes, it remained permissible nevertheless for young men to visit prostitutes in order to release what was seen as the irrepressible sex drive.[76] While it was believed that a young woman's sexuality was just as potent as a male's, the simple fact that she could become pregnant in a society which ostracized both unwed mothers and illegitimate children prevented similar outlets from developing for females. In any case, the young man's sexual experiences were typically restricted to a prostitute, for the chaperonage system of courtship did not allow the young people any privacy. The young man thus learned the feigned emotion of the *"puttana;"* an encounter with sincere emotions had to wait until the *settimana della zita,* or the "week of the bride."[77]

It is at this point that the immigrant parent's inability to understand

Anglo-American bourgeois dating practices begins to seem comprehensible. Even though such journals as the *New England Farmer* readily reflected the admission that a "young man from eighteen to twenty-five will [focus on] the object of his affection...," sociobiological theorists such as Ellen H. Richards remarked that the "joy of self-control should be taught to children."[78] In a 1904 speech given at Knoxville, Tennessee's Summer School of the South, Richards, a northeastern reformer who worked in immigrant slums, went on to argue that even though "control of self comes with [great] difficulty...patiently taught [it] does become habit."[79]

Immigrant parents quickly realized that this ideology was becoming a daily feature of American courtship practices. Jerre Mangione's parents were astounded that American parents allowed their Rochester daughters to go on unaccompanied dates. When Maureen Daniels, a girl "no more than seventeen years old" became pregnant, Italian-Americans in the neighborhood did not blame the youngster.[80] Instead, they directed most of their criticism toward Maureen's mother "for permitting Maureen too much freedom." Maureen's mother had failed to understand that sexual drives could never be tamed by self-control alone. Only sound surveillance and the threat of punitive measures could possibly contain people, especially young ones. Pietro Di Donato captured this perspective among Italian-Americans in West Hoboken when he wrote of the "volcanic" female sex drive. He tells us that when Grazia was left alone with Giuseppe, the "deed was accomplished, as mutely as the stallion is led to the heated mare...."[81]

So aside from the view that adolescents could not control sexual cravings, there also was evident the realization that a female's sex drive was just as potent as a man's. It was not necessarily more dangerous on moral grounds, however. The reluctance to permit it sexual expression at all had, at its core, the fear of illegitimacy. Such perspectives prevented agreement with Anglo-Americans who argued that sex can be rationalized.[82] Late nineteenth century feminists had been particularly vocal in this regard, and their views helped to shape American courtship practices by the turn of the century. Central to the writings of a Samuel Byron Britten or a Julia McNair Wright was the idea that passion can be controlled, rendering it harmless and incapable of inducing illegitimate sexual intercourse. In a section of her 1879 publication of *The Complete Home* entitled "when young persons should resolve upon celibacy," Wright acknowledged that "temptations are...strong," but that they can be successfully blunted by a soul "braced with religion," capable of "withstanding the onset of the world, the flesh and the devil."[83]

What made the views of feminists more palatable was the conception of a passive female, one lacking in sexual aggression. "Sexual passion," wrote one commentator in 1871, "aggressive in man, is dormant in [a] woman."[84] This writer went on.

> ...So long as she must come to him to beg her bread, to flatter her vanities, to feed her weaknesses for dress or indulgences of any kind; and just to the extent of such dependence, man will dictate the sway of sexual passion and the degree of its indulgence.[85]

As I have already suggested, *Mezzogiorno* immigrants brought an entirely different conception of the female to New Jersey and New York.

Accordingly, let us return to Mangione's Rochester in *Mount Allegro* for a moment. Antonio Ricotta, a cousin of Mangione's father, had five sons and a lone daughter. "His main worry," however, "was his daughter." The girl, Cicca, began to concern her parents when she turned fourteen. On one occasion, she attempted to go out secretly with a neighborhood boy. Incensed at the possible consequences, her father went over to see the young man. "Holding Cicca fast with one hand," Mangione wrote, "he got a stranglehold on the boy's head and bit off a piece of his ear." Despite an arrest for assault and battery and the public spectacle of newspaper headlines which blared "Man Bites Ear," Antonio refused to yield to "'American' ideas." Despite this and other setbacks in her love life, we are told that "in time Cicca came to believe it [her father's ideas] herself."[86]

This story raises crucial issues. Most obviously, there is Antonio's belief that Cicca needed to learn how to control her sexual drives. Hence, the suspicious, punitive, and vigilant nature of his relationship with Cicca. The basis of this view was the notion of the imperfectibility of human nature. That perspective also surfaced in other areas of parental doctrine. Most notable among these was in the definition of success.

Sources of Success

Before exploring how the first generation of Italian-American youth learned about attaining success, we must be clear about what constituted "success." We therefore should pay serious attention to what James Henretta called "ideological assumptions and conceptual bias."[87] The concept of "success" brought to New Jersey and New York by southern Italian peasants, and later modified by subsequent generations of workers, differed radically from dominant Anglo-American bourgeois thought. So too did the methods deemed legitimate for achieving it.

Late nineteenth-century Americans began to define success through a rejection of mere survival. One of the most prominent spokesmen in this regard was the psychologist and philosopher William James. In an 1878 article published in *The Journal of Speculative Philosophy*, James offered a critique of the Spencerian idea that survival was the highest stage of human development.[88] In this article, James celebrated those people whose qualities of heroism and recklessness enabled them to transcend the boundaries of a mere struggle for existence. At the core of his critique of Herbert Spencer's *Principles of Psychology* lies a profound uneasiness with any philosophy of crude social combat. Recklessness in this sense meant, for James, a movement past survival towards purposeful, constructive development. In the end, a new, higher form of civilization would emerge out of the complexity of a human intelligence which has progressed past the mere necessity of existence.

James, like Josiah Royce in *The Conception of God: A Philosophical Discussion Concerning the Nature of the Divine Idea as a Demonstrable Reality*, also struggled against any perspective which proved to be economically narrow and spiritually limiting.[89] Both James and Royce thus searched for a more sophisticated perspective. Inherent in their search was the assumption of progress. While neither James nor Royce applauded all Gilded Age developments, neither questioned the basic premise of a liberal society enabling individuals to develop to an undesignated end. That was the first level of Anglo-American bourgeois success—a movement past a conservative mentality focusing on individual and social preservation. They sought instead the implementation of perpetual movement and the creation of new needs.

In order to carry this out, one had to believe in the legitimacy of exercising freedom. Few bourgeois Americans felt reluctant, especially during this time, to exercise a version of individualism seemingly sanctioned by God himself.[90] Central to this belief system was a rejection of fate in lieu of desire and will. Even such a relatively cautious bourgeois propagandist as Marden challenged his readers in *Pushing to the Front* to

> ...show me a man who according to popular preju-
> dice is a victim of bad luck, and I will show you on
> who has some unfortunate crooked twist of temper-
> ament that invites disaster. He is ill-tempered,
> conceited, or trifling; lacks character, enthusiasm, or
> some other requisite for success.[91]

Marden assumed that poor traits can be overcome. Under such circumstances, fate or luck is irrelevant. Losing therefore was the unique fault of individuals all afforded an equal opportunity for a clearly defined prosperity. There was no room in this system for a rural Italian version of destiny.

A rejection of fate and an ideological longing for progress carried with it an inherent disdain for submission. Even in the emerging corporate setting of the bourgeoisie this was evident; the strain between the ideological call for personal advancement and the necessity of cooperation was never fully resolved.[92] Marden was cognizant of this tension in his 1911 essay entitled "The Salary You Do Not Find In Your Pay Envelope."[93] So too was Hall in his 1907 publication of "The Psychology of Ownership." Ostensibly discussing "primitive communism," Hall argued that it "is primarily a system of monotony revolting to an independent, virile manhood...." Three lines down, however, Hall undermined his own position when he wrote that "human society is based on mutual toleration, on each man's giving up something for the good of it all."[94]

Our concern, then, is not as much the tension between liberal individualism and cooperation as the dominant culture's denigration of submission as an end in itself. For to accept a submissive attitude was to agree with the ideal of a hierarchical community founded upon traditional sources of authority. The basic ideology of the Anglo-American middle class at this juncture, while reflecting the ideal of hierarchy, never implied the possibility of a rigid class structure maintained essentially unchanged generation after generation.[95] Not acknowledging the possibility of defeat, there was no need to rationalize subordination ad passivity.

It was thus not accidental that the children of immigrants were bombarded not with the dictums of Mardenian success, but rather, with an ideology founded upon the well known reality of subordination. "Be content to remain what your father was," one proverb expressed, "then you'll be neither a knave nor an ass."[96] Sicilian parents often adhered to the following maxim: "don't make your children better than yourself."[97] Guido D'Agostino, a second-generation boxer and novelist from New York City's "Little Italy," reiterated this point in such works as *Olives on the Apple Tree*.[98] His characters also suggested that it was easier not to dream of a better life, but rather, to accept what little pleasures life yields on a daily basis:

> ...Nick raised on his elbow and swallowed the remainder of the wine in his glass. He scowled at Giuseppe. "Is here I find every salamambitch for what I work give it to me—you know where." He directed his voice at Marco. "I have my wife and my kids and I think I doing fine."[99]

Nick has introduced us to the first component of Italian-American "success:" the ability to submit to authority in order to achieve a measure of job security. The immigrants brought with them a profound sense of fear and desperation; rational responses to the long-standing uncertainties of the southern Italian labor market. To the American of the period, ignorant of conditions in the Italian south, it seemed incomprehensible that human beings could be so "satisfied" with the low wages and unhealthy working conditions that were the typical laborers' lot.[100] But such seemingly satisfied workers were in reality resigned workers. A meager living which was steady was better than a meager living which was not. A worker of the period, Paschal D'Angelo, explained.

> ...everything was toil—endless, continuous toil, in the flooding blaze of the sun or in the splashing rain—toil. You cannot feel from the cold roads and steel tracks all the pains, the heartaches, and the anger I felt at the brutality of enforced labor. Yet

we had to live. We laborers have to live.[101]

Another laborer, Emanuel Carnevali, wrote in his autobiography that

> ...You gave me sorrow for my daily bread.
> You threw cheap words at me.
> And I found what nourishment was in them,
> And bit into them like a
> rabid dog.[102]

Workers such as D'Angelo and Carnevali socialized their children within the context of daily suppression. In other words, it would have been unrealistic to take any other route when the vision of a dramatically better future did not seem a sane one.

The children of immigrants thus worked within severe emotional constraints. Observers of the period also noted the harsh conditions of tenement and street life, which served to reinforce the feeling of limited horizons. The New York reformer Charles L. Brace, in his 1880 edition of *The Dangerous Classes of New York*, described one particularly poignant scene in the city's "Five Points" district:

> In the same room I would find monkeys, children, men and women, with organs and plaster-casts, all huddled together; but the women contriving still, in the crowded rooms, to roll their dirty macaroni, and all talking excitedly, a bedlam of sounds, and a combination of odors from garlic, monkeys, and dirty human persons.... The children I saw every day on the streets, following organs, blackening boots, selling flowers, sweeping walks, or carrying ponderous harps for old ruffians. The lad would frequently be sent forth by his padrone late at night, to excite the compassion of our citizens, and play the harp. I used to meet these boys sometimes on winter nights half-frozen and stiff with cold.[103]

For most immigrant children, it was psychologically inconceivable to plan the sort of personal advancement urged by Hall, Marden, and other bourgeois adolescent theorists—even if the rigid and solidified American class structure permitted it.[104] Personal security in the form of a steady job and home ownership thus took an early place among these people. For children who had known little more than poverty and social ostracism, it was extremely difficult to develop the sort of self-confidence necessary for dramatic advancement within the context of the American definition of "success."[105] Unable and unwilling to compete for American versions of success, the children of immigrants turned inwards in a defensive maneuver on behalf of their own egos and their own limited material resources.

Their daily lives in American exhibited the deference which helped to perpetuate a lack of self-confidence. Witness, for example, this description of a Brooklyn conversation:

> Despite their long association in America, the two men always addressed each other after the fashion of the Old World. And herein lies the clue to their relationship. My grandfather always addressed the other man and spoke of him as "Signor Pita." In fact, my grandparents never used the Pitas' first names. To this day I do not know them. In turn, Mr. Pita always addressed my grandfather as "Don Guiseppe".... Because my grandfather owned the building in which Signor Pita lived he was a don in the eyes of the tenant. Never mind that the don owned no other property than an old brownstone divided into four flats.[106]

This passage is worth exploring at some length. In the *Mezzogiorno*, forms of address among the peasantry symbolized the class position of the recipient. For instance, the propertyless *"giornaliero,"* or agricultural day laborer, was typically called by his first name.[107] Sometimes even that practice was abandoned, and the peasant was simply called "tu." Differences among dialects aside, this generally translates as a brusque "hey you." In Sicily, outright sarcasm is reported to have accompanied this address through the use of the term "Saint."[108] This last greeting poked fun at the peasant's lack of material possessions.

Agrotown landowners, whether of the artisan or the professional classes, enjoyed forms of address which were not demeaning. In both cases, this social respect was founded upon the secure ownership of land.

Artisans were often referred to as "Mastro," or "master."[109] Members of the *galantuomo* class were called "Don" or "Donna," depending on gender.[110] Landowners who were not professionals also enjoyed the use of this term.

Those immigrants who were able to secure a home acquired a social respect denied to most in Italy. They did not then need to reach beyond the working class neighborhood which was the source of that new standing. Indeed, they could not. "Success" could only be acquired, and maintained, within strict class and, to a lesser extent, ethnic boundaries.   Just as importantly, that was all that could be desired. Early on, immigrants realized that New Jersey, New York, and southern Italy all had a common theme—the quest for dignity.   Peasant parents taught working-class children that as subordinate persons, they would spend their lifetimes being treated by superiors in the workplace in a manner which embodied their commonness.[111] The only recourse was to cultivate a sense of self-worth which did not leave the immediate area of the home. Don Giuseppe could only be a "Don" within the confines of his old brownstone.

Not surprisingly, a worker such as Don Giuseppe did not call for a society of equals. His relationship with the tenant Pita was based upon a notion of authority anchored in the acquisition of property.   Further, nowhere in this account is there a recognition by Guiseppe that an acquisition of property equals a growth of individual liberty and a lack of tyranny for society at large. For Giuseppe, a consolidation of property and his own limited sense of freedom equaled the consequent ebbing of Pita's dignity and hence, Pita's growing unfreedom.   This had the effect of reproducing in America the hierarchical social view of the *Mezzogiorno*. It was never seriously believed by such workers as Guiseppe that a pursuit of self-interest would eventually produce a more just and economically beneficial civic order, and the evidence suggests that it was that very perspective which was passed on to the youngsters.[112]   It was readily accepted, though not always liked, that a pursuit of property would produce just the opposite effect, and woe to the Pita's who remained propertyless.

Anglo-American adolescent theorists of the period stressed not only the need to develop a system of internal moral restraints learned during a prolonged period of maturing, but additionally, they proposed that maturity could not be completed by a mere imitation of adults. Role models were acceptable, it was argued, but the youngster had to develop unique behavioral modifications which came from within. Marden, for instance, wrote that

> No man can really believe in himself when he is occupying a false position and wearing a mask; when the little monitor within him is constantly saying, "You know you are a fraud; you are not the man you pretend to be." The consciousness of not being genuine, not being what others think him to be, robs a man of power, honeycombs the character, and destroys self-respect and self-confidence.[113]

Marden was intent on cultivating a liberal version of individual freedom devoid of as much coercion or interference as possible. He proposed broad outlines of proper behavior, to be sure, but he was also committed to ensuring the youngster's maneuverability within those broadly defined constraints. It was no accident that adolescent theorists like Marden rejected any emphasis on a strict imitation of adult behavior.

Italian-American parents departed radically from this view. On the one hand, the imitative model of learning which they espoused effectively squelched any pretense of an internally-directed maturing process which allowed for flexibility. On another level, the rigidity of a neighborhood populated by workers like Don Guiseppe was replicated, and reinforced, through a childrearing practice which tended to deny the possibility, and the legitimacy, of individual freedom. The general parental willingness to use force and the imitative model was purposely intended to eliminate creativity and self-determination. As I have already pointed out, Italian-American parents in areas such as Newark refused to allow their children to attend certain schools for any appreciable length of time. One of their concerns was the school's refusal to fully accept the imitative model of learning. By the early decades of the twentieth century, they were increasingly turning to Roman Catholic schools and, to a lesser extent, to some secular schools which would reproduce the parental training at home in an outside institution.

In New Jersey, the first Italian-American parishes emerged in the working class enclaves of Jersey City and Newark in 1885 and 1886, respectively. Further south, in the Trenton area, St. Joseph's was founded in 1886 and St. Mary's appeared in 1887. By the early 1930s, there were approximately fifty Italian-American parishes, along with seventeen Italian missions.[114] Six Italian-American parishes alone were in Newark, four were in Paterson, three were in Jersey City, and two were in Hoboken, Union City, and Trenton. New York City, at about the same time, also witnessed the establishment of numerous Italian-American parishes and chapels, as shown below in statistics taken from the *Official Catholic Directory*:[115]

ESTABLISHMENT OF ITALIAN-AMERICAN
CHAPELS AND PARISHES
IN NEW YORK CITY, 1866–1924

BOROUGH

Brooklyn	14
Bronx	8
Manhattan	29
Queens	1
Staten Island	6

An integral part of these parishes was the parochial school. At an historical juncture in which *The Literary Digest* pointed out that Italian-Americans "have drifted into the non-churchgoing class," they were enrolling their children in Catholic schools while, simultaneously, removing them from most public cones.[116] While these Catholic schools tended to be primarily on the elementary level, which implies that parents were just as reluctant about formal education managed by the Catholic church as they were about public schools, it cannot be overlooked that parochial school enrollments were rising at a time when public school rates were dropping. Church officials, such as Bishop Wigger in the Newark diocese, anxious to make "real" Catholics out of peasant children, were willing to go along with any rationale which would bring Italian-American youngsters into Catholic schools.[117]

Parochial schools in the Newark diocese provide a striking example of the correlation between a rising parochial school enrollment and declining rates of attendance at public schools. In 1900 Fr. Felice Sandir, the acting pastor of Jersey City's Holy Rosary Church, wrote in his report of that year that

> ...an Italian parochial school is absolutely necessary
> for the spiritual welfare and improvement of the
> church. Over 500 children could attend.[118]

During the year of Sandir's report, three Italian-American parishes had a
total enrollment of 543 youngsters: Mount Carmel and St. Philip Neri's in
Newark, along with St. Michael's in nearby Orange.[119] The enrollment in
Newark occurred at the precise moment as the Board of Education reports
warning of Italian truancy.[120] But while church officials such as Sandir and
Wigger concerned themselves with the loftier notions of "spiritual welfare,"
Italian-American parents turned to parochial schools as a means of
institutionalizing the imitative model of character formation outside of the
family.

As I alluded to earlier in my discussion of the young woman Cicca in
Rochester, Italian-American teenagers were not immune to the influences
of Anglo-American practices which stood in stark contrast to those of their
parents. Indeed, the dilemma of the immigrant's children formed the basis
for Irving Child's pathbreaking 1943 publication entitled *Italian or American?*[121] Along with Caroline Ware's earlier publication of *Greenwich Village*,
Child stressed the often violent rift which developed between immigrant
parents with unalterable ideals and children compelled to deal with both
those concepts and those of their Anglo-American teachers who told them
that it was wrong to follow parental ways.

> In the school, however, the boy is subjected to
> criticism, not for his misdemeanors, but because he
> acts as he has been taught to act. If is not that the
> child disobeys, but that the very mode of conduct
> which he naturally follows is objected to. The world
> in which he has been trained is condemned by the
> new world into which he has moved.[122]

In the following passage we are shown not only the basis for the domestic
strife described by a number of novelists, but also, the growing attraction
of the parochial school:

> In the school, the child finds, with practically no
> warning or preparation, that those things which are
> taken for granted as the proper procedure in his
> home and immediate environment are not only
> undesirable but severely forbidden. It is in the
> school that the child first learns with any degree of
> definiteness that he is not an American, but an
> Italian child of the slums; it is in the school that the
> one institution which is an integral part of his
> nature and devotion—his home—is constantly
> subjected to objections.[123]

There is a plethora of evidence on the domestic strife which resulted among second generation children unable to cope with such conflicting pressures. Parochial schools, therefore, served as a way for immigrant parents to project onto relative strangers, i.e., nuns, the often harsh task of perpetuating the strict imitative model of behavior without running the risk of alienating the child's affection and, as a result, their sense of duty and obligation.

This was certainly the situation described by Leonard Covello in his autobiography *The Heart is the Teacher*.[124] Unfortunately, Covello's memory of his elementary school experiences is the closest that we can get to a lengthy recollection of a working-class Italian family's daily reaction to a specific system of education during this period which, in this case, was outside of a parochial school. From the reports of parochial school officials, however, it seems clear that Leonard's schools were operated on principles which were similar to those espoused by nuns and priests. Covello attended "*La Soupa Scuola*" and Public School 83 in Manhattan. It is the reaction of his parents, however, which is of importance to use here. Because Covello's teachers taught in a way which did not allow for individual adjustment, these immigrant parents embraced their youngsters' eduction. Covello recalled that his family had chosen "the Soup School instead of the regular elementary private school," and "by the standards I had come to know and understand in Avigliano, the Soup School was not an unpleasant experience."

La Soupa Scuola was a three-story wooden building. Squeezed between two five-story tenements, it was not impressive by American standards. But to young Leonard, it "appeared huge and impressive."

Standing with another youngster, Vito Salvatore, Leonard remembered being "ashamed to let him [Vito] know that in Avigliano our school consisted of one room, poorly lighted and poorly heated, with benches that hadn't been changed in fifty years." Initially preoccupied with the aura of such a "huge" building, Covello's interest was suddenly distracted by the actions of his father. "At this moment," Leonard recalls, "something really wonderful happened to take my thoughts from the poverty of our life in Avigliano."

Despite what Leonard's father had heard about the Soup School, he was not completely in agreement with Leonard's attendance. Neither was his mother, who "never saw the inside of a school." They seemed much more enthusiastic when Leonard, who was already laboring at itinerate menial jobs, was able to land steady work:

> ...I ran home to tell my mother and father that I had found a job and was ready to do my share in supporting the family. My mother put her hand on my shoulder. My father said, "Good. You are becoming a man now. You have grown up." I was only twelve, but I could feel that he was proud of me. And I was proud of myself because I had reached the age where I could do more than scrub floors and wash windows and look after my baby brothers. I could earn money and stand on my own two feet and help keep the family together, as I had been taught practically from the time I was born was my responsibility.

But Leonard persisted in his attempt to rise above "the worst possible jobs—jobs that paid little and were very uncertain." He yearned for "another world—beyond the tenements." School seemed to be the route to take, even though it led to such emotional outbursts as that quoted below:

> "Will you stop saying that!" my mother insisted. I don't understand. I don't understand. What is there to understand? Now that you have become Americanized you understand everything and I understand nothing.

Eventually a compromise was worked out between Leonard and his parents which began on the day of Leonard's entrance into the Soup School. Leonard remembered that his father smiled broadly upon hearing of the tactics of the school's head teacher, Mrs. Cutter. Just as Maestro Mecca in Avigliano had "cracked your hand with his ruler [making it] numb for a week," so too did Mrs. Cutter let "you have it across the back." Increasingly unable to legitimately impose the imitative model of behavior on young people simultaneously exposed to relatively free American adolescent practices, immigrant workers such as Leonard's father sought institutions outside of the family which imposed what the parents at home could not do without a perpetual struggle. In the process, parents could influence their children in the desired way without exposing themselves as harsh. Symbolically, Leonard's father made it a practice to buy candy for his son before entering the school—a habit which began on the first day. "The picture of us there on the street outside the Soup School eating candy and having a good time," Covello wrote, "will never fade." Despite the concern of Covello's mother that school would introduce unacceptable ideas, Leonard's parents came to accept their son's attendance when it proved to be a resolution of a generational conflict between competing dominant and counter-discursive world views.

In other words, Leonard's quest to become American via the route of the school was accepted by his parents because that school tended to mold adolescents in a way which was in accord with rural Italian customs, albeit in different guises. No surprisingly, the curriculum of the Soup School and P.S. 83 differed dramatically from what Gulick, Hall, and Marden called for. The young Covello, intent on becoming American, could not see that his training was of a sort which left him more Italian than ever. His parents, groping for a way to remove themselves from a generational conflict which seemed initially irresolvable, recognized the Soup School as an appropriate course of action. Covello spoke of other parents in the neighborhood who also sensed that familial conflicts rooted in a cultural clash could be resolved through selective participation in American institutions.

What did the curriculum of the Soup School look like? One is initially struck by the general atmosphere of silence, self-restraint, unquestioning obedience, and physical punishment. "You recited to the teacher standing at attention," Covello recalls. He also remembered the "Silence!" of the school, and contrasted this with "the modern child [with] his complexes and his need for 'self-expression!'" Self-expression, at least according to Covello's descriptions, were non-existent at the Soup School.

> ...Silence! Silence! Silence! This was the character-
> istic feature of our existence at the Soup School.
> You never made an unnecessary noise or said an
> unnecessary word. Outside in the hall we lined up
> by size, girls in one line and boys in another, with-
> out uttering a sound. Eyes front and at attention.
> Lord help you if you broke the rule of silence.

Covello went on, describing the situation of a relative and classmate who dared to transgress the established boundaries of behavior:

> I can still see a distant relative of mine, a girl named
> Miluzza, who could never stop talking, standing in
> a corner behind Mrs. Cutter throughout an entire
> assembly with a spring-type clothespin fastened to
> her lower lip as punishment.

All of Covello's recollections of *La Soupa Scuole* focused on such instances of regimentation and discipline. There is little discussion of academic subjects per se.[125] That was not the case for young Willard L. DeFoe of Paterson, whose school notebook can be found in his family's files at the Hackensack Public Library.[126] His notebook, which dates from about 1910, is a unique source for the study of what a nearby middle class youth was expected to receive in school. It stands in stark contrast to Covello's recollections both at the Soup School and, as we shall discover momentarily, at P.S. 83. What the notebook also suggests is the institutionalization of the bourgeois theoretical emphasis on adolescent freedom in schools with a heavy middle class population.[127]

In 1884, a writer in the *Bergen Index* condemned the "jail-like school house" of north Rutherford.[128] Readers were told that the school "has all of its windows covered with iron gratings, and reminds the passer-by of the Hackensack jail." Besides, "it does not give the building a very home-like appearance...." An integral part of a "home-like appearance," according to a local group of reformers in the Woman's Reading Club of Rutherford, was the realization that "modern educational methods [necessitate] an increasing amount of individual research...."[129] In their argument for a well-stocked library, they stated very clearly their view of what school should mean for adolescent middle-class youth. Their focus on individual discovery in lieu of mere regimentation and rote memory was later echoed in the work of Abraham Flexner, who pointed out that

> Our most recent manuals venture to leave out some of the traditional facts least appropriate for an elementary review of the past and endeavor to bring their narrative into relation...with modern needs and demands. But I think that this process of eliminating the old and substituting the new might be carried much farther; that our best manuals are still crowded with facts that are not worthwhile....[130]

Flexner proposed that a downplaying of factual memorization had particular relevance for students of history.[131] This was obviously the route that DeFoe's teachers were taking a decade before the publication of Flexner's book. Throughout DeFoe's study of "prehistoric Britain," "Roman Britain," "Britain under Saxon rule," and "Trouble in Ireland," there is a notable emphasis on thinking through a historical process rather than simply isolating dates and the reign of rulers for test-taking purposes. The young DeFoe actually seemed excited about what he was studying, and the margins of his notebook attest to his varying degrees of conceptualization and synthesis.

Look, for example, at his consideration of "Roman Britain." His teacher has challenged him to think about the relationship between uncoerced consent and the use of state force. DeFoe sketched an outline of what he concluded was the "falsity of Roman civilization," and concluded that Roman rulers failed to recognize that there was a delicate balance between "force" and "free will"—and that it was political suicide to tip that scale too much on the side of force. His teacher had lectured on Roman civil law and the excesses of the ruling elite, and it was DeFoe who had thought out for himself the process, and the ramifications of, civil consent.[132]

Such was not the case with Covello in either the Soup School or P.S. 83. Covello remembered the "constant drilling and the pressure of memorizing" which "seemed merely the continuation of my training in

Italy."[133] Unlike DeFoe, Covello's training in history and geography does not suggest the variable of independent thinking. "Geography and history I mastered easily," he wrote, "I memorized with facility." Covello himself admitted that under such a routine learning did not take place. The routine induced "discipline":

> According to modern methods and educational theories, it was rough fare. But it had its values. It may not have been the best way to train the mind, but it did teach you to concentrate on mastering difficult jobs.[134]

Precisely! Covello's parents were fully aware of what awaited most working class children. Covello tells us that it

> ...was a curious fatalistic attitude among our people in America that while they deplored their economic situation they seldom tried hard to do anything about it. Generations of hardship were behind them. Life was such. "La volonta di Dio! For them the pattern could never change...."[135]

So it would not make very much sense to inculcate anything other than the cardinal virtues of the worker: punctuality and obedience. Even the *prominenti* publication of the *History of the Italians in Trenton* had acknowledged that the lot of the worker was a grim one at best. The best that Italian-American laborers could hope for, Joseph Mainiero of *La Nuova Capitale* smugly wrote, was a

> ...vigorous, bustling wife and...numerous children; his crown jewel the happy blackeyed bambino that clung to his knees and shared with him the delicacy of a bit of bread dipped in wine...and just enough furniture to take care of the immediate needs of the family....[136]

For such people, it would prove a waste of valuable time to engage in the sort of theorizing done by DeFoe in Paterson, and their intuition about the futility of engaging in the contest for upward mobility was basically sound.

Therefore, the sensible route remained the learning of behavioral patterns conducive to jobs characterized by repetition, the liquidation of creativity, and a strict code of subordination. Employment was just there to earn money anyway, what emotional satisfaction could be found was most safely left in the old brownstone or the Cape Cod cottage later on.

Thus for Italian-American youth, "success" lie in the refusal to expect any real satisfaction in the workplace. Working situations were seen as equally deadening, it was thus illusive to try to search for a specific occupation. The personal triumph came in the acceptance of what seemed to be natural with a measure of public dignity. Even more profoundly, one had to eat. Di Donato wrote that the wheelbarrow pushed by Geremio was not loved, and that

> The stones that brutalized his palms [were not loved]. The great God Job, he did not love. He felt a searing bitterness and a fathomless consternation at the queer consciousness that inflicted the ever mounting weight of structures that he had to! had to! raise above his shoulders!

When would this end, the laborer asked himself,

> ...when and where would the last stone be? Never...did he bear his toil with the rhythm of song!
> The language of worn oppression and the despair of realizing that his life had been left on brick piles. And always, there had been hunger and her bastard, the fear of hunger.[137]

That was what working class youngsters had to learn to adapt to. To do it successfully was to ensure some measure of material security in what was seen as a very cruel and unforgiving world. When parents did periodically decide that this situation could be transcended, they did not accept the notion that success was the product of hard work, delayed gratification, and the ability to "get along."

Routes to Success

Two words best summarize what children were taught: shrewdness and cunning. This view was evident in numerous accounts of village life in the *Mezzogiorno* of the late nineteenth century.[138] Pitre's collections contain such popular expressions as "every house has its door" and "the neighborhood is a snake, if it doesn't see you it hears you"—proverbs which suggest the need to strike at an opponent's weak point in any way possible. They also imply that one should expect others to do so as well. One scholar therefore argued that in the case of women, "perhaps the chief precept to be learned was to live as a sharp practical woman, a scaltra."[139] The use of the word "practical" is important, for it suggests the repudiation of adherence to absolute moral principles. Parents stressed that children needed to acquire the habit of adapting to different situations. Hard work directed towards a definable goal was consequently seen as irrelevant.

To "succeed," then, one had to be cunning and shrewd, for no amount of perseverance could overcome the handicap of working class origins. "As a consequence," wrote Valentine R. Winsey, "many families simply succumbed to poverty as an inescapable way of life."[140] But even to maintain a poverty-level existence required the exercise of cunning and shrewdness.[141] And that was what Angelo Patri was reacting against.

In his 1922 publication of *Child Training*, Patri wrote a thinly-disguised polemic against the childrearing practices of the region's Italian-Americans; practices which had affected him as a child and in turn inspired him later on to engage in a vigorous effort to both shed its effects and to prevent other parents from engaging in the same process. Part III of his book, entitled "Building The Child's Character," is of particular importance. He challenged parents with a straightforward question: "do you want your child to be a 'good child?'"[142] He began the response with a simple dictum: "Be one yourself."[143] The most important way to achieve this, Patri argued, was to develop an Anglo-American bourgeois attitude toward work and personal advancement:

> Show him a character that you have forged in the
> fires of temptation and self-denial; one that has been
> tempered by the tears and pain of service and
> sacrifice; one that is buttressed by a purpose and

will and faith that will support it to the end.[144]

Integral to working hard and building character at the same time was the repudiation of deceit. While Patri sympathized with workers compelled by circumstances to mislead employers out of a fear of adverse repercussions, he proposed that "courage will have to be trained over the fear."[145]

But that was of course easier said than done. What the Italian-American adolescent theorist Patri failed to grasp was that deadening, unskilled labor could never be seen as "buttressed by a purpose." The only available "purpose" was the avoidance of work if at all possible. To "get one past" the foreman was one course of action.[146] The other, and by far the most typical, was the refusal to work overtime factory shifts despite the attraction of increased income. Louise C. Odencrantz, in her 1919 publication *Italian Women in Industry*, informs us of numerous young women prodded by their families to work overtime, particularly when their fathers were unemployed. For example, the

> ...father of little Louisa Trentino, seventeen years old, was a hod carrier, usually idle. Her mother and the children earned a few dollars a week making flowers at home. Louisa could increase her weekly earnings of $6.00 by 50 cents if she worked until 8:30 p.m. three nights a week. This meant that she could not attend evening classes, although she had been backward in school, nor join a club in a nearby settlement in which she was interested.[147]

Tensions thus arose between young women and parents over the issue of overtime. One young woman who cut the patterns for underwear trimmings at the rate of $4.50 per week was once paid 35 cents for working until 8:30 in the evening. Once was enough. "It is not worth while," the young operative remarked, "to kill yourself." An eighteen year old woman who worked as an operative in a kimono plant was paid 50 cents extra to work until 9 p.m.—with no time allowed for supper. She refused to do this subsequent to a three-month stint, remarking that "I can't stand it any more." Sometimes even the only inducement for working overtime—the extra wage— was not forthcoming. Carlotta Valenti worked at padding men's coats. Told to stay until a special order arrived, she had remained idle until resuming work on the order which delayed the end of her day until 9 p.m. "Yet she made no extra money," Odencrantz wrote.[148] How could parents seriously argue for the profitability of hard work when young people saw examples of work not being paid for? Besides, both parents and children were all too aware of stories like the one told below:

> A woman of twenty-two, a straw operator, summa-
> rized in her record some of the effects of such
> overwork. During four months of the year she
> worked overtime every day until 8 p.m., with no
> time for supper, In addition she was asked to come
> in for half a day on Sundays. She found the over-
> time extremely fatiguing; she used to get more tired
> in the two hours at night than during all the remain-
> der of the day. She always noticed a marked
> change in her health at the end of the first week of
> overtime, and it took her a long time to get over the
> effects at the end of the season. She was usually too
> tired to eat, and had to go to bed as soon as she
> came home at night. Even then she was often too
> tired to sleep.[149]

Di Donato, in an essay named after his mother "Annunziata," captured the feelings of parents whose attitude reflected what was really thought about experiences in the workplace. Young Paul proclaimed "Unfair! Unfair!—Our Lives—unfair!"[150] Annunziata warned her son against the necessity of working for a wage. Aware of the dangerous nature of factory and construction work and the irreversible damage it could inflict on one's health, Annunziata pleaded with Paul to look for other ways to earn money:

> "Never back to Job, son my son. We will starve, we
> will wander the streets and crowd ourselves in holes
> and corners, we will walk on our hands and knees,
> we will humble ourselves low, low rather than you
> back to Job. Oh hear me son of mine...."

Patri lamented the tendency of Italian-American parents to encourage the development of shrewdness in lieu of hard work. The young women in the New York City factories examined by Odencrantz and others from the Division of Industrial Studies at the Russell Sage Foundation came from families who accepted long work hours only during periods of unemployment. Di Donato, writing from the vantage point of West Hoboken, recalls a mother who accepted the idea of increased impoverishment rather than have her son submit to the demands of the industrial workplace. For the young people who graduated from the grammar schools of Bergen County, New Jersey in 1900, the message received was dramatically at variance with what Paul heard at home only a few miles away.

In the spring of 1900 county superintendent of schools J. Terhune addressed the graduates in what was called a "Circular of Greeting."[151] He asked "my dear graduates" to face a single question: "what time is it?" It was time, he answered, to begin looking "upward and onward." To do that, young men had to realize that

> ...success costs something; that you must determine in spite of weariness and disappointments, to persevere; and that you cannot afford to have anything to do with idlers, spendthrifts and fast-fellows. Don't believe in any genius or luck, or chance.[152]

Terhune then ushered in a common feature of the bourgeois conception of labor: delayed gratification.

> It is application that wins. We learn wisdom from failure more than from success; we often discover what will do by finding out what will not do. Assure yourselves that if you are true, faithful, upright, and intelligent, the world will want you, and you will readily find your place; though you may work unnoticed and uncommended for months, such conduct always meets its reward.

"Such conduct always meets its reward." As we have just seen in the case of one woman in a New York City factory, labor did not even necessarily equal the attainment of an overtime wage. It was this reality which Covello's father understood, and it is why parents such as he insisted upon a mode of training which did not develop intellectual and emotional qualities doomed to disappointment in an unskilled job. Terhune argued that "out of work come life and strength and growth, and even genius and virtue." But Covello's father told his son that "Nardo, in me you see a dog's life," while Paul's mother chose unemployment over dangerous work for paltry wages. Paterson's anarchist newspaper *La questione sociale* published a poem in 1895 which reflected the "dog's life":

> ...Let us weave the silk and gold:
> Our lot, our misery, our
> pain it will lighten:
> Let us weave, let us weave
> until death arrives;
> And on the cold weaving frame
> we are extended.[153]

Within the context of such a view the bourgeois idea of delayed gratification had trouble taking hold among Italian-American workers. This bourgeois ideal had not been evident among the *contadini* of the *Mezzogiorno* either. In her 1908 publication of *In The Abruzzi*, Anne Macdonell recognized that the "peasant's life is a desperate struggle to win bread from barren rock...." A peasant from Scanno sadly remarked to Macdonell's group that "the land is going out of cultivation." In Edmund Lear's journey through the Kingdom of Naples, the same impression is evident. "Almost immediately on leaving Minervino we came to the dullest possible country," he wrote in his 1847 diary.[154] "Elevated stony plains—weariest of barren undulations," he went on, "stretching in unbroken ugliness towards Altamura and Gravina." Endlessly working on uncooperative soil, people such as Verga's Compare Mosca were moved to exclaim: "cursed by the fate that brought so many troubles on us!"[155]

These observations must be taken into account in a discussion of what peasant and working class children were told about work in general, and what bourgeois theorists later termed "delayed gratification" in particular. Struggling against "natural" ecological conditions in a perpetual effort to sustain life at the most basic levels, peasants increasingly were at a loss to find meaning in work. In time, it came to be expected that there would be only frustration and futility in working the fields. This is precisely what Rudolph M. Bell implied in his study of rural Italy:

> I suggest that it was not the absolute poverty and
> exploitation that determined the peasantry's world
> view but, rather, the mode of that impoverishment
> and exploitation. Agricultural laborers who lived
> hard by a substantial segment of cittadini just
> enough above them to be objects of envy rather than
> fear or hatred tended to despise their land (Castel
> San Giorgio and Rogliano).[156]

The separation of the inner self from the laboring process was due to the open and vicious nature of class exploitation evident in the agricultural system of the south. Such manifestations of the class relation between *contadini* and *galantuomini* as exorbitant interest rates tended to undermine any reason to be any more persistent than one had to.[157] The southern ecology combined with the rural class structure to produce an emotional configuration not accustomed to the concept of working for a higher purpose which meant future improvement. When these two factors were not enough to limit the aspirations of the few ambitious peasants, then the example of what might happen from the point of view of the mafiosi did.[158]

The seeming futility of overcoming nature, debt peonage, and the strong-arm tactics of the elite was transported to America and transmitted to the generation born in New Jersey and New York. Working in the factories of the New York metropolitan area, or the cranberry bogs in southern New Jersey, parental conceptions of labor as being separate from one's self, indeed, that it is merely a commodity sold, just like "any consumer article," were reinforced.[159] Thus to prepare for work in the way that Marden or Terhune called for was to pursue the illusion that improvement was realistically attainable. Such a view would also assume that there really was a qualitative difference between different working class occupations; as if there were some which did not call for strict obedience and the acceptance of boredom and repetition. It is not surprising that Selma Berrol, in her study of immigrant school children in New York City between 1900 and 1920, found that Italian-American children in Little Italy were of the opinion that "they too could expect little practical advantage from formal education."[160] The reference was to the subject material itself, for parents did, as I have already suggested, prize those schools which, as one Italian-American woman argued,

> ...taught (young people) to respect their parents and
> relatives. They (youngsters) should never question
> their authority, nor disobey with a shrug of the
> shoulders as they are accustomed to do here in
> America. To keep quiet, listen and absorb the
> wisdom of their elders is the duty of children.
> These are the things they should be taught.[161]

Nowhere in this woman's view of adolescent training is there room for an internalized system of labor which does not have to be regulated by direct and visible outside authority. Let us return momentarily to the "Circular of Greeting." In a section of the pamphlet entitled "Perseverance," an unnamed author outlined the necessity of foregoing present pleasures for future rewards. This process, the educator assumed, was the outgrowth of an inner restraint not generally spoken of by Italian-American parents. I have provided an except from the "Greeting" below to illustrate my point:

> Even when we seem to be having a peculiarly trying
> time; when brain and nerve, courage and endurance,
> are taxed to the utmost, and it seems as if every-
> thing were so against us that it is hardly worth
> while to struggle on any longer, we can never tell
> when things may change, and the chill and gloom
> be followed by cheer and light.[162]

This passage exudes a vision not only of self-regulation, but further, of confidence. The speaker took as a given that young people would receive the full value of their labor. Indeed, it implies that the act of work itself is an uplifting experience.

I have already suggested why work in southern Italy was a traditionally alienating experience, and that this negation of the self in the workplace came to be seen as natural. Parents, therefore, socialized their children to accept this view of work. Satisfaction was thus sought in other areas of life, such as leisure activities. Our concern here is that the constraints which originally induced the perception of labor power as a barrier to emotional gratification were the same constraints which inhibited a general acceptance of Anglo-American bourgeois ideas about work. Racism and the inability to completely overcome the effects of nature, or what Di Donato referred to as "the first fleshly sense of Job," were two of the constraints not quite left behind in Italy. The third, mafiosi, also reappeared in the New World.[163]

The stultifying effects of crime were discussed by those who despised its effect on the working class the most—radical political leaders. In Paterson's *L'Era Nuova*, several long articles were devoted to the problem of working class defeatism. The authors saw the pervasive presence of organized crime as a leading contributor to a lack of initiative in the workplace. From the anarchist point of view, an unwillingness to work hard contributed to a "slovenly" political outlook which could not form the basis for serious social activism. The strategic concerns of the Paterson anarchists between 1915 and 1919 are not the central issue here, however. The point is that contemporaries recognized the lack of what Americans called a "work ethic" among Italian-Americans. And writers in *L'Era Nuova* were openly concerned that this attitude was being passed on to children.

So far I have suggested that hard work and its natural accompaniment, delayed gratification, did not generally reveal itself as a powerful motivating force among the first two generations of Italian-Americans. The reasons for this are initially identifiable, at least in part, in the agricultural conditions of southern Italy and later on, in factory conditions across the Atlantic. The conception of work passed on to Italian-American young people stood in stark contrast to the ideology and practice of adolescence found among the Anglo-American middle class. Fittingly, individualism is usually associated with Anglo-Americans. Yet, Anglo-American adolescent theorists of the period, for all of their preoccupation with self-regulation, still managed to mount a polemic against the Hooverian brand of "rugged individualism." In the process, they were laying the foundation for what William H. Whyte would decades later call the "organization man." And it was that same ideal type that Italian immigrant parents rejected early on.

Among Anglo-American families of the middle class in the late nineteenth century adolescence increasingly came to be associated with stages of schooling. In other works, to be an adolescent was to be a high school student. By the early twentieth century, college and university students were also classified as "adolescent." Writing in *The American Secondary School*, Leonard V. Koos explained that

> Pupils of secondary-school are often referred to as
> "adolescents" or as being in the "period of adoles-
> cence." In defining these terms it is customary to
> point out their Latin derivation from adolescere, "to
> grow," or "to grow up to maturity"...it is not
> uncommon to refer to [adolescence] as the "teens."[164]

Schools catering to a middle class population sought to reach a fine balance between the creative spontaneity of the individual and what Koos called "training for social cooperation." What was meant by this term? Just as importantly, how did the school institutionalize it? Educational theorists who wrote about adolescence conceptualized individual initiative within clearly limited boundaries established by an institution. Initially it was the school, and later on, it would be a corporation. Lip service was paid to the ideology of classical laissez-faire, and while liberal ideology was not completely abandoned, it was seriously modified in order to meet the organizational demands of an industrialization in full swing.[165]

Within the school curriculum itself, organized athletics began to assume a role by the turn of the century which they had not occupied before. This development was not simply the result of G. Stanley Hall's call for increased motor activity among young people. The development of organized sports served to equate routinized behavior with the normal pace of the industrial and corporate workplace.[166] This was not the routinized work of the working class, however. For in the theoretical writings of the period which are devoted to team sports there is plenty of room for individual decision-making. The modification of classical liberalism is found in a limited individualism which relegates competition to a place outside of the term. In short, team members competed against individuals on other teams. One was expected to get along with members of the same team. In his "Psychological, Pedagogical, and Religious Aspects of Group Games," Gulick thus offered a diagram of the ideal progression "Anglo-Saxon Boys' Plays" should take:[167]

ASPECTS OF GROUP GAMES

ANGLO-SAXON BOYS' PLAYS
(NEURO-MUSCULAR)

Birth

0 ————————————————————————————————————

Kicking.   Whole arm, body and hand movements.
Dropping things. Blocks. Sand Plays, digging, piling, etc.
Running, throwing, cutting and folding.   Swinging.
Shooting, guns, bows, slings, etc. Knife work. Tools of
increasing complexity.   Machinery.   Sailing.   Rowing.
Swimming. Gymnastics. Indian Clubs, etc.

7 ————————————————————————————————————

Tag. Ball games. Cross tag. Word tag. Prisoner's base.
One old cat. Throwing. Dock on a rock. Fungo. Hide
and seek. Rounders, etc. Black man. Leap frog. Track
and field sports. Marble games. "Stunts," fat, cints, hole,
etc., Foot-ball games. Care of land and animals. Hunting,
fishing.   War.   Wrestling.   Boxing, fencing.   Predatory.
Billiards. Bowling.

12 ————————————————————————————————————

Baseball. Basket-ball. Cricket. Hockey. Gangs. Houses
in woods. Pals. Predatory gangs. Hero service.

————————————————————————————————————

   In Gulick's scheme, the period of adolescence was the culmination of
a series of youth activities all leading to a necessary participation in group
activities designed to curtail unrestrained individualism. Sports such as

baseball strengthened the growing need for unified cooperation, the so-called "team spirit." Republican ideology emphasizing individualism was still an integral part of the adolescent theorists' view, but by the end of the nineteenth century it was rapidly being subordinated to an emerging bourgeois belief that the group is more efficient than the individual. In his analysis of team sports, Gulick consciously isolated this fundamental characteristic of the corporate state. The dynamics of middle class life were displayed on the playing field; to be democratic was to subdue personal ambition in an effort to create an efficient, harmonious atmosphere. One learned to play by the rules; proper behavior was defined by an older elite which in this case were umpires. Creative spontaneity was encouraged by Gulick, but it was never directed against the members of the same team.

With some minor variations, reformers and educators in New Jersey and New York attempted to impose this use of team sports as a socializing medium among Italian-Americans. In a 1910 article in the *Playground Journal*, the Playground Association of America issued an amendment to its statement of purpose.[168] Funded by the Russell Sage Foundation in New York City, Association policy was formulated there under the leadership of Gulick and other prominent adolescent theorists of the period, such as Joseph Lee and Henry Curtis. Two sentences in the Association amendment are of striking importance.

> Industrial efficiency is increased by giving individuals a play life which will develop greater resourcefulness and adaptability.

> ...People who play together find it easier to live together and are more loyal as well as more efficient citizens.[169]

In order to carry out these objectives, reformers and educators worked to construct playgrounds throughout the New York metropolitan area. Play directors were then assigned to organize working class children into teams, with directors serving as umpires and referees. As historian Dominck Cavallo put it, "the playground itself was to be a sort of outdoor social settlement."[170] Cavallo maintains, however, that "we will never know" what working class youngsters thought of the effort to socialize them to the values of cooperation. "Their reaction," he argues, "like the cloud formed by a player sliding into home plate, is dust in the wind." A careful reading of the sources which are available, however, can begin to tell us what Italian-American parents thought of American games which they did not see as serving any useful purpose. While their reactions were not to the Playground Association specifically, they were directed towards the ideals stated in the Association's purpose and institutionalized in school athletics.

I have already emphasized the Italian-American parents' use of the imitative model of child-rearing. Thus the "adaptability" spoken of by Association leaders was inappropriately forced into an Italian-American procrustean bed. But one does not have to dwell on the purpose of playground sports to uncover the basis for the parental rejection of team sports. For it was the very act of playing, regardless of the play director's intentions, which alienated working class parents from school athletics.

> Why, these boys and girls—particularly the boys—do nothing but play ball, morning noon and night. The school should give our children definite tasks to do in the home. But one cannot expect very much from the school because it is the school that encourages play.

One Italian-American mother remarked that

> They accuse my boy of having lost interest in learning, but I don't blame him. How can he learn when they compel him to play more than to study? Imagine they called me to school to explain why my son does not want to attend his playing lessons! I did not go, because I brought up my boy well.[171]

This mother's attitude was a long-standing one in southern Italy. Lacking a concept of adolescence, children simply ceased to play when they became adults. In a subsistence economy, adult peasants worked. The harsh conditions of working class life in America did not soften this view. Indeed, given the addition of new obstacles to overcome, such as language differences and a sense of isolation in unfamiliar surroundings, older ways of doing things tended to be reinforced, not abandoned. This explains why parents during this period also rejected a central guiding principle of the play director—that team members must display loyalty towards one another.

In rural Italy, the peasant's conception of loyalty traveled upwards towards the land owner or his hired representative, the overseer. Peasants did not generally see themselves as owing loyalty towards those on the same class level. In his travels through Calabria, Douglas observed that "out of envy they pine away and die; out of envy they kill one another."[172] Pitre's collection of proverbs reveals the pervasive attitude of distrust between peasants, as do the writings of Giovanni Verga and the few testimonies of immigrants available to us.[173] We have already seen how the competitive nature of social interaction between peasants manifested itself in the struggle for status during the funeral process. Even during times of revolt, in which peasants felt that the landowners were not fulfilling that expected sense of duty towards their subordinates, the distrust between members of the same class was not softened. In fact, new opportunities inspired fresh sources of distrust. Such social upheavals as those evident between 1860 and 1893 served to intensify the cynical view of friendship quoted below; a perspective totally devoid of the social dynamic and socialist values urged so passionately by radicals of the time:

> They judge friends with the following yardstick. "Can they help you to get a good job? Can they entertain you in their own home? Do they have money or are they just going to sponge on you?" If friends meet these requirements, the friendship still has to remain coldly distant; because sooner or later you'll find that these friends will take advantage of you and get you into trouble.[174]

The Sicilian woman who expressed this view was not the sort to either lend herself unselfishly to political activism or to a corporate setting which demanded unquestioning devotion. From the perspective of child-rearing, the evidence suggests that parents reiterated a corporate or cooperative sense of the individual only with familial boundaries. Loyalty to outsiders was directed upward towards anyone capable of improving the individual's and hence the family's social standing.[175] Persons in the same class were hardly in a position to provide that sort of service.

As a result, an integral aspect of either a liberal or a radical vision was missing among Italian-American children. That variable was an optimism which grew out of either a belief in the victorious, autonomous individual or, in this instance, the collective class power of trusting comrades. Patterns of industrial authority in America were not qualitatively different from those in rural southern Italy. They thus served to reproduce the structure of personal relations evident in the villages of the south. The old belief that people generally cannot be trusted was reformulated in America. Loyalty, a product of necessity, was reserved for those powerful people capable of easing the struggle to survive. Dependence and obligation thus remained part of nature, safely keeping class unrest within confines deemed appropriate by ruling elites. This is what writer Angelo P. Bertocci had in mind in his "memoir of my mother:"

> ...For my mother...understood neither the theory nor the ethics of trade-unionism nor was she conscious of laboring-class solidarity. For her, with her Italian peasant fatalism, a job was a job, one got as much as one could, but one took what one got; the world was divided between i patroni and the poor, and the poor invariably got the worst of it anyway. So take hold when and where you can and have sense enough to know when you are reasonably well off.[176]

CHAPTER FOUR NOTES

1. Joseph Kett, "From Nurture to Adolescence," in *Rites of Passage: Adolescence in America, 1790 to the Present* (New York, 1977), p. 113.
2. See Hall's classic *Adolescence: Its Psychology and Its Relations to Physiology, Anthropology, Sociology, Sex, Crime, Religion and Education*, Volumes I and II (New York, 1924); Orison S. Marden, *Pushing to the Front*, Volume II (Petersburg, New York, 1911); and George F. Bowne and Roy M. Jacobus, *Troop Meeting Programs* (Newark, New Jersey, 1926). Bowne was the scoutmaster of Troop 36 in Newark, while Jacobus was the Assistant Scout Executive in that city. This small book was privately published, and it is located in the files of the Bergen County Historical Society in Hackensack, New Jersey.
3. Kett, *Rites of Passage*; and Dominick Cavallo, *Muscles and Morals: Organized Playgrounds and Urban Reform, 1880–1920* (Philadelphia, 1981). Donald R. Raichle's "The Great Newark School Strike of 1912," *New Jersey History*, Spring/Summer 1988, pp. 1–17, is appropriate here. Also refer to Robert H. Wiebe's *The Search for Order, 1877–1920* (New York, 1969), for a wider synthesis of this trend. For an overview of the historiographical debate which Wiebe has been at the center of, see Daniel T. Rodgers, "In Search of Progressivism," in *The Promise of American History: Progress and Prospects*, eds. Stanley N. Katz and Stanley I. Kutles (Baltimore, 1982), pp. 113–132.
4. In Leonard Covello's "Early Maturity of Children," in *The Social Background of the Italo-American School Child: A study of the Southern Italian Family Mores and Their Effect on the School Situation in Italy and America* (Totowa, New Jersey, 1972), p. 229. For a broader treatment, see David I. Kertye and Richard P. Saller, eds., *The Family in Italy from Antiquity to the Present* (New Haven, Connecticut, 1991).
5. See the summary of Covello, "Early Maturity of Children," in *The Social Background of the Italo-American School Child*; pp. 229–237. Also refer to the oral testimony of an immigrant from Apulia in Richard N. Juliani's "American Voices, Italian Accents: The Perception of Social Conditions and Personal Motives by Immigrants," *Italian Americana*, 1, 1974/75, p. 10.
6. Covello, "Early Maturity of Children," p. 230.
7. Ibid., p. 232. Basic introductions to southern Italian linguistic structures are Michele Castagnola's *Dizionario Fraseologico Siciliano Italiano* (Vito Cavallotto Editore, 1980); Sandro Attanasio, *Parole Di Sicilia: Frasi, espressioni, detti, paragoni, proverbi e "vastasate"* (Mursia, 1977); Giovanni Pansa, *Saggio Di Uno Studio Sul Dialetto Abruzzese* (Lanciano, 1885);

Giorgio Piccitto, *Vocabolario Siciliano* (Palermo, 1977); Vincenzo Nicotia, *Dizionario Siciliano-Italiano* (Catania, 1883); G. B. Pellegrini, *Saggi Di Linguistica Italiana: Storio, Struttura, Societa* (Borginhieri, 1975). Also see Caterina de Bella's *La Poesia Dialettale in Calabria* (Florence, 1959).

8. Covello, "Early Maturity of Children," p. 232.
9. Ibid., pp. 230–232.
10. See the summary of Covello in "The Primary Family Group," p. 230; the background material in George Psathas, "Ethnicity, Social Class, and Adolescent Independence from Parental Control," *American Sociological Review*, 22, 1957, p. 415; Selma Berrol, "Turning Little Aliens into Little Citizens: Italians and Jews in New York City Public Schools, 1900–14," in *The Interaction of Italians and Jews in America* (New York, 1975), pp. 32–41; and Lydio F. Tomasi, "First-Generation Southern Italian Family in American," in *The Italian American Family: The Southern Italian Family's Process of Adjustment to an Urban America* (Staten Island, New York, 1972), p. 24.
11. In Kett, "From Childhood to Adolescence," in *Rites of Passage*, p. 135.
12. Foerster, "South Italy. People and Emigration," in *The Italian Emigration of Our Times* (Cambridge, Massachusetts, 1919), p. 85.
13. Zanotti-Biano, *La Bascilicata* (Rome, 1926), p. 45.
14. In Covello, "Economic Exploitation of Children," p. 229.
15. Pitre, *Biblioteca della Tradizioni Popolari Siciliane: Proverbi Siciliani*, Volumes 8–11 (Palermo, 1990).
16. Mary F. Matthews has astutely observed that

> Amidst such poverty as the early immigrants experi-
> enced, deferred gratification would have had little
> appeal; the immediate opportunity for employment
> would be far more desirable than the expense of a
> prolonged education.

Matthews, "The Role of the Public School in the Assimilation of the Italian Immigrant Child in New York City, 1900–1914 (Ph.D. dissertation, Fordham University, 1966), p. 282. For a discussion of the New York City school's failure to take into account the complexity of different immigrant backgrounds, see Francesco Cordasco, "The Children of Immigrants in the Schools: Historical Analogues of Educational Deprivation," *Kansas Journal of Sociology*, Fall 1970, pp. 143–155.

17. In the statistical table below, drawn from the 1940 United States

census, the average educational level of Italian-Americans 25 years and older in Health Area 21 of East Harlem stood at 6.3:

HEALTH AREA 21

NUMBER OF SCHOOL YEARS COMPLETED		% OF TOTAL POPULATION (EAST HARLEM)
No schooling at all		18.96
Grade School	1–4 yrs.	21.39
	5 or 6 yrs.	12.29
	7 or 8 yrs.	32.76
High School	1–3 yrs.	6.68
	4 yrs.	2.85
College	1–3 yrs.	0.77
	4 or more years	0.96
Not reported		3.34
TOTAL		100.00
Median School Years Completed		6.3

The oral testimonies of workers and New York City school officials in the period before 1920 is also illuminating:

> His wife and their two children were required to work hard. Josephine, the girl, helped a great deal though she was only eight years old…. When Josephine was ten years old, the father forbade her to go to school. In his estimation, she could read and write, and that was good enough for any Italian girl. The father insisted that she was big enough to give real help to her parents. …Josephine is forty-two years old today, married, a mother of five, and almost illiterate.

Another interview revealed that

> One woman (twenty-four years old) of the T-family,

who was born in 1914 in East Kingston, New York, told me she had never been to school because her mother did not believe girls should be educated except at home and in church. When the truant officer came around, the little girl would hide and the mother would tell the officer that she had only three children although she really had ten. The officials, moreover, were very lax in their duties, and the Italians were able to keep their children home from school so that they could work them all day long at household tasks. This American-born woman still cannot speak good English.

And still another respondent remembered that

My mother was born in America. She had only two years of elementary school....

Finally, a New York City public school teacher recalled that

This was years ago.... I was amazed at the frank statements by Italian pupils who when absent from school gave as an excuse, "My mother told me to stay home," or "My parents cannot afford to send me to school every day," or anything to this effect....
In my conversations with the parents I became convinced that they did not uphold the worth of education nearly as much as the worth of the child's earning power to eke out the parental income.

Refer to Covello, "Opposition of the Contadino Family to Compulsory School Attendance," and "Conspicuity of Italo-American Children in the Public Schools of New York City," in Eugene Bucchioni and Francesco Cordasco, eds., *The Italians: Social Backgrounds of an American Group* (Clifton, New Jersey, 1974), pp. 520 and 529–530.

18. In Covello, "Influence Upon the School Situation in America," p. 283.
19. Ibid.
20. Irwin, "Michelangelo in Newark," *Harper's Magazine*, September 1921, pp. 446–454.
21. Ibid.
22. Ibid.

23. Report on the Seventh Avenue School, in *Annual Report of the Board of Education* (Newark), 1890–1914, p. 255.

24. Especially given the efforts of Anglo-American bourgeois ideologists in the schools of the period. For a general discussion of this trend, though the evidence is drawn from neighboring Pennsylvania, consult William Issel, "Americanization, Acculturation ad Social Control: School Reform Ideology in Industrial Pennsylvania, 1880–1910," *Journal of Social History*, Summer 1979, pp. 569–590.

25. Bushnell, "In Development," in *Nature and the Supernatural, As Together Constituting the One System of God*, 3rd edition (New York, 1858), p. 233.

26. "We Have No Faith," in *Nature and the Supernatural*, p. 232.

27. "In Development," p. 233.

28. "Dedication of a New School House at Carlstadt," *New Jersey Citizen*, 27 February 1874, n.p. Also see the file marked "Education" in the archives of the Bergen County Historical Society, Hackensack Public Library, Hackensack, N.J.

29. Ibid. Also interesting is an unpublished report written by Reeves D. Batten, who served as Lyndhurst High School principal in the mid-twentieth century. Entitled "Bergen County Schools," it is located in the aforementioned file.

30. "Dedication of a New School House at Carlstadt," n.p.

31. "Leonia School," *Bergen Index*, 9 September 1879, p. 1.

32. *Annual Report of the Board of Education* (1890–1914), p. 99.

33. "Self-Reformation," p. 234.

34. *Annual Report of the Board of Education*, p. 99.

35. The "common school course" notebook of Wygarst, located in the "education" file at the archives of the Bergen County Historical Society.

36. "Business Virtues," in the *Common School Course*, p. 5. A good introduction to Smiles is that of Asa Briggs, "Samuel Smiles and the Gospel of Work," in *Victorian People: A Reassessment of Persons and Themes, 1851–1867* (Chicago, 1972), pp. 116–139.

37. *Common School Course*, p. 6.

38. "County Commencement. Annual Exercises of the Public Schools of Bergen," June 5, 1883, document in the "Education" file of the Bergen County Historical Society.

39. Ibid., p. 1.

40. In Covello's "The Gravitation Toward Parental Patterns at the High School Age Level," in *The Social Background of the Italo-American School Child*, p. 347.
41. "Work of Children on New Jersey Truck Farms," *Monthly Labor Review*, May 1924, p. 115.
42. Ibid., p. 116.
43. Mosso, *Vita moderna degli Italiani* (Milan, 1906), p. 32.
44. In Richard Gambino's "The Family System," in *Blood of My Blood: The Dilemma of the Italian-Americans* (Garden City, New York, 1974), p. 3.
45. Di Donato, *Three Circles of Light* (New York, 1960), p. 188.
46. Ibid., p. 198.
47. In Andrew Rolle, "La Famiglia: Reaching Out," *The Italian Americans: Troubled Roots* (New York, 1980), p. 135.
48. Oral interview of George Hewitt, April 26, 1986. According to Hewitt, the Bunker Hill section of Paterson had a high concentration of Italian-Americans who frequently referred to the school in the way I have noted.
49. *Annual Report of the Board of Education*, p. 455.
50. Miles, "The Italians of Newark" (M.A. thesis, Columbia University, 1926), n.p.
51. *Marzulli, Gl'italiani di Essex Note storiche e biografiche, con l'agguinta di un Business Directory* (Newark, 1911).
52. Churchill, "Education," in "The Italians of Newark: A Community Study" (Ph.D. dissertation, New York University, 1942), p. 157.
53. See Leonard P. Ayres, *Laggards in Our Schools* (New York, 1909).
54. Gulick, "Psychological, Pedagogical, and Religious Aspects of Group Games," *Pedagogical Seminary*, March 1899, p. 139.
55. Covello, "The Punitive Element in the Education of the Contadino Child," p. 270.
56. Covello, "Corporal Punishment," p. 272. These feelings were also sometimes directed to young brides by their husbands. In Michael De Capite's *Maria*, sixteen-year-old Maria is introduced to sex on her wedding night through the following procedure:

> She stood by a window overlooking the hill. The
> questions in her mind now changed to fear. She heard
> Dominic's movements, but did not dare to look his

way.

"What are you standing by the window for?" His voice cut like a sudden chill. "Aren't you going to undress?" His voice was dry and harsh.

Mechanically Maria's hands unbuttoned her white wedding gown. When she knew it was loose on her body she clutched it close to her bare arms.

"Well," Dominic said again, annoyed, "you can't stay there all night...."

Dominic rose from the bed. In his bare feet he took long strides to where she was standing. He peered into her wet eyes, and then with one swift movement, raising his open hand, he struck her across the mouth.

He picked Maria up and carried her to the bed.

De Capite, *Maria: A Novel* (New York, 1943), p. 20.

57. In Covello, "Corporal Punishment," p. 272.
58. Part of this Sicilian tale went as follows:

Once upon a time in Messina there was a mother with a son named Nick, who spent all his time, day and night, swimming in the sea. His mother was constantly calling to him from the shore, "Nick! Oh, Nicke! Come out of the water, will you? You're no fish, are you?"

But he would always swim farther out. From so much yelling, the poor mother got a kink in her intestines. One day when he'd made her scream herself hoarse, she pronounced a curse on him. "Nick, may you turn into a fish!"

Obviously heaven was listening that day, for the curse took effect....

See "Nick Fish," in *Italian Folktales*, ed. Italo Calvino (New York, 1980), p. 521.

59. In Covello, "'La Maledizione'—The Curse," p. 271.
60. Ibid.
61. Giovanni Verga, "Stinkpot," in *The She-Wolf and Other Stories* (Berkeley, 1962), pp. 108–114. This story dates from about 1880.

62. Ibid., p. 109.
63. Covello, "'La Maledizione'—The Curse," p. 271.
64. Ibid., pp. 271–272.
65. "Lack of Penal Measures in the High School as a Source of Complaint," in *The Italians: Social Backgrounds of an American Group*, p. 561.
66. Ibid.
67. Ibid., p. 562.
68. Ibid., p. 563.
69. Ibid., p. 562.
70. See especially the summaries of Covello, "The Role of Children in the Marriage Unit," pp. 223–229; and Foerster, *The Italian Emigration of Our Times* (Cambridge, Massachusetts, 1919), pp. 85, 102, passim.
71. Jerre Mangione, "Sicilian Virgin," in *Mount Allegro: A Memoir of Italian American Life* (New York, 1981), p. 152.
72. Ibid.
73. Ibid., p. 153.
74. Donna R. Gabaccia, "Agrotown Social Patterns," in *From Sicily to Elizabeth Street: Housing and Social Change Among Italian Immigrants, 1880–1930* (Albany, 1984), pp. 46–48.
75. *Annuario Statistico Italiano*, Volume I, in Phyllis H. Williams, "Marriage and the Family," *South Italian Folkways in Europe and America: A Handbook for Social Workers, Visiting Nurses, School Teachers, and Physicians* (New York, 1969), p. 74.
76. Gambino has written that

> The only departure from premarital chastity even surreptitiously permitted were young men's relations with the town whore, or in larger towns and cities their visits to the local government-supervised whorehouse, called by the familiar Italian word bordello....
>
> Although a mother would attempt to keep her son away from the local *puttana* or bordello from fear of disreputable company and venereal disease, mature men sometimes encouraged younger men to indulge. In a society where single women were closely chaperoned, for most young men the prostitute presented the only accessible sexual experience.

See Gambino's "Sex," in *Blood of My Blood*, pp. 187—188. Also refer to
Mary Gibson's "Prostitution and Feminism in Late Nineteenth-Century
Italy," in *The Italian Immigrant Woman in North America*, ed. Betty Boyd
Caroli (Staten Island, New York, 1977), pp. 24–30.

77. Gambino, "Sex," p. 199. Gambino has argued that the newly married
couple

> ...spent some period of time in total seclusion, usually
> in their new home but on occasion in a different place
> provided by family or close friends. The period was
> equivalent to a honeymoon...it typically lasted one
> week and a groom was expected to pamper his
> bride....

Verga, writing about the southern Sicilian village Vizzini in 1888, tells
us of events subsequent to *settimana della zita*:

> He was a peasant, but he had the subtle shrewdness of
> a peasant too! And he had his own pride, even he.
> The pride of a man who has managed to earn with his
> own hands, and his own work, the fine linen sheets in
> which they both slept turning their backs on one
> another....

In *Mastro-Don Gesualdo* (New York, 1955; reprint ed., Westport,
Connecticut, 1976), p. 272.

78. "Men's Love Letters," *The New England Farmer*, 7 April 1883, n.p.; and
Richards, *The Art of Right Living* (Boston, 1904), p. 20.

79. Ibid.

80. "Sicilian Virgin," pp. 154–155.

81. Ibid., p. 155; and Di Donato, *Three Circles of Light*, p. 46. Di Donato's
father suggested the presence of powerful female sex drives that called
for male caution.

> ...I would not venture my lovely hide with that lupa
> unless she was first depilated, deodorized, muzzled,
> and chained, hand and foot like a cave she-wolf to the
> bedstead! (p. 46)

82. See the fine summary of William Leach, "Sexual Ownership and the Rationalization of Sexual Desire," in *True Love and Perfect Union: The Feminist Reform of Sex and Society* (New York, 1980), pp. 81–98.

83. Wright, *The Complete Home: An Encyclopedia of Domestic Life and Affairs* (Philadelphia, 1879), p. 19.

84. "The Woman Question—'Sex in Politics'," *Springfield Republican*, 30 June 1871, in Leach, "Sexual Passion: Benign and Harmless," pp. 93–94.

85. Ibid.

86. Mangione, "Sicilian Virgin," p. 159; pp. 161–162; and p. 165.

87. Henretta, "The Study of Social Mobility: Ideological Assumptions and Conceptual Bias," *Labor History*, 18, 1977, pp. 164–178. Also useful is Henretta's "Social History as Lived and Written," *American Historical Review*, December 1979, especially p. 1,310.

88. "Remarks on Spencer's Definition of Mind as Correspondence," in the *William James Reader*, ed. Gay W. Allen (New York, 1972), pp. 3–15.

89. Royce, *The Conception of God* (New York, 1897).

90. At least ideologically, what began with Herbert Spencer culminated in 1922 with Herbert Hoover's argument that

> It is in the maintenance of a society fluid to these human qualities that our individualism departs from the individualism of Europe. There can be no use for the individual through the frozen strata of classes, or of castes, and no stratification can take place in a mass livened by the free stir of its particles. This guarding of our individualism against stratification insists not only in preserving in the social solution an equal opportunity for the able and ambitious to rise from the bottom; it also insists that the sons of the successful shall not be any mere right of birth or favor continue to occupy their fathers' places of power against the use of a new generation in process of coming up from the bottom.

"Philosophic Grounds," in *American Individualism* (Garden City, New York, 1922), p. 20.

91. Marden, "The Will and the Way," p. 475.

92. Thus generations later William H. Whyte, Jr. could write that "since the

war the younger generation of management haven't been talking of self-reliance and adventure with quite the straight face of their elders." See Whyte's "The Decline of the Protestant Ethic," in *The Organization Man* (Garden City, New York, 1956), p. 20. Also refer to the broad theoretical overview of Michel Crozier, in *The Bureaucratic Phenomenon* (Chicago, 1964), especially Part Three, "Bureaucracy as an organization System." Also relevant is George Cotkin's *Reluctant Modernism: American Thought and Culture, 1880–1900* (New York, 1991).

93. "The Salary You Do Find in Your Pay Envelope," pp. 525–539.
94. Hall, *Aspects of Child Life and Education* (Boston, 1907), pp. 241–286; and p. 248.
95. See the still able summary of Louis Hartz, "The New Whiggery: Democratic Capitalism," in *The Liberal Tradition in America: An Interpretation of American Political Thought Since the Revolution* (New York, 1955), pp. 203–227.
96. In Rolle, "La Famiglia: Reaching Out," in *The Italian Americans*, p. 134.
97. Ibid.
98. D'Agostino, *Olives on the Apple Tree: A Novel* (New York, 1940). For broad considerations of Italian-American novels and novelists, refer to Rose B. Green, *The Italian-American Novel: A Document of the Interaction of Two Cultures* (Rutherford, New Jersey, 1974); and John M. Cammett, ed., *The Italian American Novel*, Proceedings of the Second Annual Conference of the American Italian Historical Association, October 25, 1969.
99. *Olives on the Apple Tree*, p. 27.
100. In a poem about Italian-American children written at the turn of the century, Florence Wilkinson dreamed of a day when young Italian-American laborers would be neither resigned nor satisfied:

"The Flower Factory"
Lisabetta, Marianina, Fiametta, Teresina,
They are winding stems of roses, one by
one, one by one —
Little children who have never learned
to play: Teresina softly crying that her
fingers ache to-day, Tiny Fiametta

nodding when the twilight slips in, gray.
High above the clattering street, ambulance
and fire-gong beat, They sit, curling
crimson petals, one by one, one by one.

Lisabetta, Marianina, Fiametta, Teresina,
They have never seen a rose-bush nor a
dewdrop in the sun.
They will dream of the vendetta, Teresina,
Fiametta, Of a Black Hand and a face
behind a grating; They will dream of
cotton petals, endless, crimson, suffocating, Never of a wild-rose thicket nor the
singing of a cricket, But the ambulance
will bellow through the wanness of their
dreams. And their tired lids will
flutter with the street's hysteric screams.

Lisabetta, Marianina, Fiametta, Teresina,
They are winding stems of roses, one by one,
one by one. Let them have a long, long
play-time, Lord of Toil, when toil
is done! Fill their baby hands with
roses, joyous roses of the sun.

In Antonio Mangano's *Sons of Italy: A Social and Religious Study of th*
Italians in America (New York, 1917), p. 98.

101. In Alberto Giovannetti, "Padroni and Banchisti," *The Italians of Americ*
(New York, 1979), p. 167.

102. Carnevali, "Annie Glick," in *The Autobiography of Emanuel Carneval*
compiled by Kay Boyle (New York, n.d.), p. 167.

103. Brace, *The Dangerous Classes of New York* (New York, 1880), p. 19<
Also see Paul Boyer's *Urban Masses and Moral Order in Americ*
1820–1920 (Cambridge, Massachusetts, 1978).

104. Examples of the lack of social fluidity in America, especially durin
the nineteenth and early twentieth century, abound. Refer to Thom<

Kessner's *The Golden Door: Italian and Jewish Immigrant Mobility in New York City, 1800–1915* (New York, 1977); John Bodnar, *Immigration and Industrialization: Ethinicity in an American Mill Town* (Pittsburgh, 1977); and Clyde and Sally Griffin, *Natives and Newcomers: The Ordering of Opportunity in Mid-Nineteenth Century Poughkeepsie* (Cambridge, Massachusetts, 1978).

105. Maria Sermolino, a northern Italian immigrant whose family settled in Manhattan around 1892, remembered her indignation over being confused with *"caffone"* from the south. She suffered on city playgrounds the sort of treatment given daily to children of immigrants from the south:

> At school...my playmates skipped away chanting, "Mary" (my teachers had thus anglicized my name) "is a dirty Eyetalian, Mary is a dirty Eyetalian...."

Sermolino, *Papa's Table d'Hote* (New York, 1952), p. 87.

106. Gambino, "L'Vomo di Pazienza—The Ideal of Manliness," p. 142.

107. Refer to the summary of Covello, "The giornaliero," p. 79.

108. Ibid.

109. Ibid., "The Artigiano," p. 93. Also consult the "Biographical Note" in Verga's *Mastro-Don Gesualdo* (Westport, Connecticut, 1976), p. vii.

110. *Mastro-Don Gesualdo*, p. vii; and Covello, "The Professional Class," p. 100.

111. Some parents told of the poor results when efforts to break out of the working class were attempted. One mother in New York City commented that

> ...my daughter wanted to be a teacher. I sacrificed everything to send her to high school and college. I did not send her to a factory or a shop to help along with the family income, much as the family needed it. And now after all the worries and sacrifices, she can't get a job in any school....
>
> Well we did send our children to high school and college and followed the American way and chi mi conchiude? Did they make anything out of it? We

> should have followed i buoni costumi del nostro
> paese. Send them to work soon to help out the
> family and then arrange for them to sistemarsi.
> Everybody would have been much better off. I stay
> awake nights thinking of the terrible mistake my
> husband and I made.

This feeling of commonness began in the school system itself, as young Maria remembered.

> The one day in the year they marched down to the
> basement where heaps of old clothes were stacked.
> From them they were allowed to take whatever fitted
> their bodies. Maria always remained in the back-
> ground of the rush, until Mama Rosalie threatened to
> beat her if she came home with her hands empty
> again.   And one day she allowed herself to be
> carried along with the others, and when she came
> out she had a pair of shoes twice her size.

Covello, "The School as a Social Institution," p. 317; and De Capite's "Little Italy," in *Maria*, p. 4.

112. For example, see Edward Corsi's "Pathways of a Youthful Immigrant," *In the Shadow of Liberty* (New York, 1935).

113. "Stand for Something," p. 568.

114. See the summaries of Silvano Tomassi, *Piety and Power: The Role of Italian Parishes in the New York Metropolitan Area, 1880–1930* (New York, 1975); Carmine A. Loffredo, "A History of the Roman Catholic School System n the Archdiocese of Newark, New Jersey, 1900–1965" (Ed.D. dissertation, Rutgers University, 1967); Paul V. Flynn, *History of St. John's Church, Newark: A Memorial of the Golden Jubilee of Its Consecration, in the Eighty-second Year of the Founding of the Parish, with a Retrospect of the Progress of Catholicity* (Newark, 1908); and John K. Sharp's *History of the Diocese of Brooklyn, 1853–1953* (New York, 1954).

115. In Tomasi, "The Emergence and Growth of Italian American Parishes," p. 99.

116. "Catholic Italian Losses," *The Literary Digest*, 11 October 1913, p. 636. Loffredo, writing about the Newark diocese, which was heavily populated by Italian immigrants, points out that "between 1900 and

the end of the First World War, there were thirty-three parochial elementary and secondary schools built and/or opened..." (p. 128).

117. Yet he was personally not the sort of role model which immigrant parents preferred. As I suggest in my consideration of *Mezzogiorno* religion, Wigger's martyr-like version of Catholicism was seen as utterly inappropriate in a world demanding even a small amount of material wealth as the basis for social standing and respect. An excerpt from Wigger's diary gives us some insight into his life:

> I will be away all the week. Mr. J. J. Keane, of Jersey City, accompanies me, and pays all expenses. Had he not invited me and kindly volunteered to pay all expenses, I could not have gone, I am so poor. When I was only a simple Priest I was always more or less in debt. Only once did I succeed in laying by $100. In less than three months all had disappeared. Since I have been Bishop things are worse even. My personal debts are larger than formerly. There is some comfort in knowing that I have not spent much on myself; I have never done that. The money has been given to others, generally in charity.

See Flynn, "The Third Bishop of Newark," p. 157. Also see Carl D. Hinrichsen, "Immigration Old and New," in "The History of the Diocese of Newark, 1873–1901" (Ph.D. dissertation, Catholic University of America, 1962), p. 322.

118. In Hinrichsen's "Immigration Old and New," p. 322.

119. Taken from the 1901 *Catholic Directory*, in Hinrichsen, p. 323.

120. *Annual Report of the Board of Education* (1904), p. 455.

121. Child, *Italian or American? The Second Generation in Conflict* (New York, 1970).

122. Bromsen, "The Public School's Contribution to the Maladaptation of the Italian Boy," in *Greenwich Village, 1920–1930: A Comment on American Civilization in the Post-War Years*, ed. Caroline Ware (New York, 1965), pp. 455–456.

123. Ibid., p. 456.

124. Covello and Guido D'Agostino, *The Heart is the Teacher* (New York, 1958).

125. The classic revisionist work which emphasizes the correlation between the school's purpose and the needs of an emerging industrial order is Samuel Bowles and Herbert Gintis, *Schooling in Capitalist America* (New York, 1976).

126. Notebook of DeFoe in the file marked "Education." Also see the family file marked "DeFoe."

127. In an essay entitled "Social Organization and Control," Thomas H. Briggs lamented that

> Unfortunately, a few individual high school teachers, as perhaps would happen anywhere, ridiculed these attempts [at intellectual self-direction] and discouraged anything except obedience to explicit directions emanating from themselves.

In *The Junior High School* (New York, 1920), pp. 250–251.

128. "Jail-Like School House," *Bergen Index*, 11 January 1884, n.p.

129. *The Free Public Library of Rutherford, 1894–1924* (n.p./n.d.), p. 15. This small book is particularly valuable for its collection of the Club's correspondence, including personal letters, dating from the spring of 1894.

130. Flexner, "A Modern School: Current Education," in *A Modern College and a Modern School* (Garden City, New York, 1923), pp. 112–113.

131. Ibid., pp. 111–113. In this regard, Flexner relied upon the judgment of James Harvey Robinson, progressive professor at Columbia and author of *The New History* (1912).

132. DeFoe notebook, p. 5.

133. Covello, *The Heart is the Teacher*, p. 41.

134. Ibid., p. 42.

135. Ibid., p. 29.

136. Mainiero, "The Incoming Tide," in *History of the Italians in Trenton* (Trenton, 1929), p. 33.

137. Di Donato, *Christ in Concrete* (New York, 1939), p. 18.

138. This showed up repeatedly in oral testimonies, particularly with respect to the concept of friendship. A woman who emigrated from Messina, Sicily explained that friends were appraised from the perspective of what they could give in a material sense. She recalled

that her family reinforced this view.

> My sister-in-law looks favorably on the cummari
> [Sicilian for "commare"] who often brings her lovely
> gifts; she is ready to condemn the cummari who
> used to bring her nice gifts....

A male immigrant from Apulia also expressed the same perspective
as the woman quoted above.

> ...a friend is a person who can help you when you
> are in trouble, a person in whom you can confide
> family matters, and who can give you advice pertain-
> ing to family problems. In short, a friend must be
> able to render some service to you. He should be in
> a position to reciprocate with a gift when you give
> him one, and to return a favor with a better favor.
> A person who cannot perform all these duties cannot
> be called a real person.

In his analysis of the southern Italian village Montegrano forty years
later, Edward Banfield, in his very controversial book, found that this
view was still intact.

> In the Montegrano view, the conditions of life—the
> brutal and senseless conditions of life—determine
> how men will behave. In so fearful a world, a
> parent must do all he can to protect his family. He
> must preoccupy himself exclusively with its *interesse*.
> The *interesse* of the family is its material, short-run
> advantage. The tireless and cunning pursuit of
> advantage cannot be depended upon to secure the
> welfare of the family: the threat of calamity hangs
> over all, even the unsleeping. But, little as it may
> count against the overwhelming uncertainties of the
> universe, the pursuit of *interesse* is at least some-
> thing—perhaps the only thing—the individual can
> do to give a measure of protection to his family.

See Covello, "Friendship," p. 190; and Banfield, "Ethos in Practice," in *The Moral Basis of a Backward Society* (Glencoe, Illinois, 1958), p. 115. Also examine Giovanni Verga's *House by the Medlar Tree* (Berkeley, 1964); along with Norman Douglas, "Reposing at Costrovillari," in *Old Calabria* (London, 1915), p.124.

139. Gambino, "La Serieta—The Ideal of Womanliness," p. 166.

140. This is a strong theme which runs throughout Winsey's work, "A Study of the Effect of Transplantation upon Attitudes toward the United States of Southern Italians in New York City as Revealed by Survivors of the Mass-Migration, 1887–1915" (Ph.D. dissertation, New York University, 1966).

141. See the discussion of the "ways in which a smart fellow working at Gonfarone's could make money," in Sermolino, *Papa's Table d'Hote*, pp. 75–77.

142. Patri, "A Good Child?," in *Child Training* (New York, 1922), p. 199.

143. Ibid. "Be assured," Patri went on, "that is the only way you will ever be able to teach him your idea."

144. Ibid., p. 200.

145. "The Lie," p. 212.

146. Sometimes even this passive resistance was transformed into open rebellion when the basic necessities of life, i.e., food and shelter, were not forthcoming. See Cesidro Simboli, "When The Boss Went Too Far," in Francis A. J. Ianni; Wayne Moquin; and Charles Van Doren, eds., *A Documentary History of the Italian Americans* (New York, 1974), pp. 146–149.

147. Odencrantz, "Attitude of Workers," p. 100.

148. Ibid., pp. 98–99.

149. Ibid., p. 99.

150. *Christ in Concrete*, p. 299.

151. *Superintendent's Annual Circular of Greeting to the Grammar School Graduates of Bergen County, New Jersey, Class of 1900*. This book is located in the "Education" File of the Bergen County Historical Society archives, Hackensack Public Library.

152. Ibid., p. 3.

153. A. Agresti, "Chant of the Weaver," *La Questione Sociale*, 30 December 1895, p. 3.

154. "September 23," in *Edward Lear in Southern Italy: Journals of a Landscape*

Painter in Southern Calabria and the Kingdom of Naples (London, 1964), p. 188.

155. Verga, *The House by the Medlar Tree*, p. 254.

156. Bell, "Work," in *Fate and Honor, Family and Village: Demographic and Cultural Change in Rural Italy since 1800* (Chicago, 1979), p. 115.

157. See the summary of government reports by Gambino, who tells us of interest rates ranging from 400% to 1,000%, in "Reasons For Leaving," pp. 53–54.

158. See Anton Blok's *The Mafia of a Sicilian Village, 1860–1960: A Study of Violent Peasant Entrepreneurs* (New York, 1974).

159. This is the point of Georg Lukacs in "Reification and the Consciousness of the Proletariat," in *History and Class Consciousness: Studies in Marxist Dialectics* (Cambridge, Massachusetts, 1971), especially p. 87. Also refer to Victor Zitta, *Georg Lukacs' Marxism: Alienation, Dialectics, Revolution. A Study in Utopia and Ideology* (The Hague, Netherlands, 1964); and Istvan Eorsi, ed., *Georg Lukacs: Record of a Life. Autobiographical Sketch* (London, 1983).

160. Berrol, "Immigrants at School: New York City, 1900–1910," *Urban Education*, October 1969, p. 227.

161. In Covello, "Intellectual Interests of the Contadino in Relation to High School Education," p. 318.

162. *Circular of Greeting*, p. 17.

163. See Thomas M. Pitkin and Francesco Cordasso, *The Black Hand: A Chapter in Ethnic Crime* (Totowa, New Jersey, 1977); American Italian Historical Association, "An Inquiry into Organized Crime," *Third Annual Conference Proceedings* (Staten Island, New York, 1971); Humbert S. Nelli, *The Business of Crime: Italians and Syndicate Crime in the United States* (New York, 1976); and S. Merlino, "Comorra, Maffia and Brigandage," *Political Science Quarterly*, VIII, 1893, pp. 677–721.

164. Koos, "Secondary-School Pupils—Physical and Mental Growth," in *The American Secondary School* (New York, 1927), p. 49.

165. This led to conceptual muddles not effectively transcended by either the era's participants or the legions of historians who would subsequently attempt to define "progressivism." For scholars such as Peter Filene, the era's striking paradox eliminated the possibility of even defining Progressivism itself. See "An Obituary For 'The Progressive

Movement'," *American Quarterly*, 22, 1970, pp. 20–34.

166. Cavallo, *Muscles and Morals: Organized Playgrounds and Urban Reform, 1880–1920* (Philadelphia, 1981); and Benjamin Rader, *American Sports: From the Age of Folk Games to the Age of Spectators* (Englewood Cliffs, New Jersey, 1983). See Rader's chapter entitled "The Quest for Order," pp. 124–144.

167. Gulick, "Psychological, Pedagogical, and Religious Aspects of Group Games," p. 137.

168. Cavallo, "Institutional Phases, 1880–1920," p. 37.

169. Ibid., p. 37.

170. Ibid., p. 42.

171. In Covello, "Recreational Education of the School as a Source of Complaint," p. 326.

172. "Reposing at Castrovillari," p. 127.

173. All of the immigrant narratives which I have read constantly reiterate this theme. Look, for instance, at the observation of Sermolino's father:

> As papa tossed and turned in his bed that first night at the Hotel Campidoglio he could not free his mind of the lurid tales he had heard on the long voyage across the Atlantic. There were stories of immigrants beaten and robbed, of men and women kidnaped and shipped to faraway places....

Sermolino, "Three Who Eloped," pp. 22–23.

174. In Covello, "Friendship," p. 190.

175. This is most obvious in the attitude towards the *promenenti*, or what was sometimes termed the *"bossismo."* Rudolph Vecoli has captured this process in an interesting essay:

> Few of the immigrants had participated in the electoral process before coming to America, and they learned their first lessons in politics from ward-heelers. By the 1880s the naturalization mills of Jersey City and Newark were turning out Italian voters, many of whom regarded the ballot as a commodity to be sold for as little as a glass of beer.

> As the Italian vote become considerable, a system of "bossismo" was established whereby the Italian leaders delivered the vote in exchange for petty political positions. With the exception of the radicals and a few others, the immigrants were not much concerned with political issues. Political affiliation was determined by the loyalty to the "boss" was got them jobs, provided food and coal, interceded with the police, and helped them in other ways.

Vecoli, "The Italian People of New Jersey," in Barbara Cunningham, ed., *The New Jersey Ethnic Experience* (Union City, New Jersey, 1977), pp. 283–284.

176. Bertocci, "Memoir of my Mother," *Harper's Monthly Magazine*, June 1937, p. 9.

5

THE COMPLEX PATTERN OF MODIFIED PARENTAL CONTROLS THROUGH THE POSTWAR PERIOD

Long ago...in a "reversal of the generations," immigrant children came to interpret the new society to their parents.

> Andrew Rolle, *The Italian Americans: Troubled Roots*

The More Sophisticated System of Parental Control

Marie Concistre observed the pattern noted in the epigraph above while conducting anthropological field research for her 1943 Ph.D. dissertation at New York University.[1] While it appeared to Concistre that first and second generation Italian-American parents in East Harlem were loosening their control over teenage girls by allowing them the unprecedented freedom to go on dates unaccompanied by a family member serving as chaperone, a closer examination reveals that parents were in the process of constructing new and far more subtle mechanisms for youth control. Dating, the selection of a spouse, and the desirability of formal education were all areas of adolescent life in which changes appeared to be underway.[2] But underneath the tactics, moral rationales and clearly conceptualized objectives remained untouched. Not surprisingly, both the tactics and the objectives remained as stark contrasts to the trends evident among Anglo-American youth during this period. Further, one is still hard-pressed to isolate a clearly delineated period of "adolescence" in Italian-American communities through the postwar period. The control of young people evident in Italian-American families was only one of several stages of community-sanctioned restraints designed to curb the frailty of "human nature" evident throughout life. Accordingly, all of life was laden with authoritarian guidelines. The strategy employed was the only issue up for discussion.

The dominant discourse of the Anglo-American bourgeoisie during this period reveals a different perspective. The earlier trend towards the chronological delineation of adolescence intensified.[3] The clearest institutionalization of this was the prolific growth of high schools.[4] It was in the secondary school that young people were expected to internalize the values of the liberal capitalist order. Indeed, for middle class youth by the 1920s, the secondary school served as the primary point of contact between teenagers and adults. For Italian-American youth, the workplace still served as this conduit.

Italian-American parents were forced to consolidate their socialization efforts at home early on, fully aware that a diverse group of people in the workplace would influence their children in undesirable ways.[5] Attitudes toward work, dating, and marriage which were decidedly non-southern Italian would all be learned and possibly adopted by Italian-American youth. Adolescents in Anglo-American middle class high schools, however, entered an environment which served to reinforce the values evident in the communities and homes of their students.

Helen and Robert Lynd proposed this argument in their important 1929 study *Middletown: A Study in Modern American Culture.*[6] They found that it was becoming increasingly difficult to draw a clear line between the home and the school. "Today the school is becoming not a place to which children go from their homes for a few hours daily," the Lynds wrote, "but a place from which they go home to eat and sleep." An integral part of both home and school was the spirit of cooperation, or "boosterism," which emphasized the almost complete subordination of the individual to the group in a visibly enthusiastic way. This process of social immersion was learned in middle class secondary schools via the advent of such activities as the "pep rally." For middle class parents of the 1920s and 1930s, the function of adolescence was to inculcate a spirit of Rotarian community service imperative for a young man "on the make."

In a privately published history of Bergen County schools published sometime in the 1930s, Reeves D. Batten, principal of Lyndhurst High School, pointed out that thirty years before there were

> ...no such things as...school bands, football teams, basketball teams, shower baths, athletic fields, stadiums, etc.[7]

This was hardly a trivial point. Batten isolated a new and prominent feature of the middle class secondary school—athletics. Having grown from a spontaneous and relatively unorganized recreational activity of the mid-nineteenth century into a routinized and rigidly structured one by the 1920s, youth sports, as institutionalized in the high school, became the training grounds for developing the middle class desire for physical prowess, leadership, and exclusionism. Just as importantly, membership on the team began to mean a personal attractiveness which would not be there otherwise.[8]

It was also during the 1920s and 1930s that the New York metropolitan region, like America at large, witnessed the appearance of a post-high school institution which further extended the period of middle class youth training. The Junior College of Bergen County, for example, was incorporated in the summer of 1933 for the express purpose of answering "the problem of how to complete secondary education."[9] While decades later the area's junior colleges would be, as one critic argued, a "social defense mechanism that resists basic changes in the social structure," institutions which reinforce in the minds of its working and lower middle class students perceptions of always having "been second best," early community colleges such as that found in Bergen County were havens of bourgeois training.[10] As in the case of the high school, the early junior college was a school designed to teach the social graces necessary for effective competition in an increasingly organizational, bureaucratic society. Academic subjects per se were thus portrayed as relative appendages to the important task of developing social graces. In a sense, the middle class saw all of its young people in the way that it saw its athletes—in training. "Leisure" profitably pursued was an integral part of this child-rearing process, as the 1936–1938 catalog of the Junior College of Bergen made clear.

> The ability to employ leisure time wisely constitutes one of the greatest values to be gained from education. Each student finds opportunity apart from his or her program of work to participate in music, art, home economics, dramatic, athletic or social pursuits. A hall is made available for one party a month, if the student body so desires. Informal groups may be formed for the discussion of such subjects as arouse a concerted interest, from philosophy and chemistry to current events and gardening.[11]

Note the school's emphasis on becoming superficially proficient in a wide range of subjects, all known just enough to facilitate the art of conversation so espoused by the era's middle class spokesmen.[12] Even more tellingly, the catalog's writer subsequently warned against taking academic courses which would interfere with the cultivation of this art:

> In fact, we recommend that the student take not to exceed fifteen hours of academic work which will give him the required sixty hours for graduation at the end of the two year period and fill in the rest of his program to a total of eighteen hours with such subjects as Art, Foods, Clothing, Music and Dramatics. Many times these so called extras or frills will be of as much value in later life as the subject matter contained in academic courses.[13]

Thus the growing bourgeois emphasis on secondary and even junior college education was much more than a mere remedy for teenage unemployment, particularly in the depths of the 1930s. Not that this was not one consequence of public policy. But the underlying rationale, more than anything else, remained an insistence upon a prolonged period of institutional socialization between the ages of fourteen and twenty-two. The values of Babbitt-like boosterism taught in the home were continued in the school. Otherwise stingy taxpayers in the developing suburbs of northern New Jersey were willing to pay for what was now seen as crucial. Frances

A. Westervelt, a member of an old and prosperous Bergen County family, who served as the curator of the elite Bergen County Historical Society in 1923, pointed out that the following high schools all opened in 1922 alone. The cost of each building was recorded as follows:[14]

NEW BERGEN COUNTY HIGH SCHOOLS, 1922

Park Ridge	$265,000.00
Tenafly	$300,000.00
Westwood	$150,000.00
Closter	$ 75,000.00
Rutherford	$325,000.00

Despite the growing Anglo-American bourgeois insistence on prolonging both the qualitative and quantitative aspects of adolescence, Italian-American parents continued to reject the very idea of adolescence itself. Accordingly, the secondary school, not to mention the junior college, was generally dismissed as an institution irrelevant to the reality of young people who had become adults by, at the absolute latest, fifteen or sixteen years of age. In a 1940 guidance counselor report in an East Harlem high school we thus find that

> ...Anthony V., sixteen years old, attending public school, who formerly was an obedient boy and a regular attendant at school has started to show a truancy pattern and a defiant attitude toward school.... Father feels that the son should be given a mechanical education if school is to be of any use to Anthony. Otherwise, the father feels that the boy is very mature and that naturally his mind is set on going to work and not on attending school.[15]

Other Italian-American parents in East Harlem also rejected the high school fixation with adolescence. Leonard Covello, a principal at Benjamin Franklin High School from 1934 to 1956, recalled that

> In a recent interview with a mother and her son who had been a truant and was failing all his subjects, I

> turned to the boy and said to him: "Why you are a
> full-grown man. Just think of it, sixteen years of
> age..." and before I could finish, the mother inter-
> rupted and said, "Why he should have been a man
> and acted like a man when he was thirteen years of
> age. His father went to work when he was nine
> years old...."[16]

Covello also tells us about someone he names only as "L.V." "L.V.,"
a student at Benjamin Franklin in 1943, was fourteen and a half years of age
when he became disruptive in the classroom, openly defying the teachers,
and embroidering his behavior with verbal obscenities. When L.V.'s mother
met with a representative for the school, she defended her son's behavior.
In a response which would have absolutely shocked an administrator
ignorant of southern Italian peasant culture, she attributed L.V.'s behavior
to maturity. She told Covello that

> I don't mind if he goes to school. I would be very
> proud to have a learned man in our family. But then
> again, I am against his being tortured. The teachers
> have no sympathy for him; they don't realize that it
> is hard for Leo to sit in class with babies around
> him...Leo is coming of age, he is almost fifteen years
> old; the teachers should know that....[17]

Other sources also reveal the Italian-American refusal to acknowledge
adolescence. In Concistre's sample survey of one hundred Italian-American
families in East Harlem in 1934, she found that 37% of the parents in Cohort
A did not care if their sons attended high school.[18] Cohort B parents
registered a higher rate of approval, though it was still decidedly less than
half: 46%. With respect to daughters, the percentages were about the same.
Cohort A parents registered a 38% approval rate, while those in Cohort B
amounted to 43%. In all cases, a trade school of some kind was seen as the
most viable option if an educational institution was considered at all. A
trade school in America was analogous to an apprenticeship in the
Mezzogiorno, as some parents argued.

An important component of the Anglo-American conception of
adolescence was the development of abstract reasoning. A spontaneous sort

of "creativity" was accordingly spoken of by parents, school officials, and child psychologists alike.[19] Conversely, Italian-American parents persisted in their dismissal of such talents as irrelevant to the demands of working-class life. In October of 1925, Theresa S. Koldin and Dorothy W. Seago found out just how pervasive this sentiment was. In a study conducted under the auspices of New York City's Vocational Service for Juniors, the two set out to compare the cognitive processes of twelve-year-old sixth graders who were either Italian-American or Jewish.[20] During the academic years of 1923–24 and 1924–25, 2,259 of these pupils were tested. All of the students were from the working class districts of Manhattan's lower east side. The goal of Koldin and Seago was straightforward: "Are Jewish children superior to Italians in the understanding and use of language and in abstract-verbal reasoning...?" Adjusting for language difficulties evident among children of both groups, Koldin and Seago concluded that the

> ...superiority of twelve-year-old Jewish boys in the
> 6B grade over Italians of the same sex, age and grade
> is most marked in mental functions involved in the
> use and comprehension of language and in abstract-
> verbal reasoning. It is less marked in mental func-
> tions involved in concrete non-verbal reasoning.

Initially, the peasant and, later, his or her working class descendants in New Jersey and New York, drew a clear correlation between formal education and the acquisition of material possessions—especially a house. What would be the point of embarking upon a costly and time-consuming pursuit of a diploma when a trade could be learned at so much less expense—and accomplish the same results? Trades such as masonry, tailoring, or baking did not require the abstractions of political theory or a knowledge of the finer points of plane geometry. Instead, a trade led to immediate, tangible results. Even in the work of an unskilled laborer there was the immediate revelation of a task rewarded with an obvious testimony to self-worth—a pay envelope. There was no necessary reason for an extended period of youthful self-discovery.

This ideology combined with the structural imperatives of occupational stagnation during the first several decades of the twentieth century. Young Italian-American men entered occupations in which both intellectual abstractions and the high school emphasis on developing organizational men were irrelevant. While the number of unskilled laborers decreased dramatically between 1916 and 1931, well over half of the occupations by the later date were still devoid of the very qualities emphasized by the era's secondary schools and junior colleges. A list of these jobs is shown below.[21]

LEADING OCCUPATIONS: ITALIAN-AMERICAN BRIDEGROOMS, NEW YORK CITY, 1916 AND 1931

		1916	
RANK	OCCUPATION	NUMBER	%
1	Laborer	2,389	32.5
2	Tailor	498	6.8
3	Barber	342	4.7
4	Shoemaker	255	3.5
5	Driver	200	2.7
6	Carpenter	152	2.1
7	Clerk	117	1.6
8	Machinist	115	1.6
9	Cook	104	1.4
10	Waiter	104	1.4
11	Presser	89	1.2
12	Coal Dealer	85	1.2
13	Painter	78	1.1
14	Chauffeur	76	1.0
15	Ice Dealer	73	1.0
16	Piano Maker	71	1.0
17	Mechanic	70	1.0
18	Fruit Dealer	68	.9
19	Butcher	66	.9
20	Longshoreman	64	.9
21	Salesman	64	.9
22	Baker	56	.8
23	Printer	55	.7
24	Bricklayer	50	.7

25	Mason	49	.7
26	Plasterer	48	.7
27	Musician	47	.6
28	Grocer	43	.6
29	Cigar Maker	39	.5
30	Operator	34	.5
31	Bootblack	33	.4
32	Merchant	33	.4
33	Electrician	27	.4
34	Hatter	27	.4
35	Cabinet Maker	25	.3
36	Candy Maker	25	.3
36 Leading Occupations		5,671	77.4
All Other Occupations		1,315	17.8
Unknown		355	4.8
TOTAL		7,341	100.0

1931

RANK	OCCUPATION	NUMBER	%
1	Laborer	402	10.6
2	Chauffeur	224	5.9
3	Barber	186	4.9
4	Tailor	140	3.7
5	Shoemaker	108	2.9
6	Clerk	105	2.8
7	Painter	99	2.6
8	Mechanic	94	2.5
9	Salesman	92	2.4
10	Baker	79	2.1
11	Plasterer	76	2.1
12	Carpenter	71	1.9
13	Cook	60	1.6
14	Presser	60	1.6

15	Butcher	59	1.6
16	Ice Dealer	55	1.5
17	Waiter	54	1.5
18	Printer	50	1.3
19	Bricklayer	46	1.2
20	Driver	46	1.2
21	Operator	43	1.1
22	Ice Man	41	1.1
23	Machinist	40	1.1
24	Plumber	33	.9
25	Electrician	31	.8
26	Cabinet Maker	22	.6
27	Upholsterer	20	.5
28	Grocer	19	.5
29	Fruit Dealer	18	.5
30	Fruit Store	18	.5
31	Laundry Worker	18	.5
32	Restaurant Worker	18	.5
33	Auto Mechanic	17	.5
34	Contractor	17	.5
35	Cutter	17	.5
36	Mason	17	.5

36 Leading Occupations		2,495	66.3
All Other Occupations		1,415	33.2
Unknown		20	.5
TOTAL		3,930	100.0

Thus in New Jersey and New York, adulthood became evident through the acquisition of "working papers" which, in the first several decades of the twentieth century in the New York metropolitan area, could be legally secured at the age of fourteen.[22] At that point parents spoke of their "adult" children. One father proudly boasted that

My oldest son C [the identity of the respondent was

> kept confidential] was always a very obedient son.
> I cannot remember a single instance when we had
> reason to complain about him. He was always a
> hard worker and gave us every penny he earned.
> Even while in school, he managed to bring home
> from two to seven dollars a week. At the age of
> fourteen he began to lose interest in school. We
> could see he was not made to be a scholar so I got
> him a job at the docks....[23]

This same father held a different view of another son of his, one who insisted upon going to high school and not obtaining working papers.

> ...that fellow is different. I begged him, my wife
> begged him to work with his brother at the docks
> where they pay a man's wages. But no, his mind
> was set to continue school after he was fifteen years
> old. Now he has the diploma. What good is it to
> him? What good is it to his parents? While he was
> a boy he gave very little to his mother. Then for
> three years that he went to high school, all he gave
> us was twenty-two dollars....[24]

Aside from an uneasiness over the intellectual abstractions taught in the classroom, Italian-American parents of the first two generations generally had a very hard time accepting the integral role of organized athletics in a school setting. Again, this perspective was also rooted in the conception of what it meant to be a student in southern Italy. Secondary school pupils there were expected to approach their studies with professional commitment and seriousness.[25] To attend school in nineteenth-century Naples or Palermo was to be absolutely certain concerning one's calling. In effect, secondary education, as well as university work, was seen by the lower middle class as just another form of training undertaken by an adult. Play, be it football, baseball, or any other sport, was seen as a simple waste of time better put to use elsewhere. Again, we can detect the insistence upon a clearly recognizable prize which brought equally clear financial rewards.

Not understanding the real objectives of early athletic directors, Italian-American parents condemned what they viewed as childish behavior unbecoming adults. "I always thought of the school as a place where one has to study," declared one mother in East Harlem. "But play?" she asked quizzically.[26] Not only did parents view such behavior as undignified for a man in training for a trade or profession, but just as importantly, American team sports struck them as invitations to physical injury. Life is fraught with enough hardship, parents reasoned, so why invite more unnecessarily?[27]

Within this context let us return momentarily to the writings of the Italian-American adolescent theorist Angelo Patri. Patri was a rare man among his contemporaries. His parents had emigrated from the Salerno area sometime around 1883, settling in New York City.[28] Gaining an almost unheard of college education, Patri became the first Italian-American to be named a principal of a public school in the United States. City authorities assigned him to Public School 45 in a section of the Bronx inhabited chiefly by Italian-Americans. His school stood as a veritable testament of opposition to what he most detested about Italian-American childrearing practices: the imitative model of learning and the school's concept of the student. In a 1938 Federal Writers' Project entitled *The Italians of New York*, WPA writers characterized P.S. 45 as

> ...one of the country's model educational institutions. In this school young American-born Italians have exceptional opportunities to experiment according to their abilities and inclinations, and to learn arts, trades and the elements of professions for which they may have special aptitudes. Permanent exhibitions of paintings, sculptures, and handicraft products...are further evidences of Mr. Patri's talent as an educator.[29]

While Patri was still obliged to placate the parents of the area with a book-printing plant, his overall insistence on creativity was a clear departure from traditional peasant emphasis. Patri's interest in combating parental rejections of intellectual abstractions and artistic experimentation extended to the playing field as well. For him, organized athletics were an important part of the school's curriculum.[30] "Loosen up the rigid school," he asked Italian-American parents in 1925.[31] "Let go," he asked, "of the cherished belief that the school must be a silent place." He then went on to depict his ideal school. In his idealization, so radical in the Italian-American community of the Bronx, we can detect his sense of desperation in not being listened to by the very people he so wanted to reach:

> Pile up the experiences and make them as vivid as may be. Excursions, play spaces, music rooms, woodworking shops and quiet classrooms, busy laboratories, a library, an auditorium, a swimming pool and a toy room are all needed by the school....
>
> Every child must be allowed to work out his own salvation, travel at his own rate and in his own characteristic way.
>
> The right sort of school will make provision for a program so fluid that no child can suffer because of the rigidity of grading. Promotions will occur whenever the child is ready. There will be no formal promotion day.[32]

But Italian-American parents in the Bronx were not persuaded. Nor were their counterparts in Newark, as an examination of the Board of Education's truancy rates among Italian-American students during the 1920s attests.[33] In Paterson, a review of the Board of Education reports for the period also reveals the same trend towards truancy among Italian-Americans in the city's "Dublin" district,[34] an area of Paterson near the Passaic River, largely comprised of textile mills. It contained, in the 1930s, four of the city's elementary schools. Each of these had enrollments in which more than half of the student body spoke only Italian.[35]

Given their perspective, Italian parents were compelled to devise unprecedented guilt mechanisms which, on the surface, proved to be a radical departure from the openly imitative model of behavior. These tactics, which are most detectable in the texts of novelists, autobiographies, and participatory observations recorded by anthropologists and sociologists, were typically evident in dating rituals and the early stages of spousal selection. Just as in the earlier outlook of the peasants and the early working class, the context for these rituals was the conservative view of human nature. With this in mind, let us return to the important writings of Concistre in East Harlem.

Through an examination of her observations in the 1930s and early

1940s, a complex historical divergence between Italian-American child-rearing practices and those of the Anglo-American bourgeoisie begins to emerge. As we have already seen, earlier theorists of adolescence such as Marden and Gulick emphasized the necessity of self-direction and spontaneous creativity. They also assumed the possibility of young people achieving moral perfection—"morality," of course, being defined as a complex arrangement of eternal "truths." As a result, it was expected that adolescents, having been properly taught what is right and what is wrong, could then go out unaccompanied into the world without transgressing standards of decency. In short, a process of internalization had been completed.

But as scholars such as Paula Fass and Joseph Kett have convincingly demonstrated, the advent of such technological variables as mass-produced automobiles in the 1920s forced middle-class parents to confront the possibility that, theories of moral perfectibility aside, young people were inclined to engage in what were generally considered immoral activities: especially illicit sex and the consumption of alcoholic beverages. Kett thus argued that

> The behavior of flaming youth stood poised between
> conventionality and unconventionality, marked by
> what David Matza has called drift. "Drift," Matza
> has written, "stands midway between freedom and
> control. Its basis is an area of the social structure in
> which control has been loosened."[36]

It was precisely this "drift" that middle class parents and educators in New Jersey and New York sought to counter in full force by the 1920s. In effect, often without publicly acknowledging it, they surrendered an earlier belief in the internalization of moral restraints. The perfectibility of the adolescent was still possible, but it would have to come about through prolonged institutional coercion.[37]

It was at this historical juncture that Italian-American parents in East Harlem were abandoning the older imitative models of childrearing. The firm belief in unquestioning obedience was as strong in the second and third generations as it had been in the first. The difference, however, was one of strategic emphasis. Unable and unwilling to construct their own institutional extensions of the home and community, parents came to rely on the internalization methods being abandoned by the middle class. Older forms of coercion, especially constant supervision and threats of physical punishments, gave way to the new spectacle of guilt. From this perspective, the seemingly radical shift in dating and spousal selection rituals become comprehensible. On a more subtle level, they reveal the strong element of continuity lying underneath the surface changes. We thus find out that 87 out of 100 parents questioned by Concistre in the early 1940s insisted that in accordance with American custom, a young woman should be permitted to select her husband.[38] The formal practice of marriage arrangement was thus being discarded. Parents were therefore able to seemingly accede to American customs without really relinquishing an older insistence on strict supervision.

Therefore, a key element in this regard was the illusion that young people were in fact making free choices. As a result, the older manifestations of chaperonage, in which parents, grandparents, or older brothers accompanied the daughter on a "date," began to break down.[39] Fully half of the mothers questioned by Concistre allowed their daughters to select a boyfriend, as long as he visited the daughter at home in the company of family.[40] Fifty-one percent of the mothers would, or would have, allowed their daughters to go out of the house with a boyfriend as long as the couple remained in a group of young people. Sixty-four percent of the mothers only allowed their daughters to go on a date completely unaccompanied when such an outing was with the fiancé.

This same group of mothers also endorsed modified supervision for young men. A whopping 93% of the mothers interviewed insisted upon some sort of "supervision" for young men "under age or living at home." "Under age" ranged from sixteen to twenty-one years old. The sort of control evident among young women was not confined merely to the 16–21 male age group, as Concistre remarked that some mothers expressed "the opinion that such supervision should last as long as the boys are in the home or until they marry."

Young Sirola in George Cuomo's novel *Family Honor* also experienced this new form of supervision. Cuomo is a third-generation Italian-American who was born in the Bronx in 1929.[41] A prolific novelist, he has recorded his impressions of life in the Bronx in a variety of guises.[42] But it is in his depiction of the young man Sirola, and specifically, Sirola's courting practices, that we are able to glimpse at a relatively hidden world. The problem for Sirola's family was that the young man's sexuality might lead to a disastrous marriage or unwanted pregnancy—or both. Unable to completely counteract the influence of an Anglo-American culture which endorsed dating, Sirola's family sought to provide him with a young woman who would conduct herself with a restraint not displayed by the neighborhood's Dorrie, Janie, or Bridget.

Accordingly, "the whole family, scoured the neighborhood for acceptable girls." "Acceptable" meant Italian. Aunt Serafina encouraged him to date a "tantalizingly...Italian girl from across Tremont." "'Nice, nice,'" his middle-aged aunt repeated." "'A good big girl,' Aunt Serafina said, 'you'll like her.'" Cuomo wrote that on their date the

> ...two of them sat like a pair of wrapped mummies
> at the Belmont Theater while Sirola imagined himself
> crawling up to her under the sheets. He said good
> night in front of her apartment without even touch-
> ing her hand. She was too neatly starched, too
> awesomely pious, and gave every indication of
> believing that beneath their layers of clothing human
> beings were as smooth as china dolls.

Cuomo's literary characterization of this new mode of supervision implies that it was effective. Just as importantly from a parental point of view, it served to facilitate marriage between Italian-Americans. As a number of scholars have discovered, the long-term trend among this group towards endogamy was powerful indeed.[43] This trend was also evident in smaller statistical samples, as the work of Valentine R. Winsey reveals.

In the early 1960s, Winsey conducted a series of fascinating interviews at East Harlem's La Guardia House.[44] She spoke with seventy-nine elderly Italian-Americans who frequented this settlement house, where they enjoyed a subsidized lunch program and the fellowship of others with a similar class and ethnic background. The population interviewed by Winsey in such depth were all descendants of immigrants who arrived at Ellis Island between 1900 and 1915. In their lengthy discussions with Winsey, they noted an internalization process in their youth which led to 85% of them marrying "Americans born of Italian extraction."[45] One 67-

year-old respondent, who was a retired bottle filler with the Borden milk company, recalled that as a young worker in a silk mill, he was influenced to look for an Italian-American wife devoid of romantic illusions; one who understood the paramount importance of "the house and the boys."[46] For after all, marriage was, "you understand—not for love."

In the end, therefore, marriage in America, like marriage between the peasants of the Italian south, focused as much on practicality as it ever had. The difference in America was the tendency of parents to allow room for some romance through modified dating patterns. Despite this modification, however, the needs of young people were still subordinated to the perceived reality of having to adapt to a hard working-class life. Italian-American youth were therefore not the focus of a long-range family program designed to develop all of their capacities to the fullest.[47] This was also true for those few young people who desired higher education.

The Lack of a Child-Centered Family

Looking back on his thirty-five years as a New York city resident, a 76-year-old man from Campobasso recalled a proverb which he has "always lived by;" one that he initially learned in his youth. *"Fa bene, ascoltaci; fa male, pensarci"* ("Do good, and listen, do evil, and think").[48] Such proverbs were concrete manifestations of the long-standing repudiation of abstract conceptualizing which I have already suggested. As in the case of chaperonage, surface modifications should not be confused with the continuity of underlying premises. It is true that from 1920 on, a growing number of Italian-Americans in New Jersey and New York were attending local colleges and universities, though in absolute percentages, their number still constituted a very small group indeed. In Newark in the early 1940s, for example, Italian-Americans constituted a fifth of the city's total population.[49] Yet they made up no more than 12% of the Newark State Teacher's College total student population. At the University of Newark, which later became the Newark College of Arts and Sciences—Rutgers University, there were 70 Italian-American students. They thus constituted 8.4% of the university's student population.[50]

ITALIAN-AMERICAN REPRESENTATION AT THE
UNIVERSITY OF NEWARK AS OF NOVEMBER 1, 1941

School	Both Parents Italian	One Part Italian
Business	25	14
Arts & Sciences	22	2
Law	7	0
TOTALS	54	16

But absolute numerical representations do not fully address my concern in this section. All too often, scholars such as Charles W. Churchill, who initially compiled these statistics, saw the rise in Italian-American enrollments as a sign that assimilation was taking place. Even more dramatically, they have been quick to conclude that growing college enrollments meant the advent of American-style adolescence and a break with rural Italian notions concerning education. Churchill, for instance, noted without elaboration that when "questioned as to the amount of schooling necessary to get a good job...40 percent thought college would be needed."[51]

Instead, formal education was understood, from a parental perspective, as an investment in the future. But unlike the Anglo-American middle class, the investment was not in the young person's future, but rather, in that of the parents. With a perspective not qualitatively very different from the Agrigento peasant who said that "a father with many children is like a king with many vassals," a Sicilian emigrant in New York City pointed out that in America

> ...a parent has to wait long years till everything that was spent on the child comes back.... Some parents even keep track of what the upbringing of a particular child costs them, and they tell the amount to the son or the daughter so that they know how much is

> expected from them....
>
> I, myself, don't think much of giving an education to a girl for there is no chance to be repaid. Everything she earns in later life belongs to her husband. With a boy it is different. One can take a chance even on his going to school for, if he is an obedient son, he will return the cost of his upkeep with interest....
>
> But as I say, you have to wait and be watchful all the time.[52]

In order to facilitate a return on their investment, those Italian-American parents who endorsed the idea of post-grammar school training insisted upon career tracks which culminated in particular occupations. Throughout the process of career selection, the desire of the young person was subordinated to the immediate material and status concerns of the parents. Like the Sicilian quoted by Covello, the Rochester parents of writer Jerre Mangione were intent upon selecting work which would bring a return on their investment.

Young Jerre remembered that his parents viewed college in the following way:

> ...America bella! Here a poor Sicilian who earned his bread shining shoes could, by shining more shoes, send his son through college and see him become an avvocato or dottore. It was wonderful because then, presto, the poor Sicilian was no longer poor. He could stop shining shoes and he and his wife could live comfortably for the rest of their lives, confident that the son for whom they have made so many sacrifices would support them and honor them. Not only that—but they would enjoy a great deal more "respect" among their paesani....[53]

From this passage in Mangione's autobiography, it is clear that Jerre's parents viewed their son's education as a form of security for themselves. Despite the fact that this lofty ambition "dazzled" their neighbors, the Mangione family early on "started conditioning me [Jerre] for those professions even while I was still young enough to want to be a streetcar conductor more than anything else in the world."

Jerre soon outgrew his earlier ambition to be a streetcar conductor. Accordingly, he began to follow the path set by his parents and uncle. His family soon became dismayed with Jerre when they realized he had become too American in his views on morality. They attributed this development to his public school education. As a result, Jerre recalls that "it was obvious to everyone that I would never make an avvocato." "My Uncle Nino," he added, "pointed out that I was far too sensitive and too honest. So my mother told me I would be a doctor." But after a physician had failed to prevent the death of Giuseppina, Mangione's younger sister, Jerre "refused to become a doctor."

His parents and Uncle Nino, having exhausted the first two career possibilities for Jerre, subsequently turned to the third level of the occupational hierarchy: "*farmacista*." This time Uncle Luigi stepped in to help "by suggesting" this career really suited Jerre. Luigi quickly went on to point out the numerous benefits of being a druggist. In terms of prestige, Jerre's parents would be honored through their son's use of the title "Farmacista," rather than a mere "Mr." Luigi then argued that pharmacists "were respected almost as much as doctors and they had a far easier time." He reassured Jerre's parents that the pharmaceutical business was a "profitable" one; in which druggists "collected their money on the spot." He then cited another advantage:

> A pharmacist could charge you anything he wished
> for a few grains of powder or a little medicine and
> no one would ever dare complain for fear he would
> put poison in the medicine you bought the next
> time.[54]

It was decided that Jerre would be a pharmacist.

Eventually, Jerre lost interest in being a pharmacist. A long struggle thus set in between Jerre and his parents which culminated at age eighteen. Working his way through high school, Jerre's "curiosity about the outer American world" became more intense. Working at one point in the public library, his interests grew to include a wide variety of subjects. Although by now rejecting the idea of being a pharmacist, he nonetheless wished to attend college. Despite his parents' earlier desire to see their son acquire a profession, they had by now grown suspect of what Jerre was being taught. In an essay entitled "Growing Up Sicilian," Jerre wrote that

> In his thunderings against our teachers my father
> must have sensed that the philosophy they drummed
> into us was diametrically opposed to that of his
> people. There was nothing fatalistic about it; con-
> stantly our teachers talked of freedom, free enter-
> prise, free will, and stressed the ability of the indi-
> vidual to change and improve his situation.[55]

When eighteen-year-old Jerre announced in the fall of 1928 that he was going to Syracuse University to learn how "to write for a living," the worst fears of his parents and close relatives were confirmed. Mangione wrote that

> My relatives were nettled to hear that instead of
> studying medicine, law, or pharmacy I planned to
> study no particular subject but a number of subjects,
> with the idea of equipping myself for newspaper
> work. My Aunt Giovanna threw up her hands. 'Ma
> chi si stupidu!' she said.[56]

Jerre's mother "was not sure what I was talking about when I told her I was going to write for a living." "She looked worried," Mangione wrote, "and said she should never have permitted me to read so many books." But soon a solution was reached, as Jerre described.

> Could I not become a teacher instead; or at least
> train to be a teacher, so that I would have something
> to fall back on it I couldn't earn a livelihood as a
> writer? Maestro. It was obviously the fourth item
> on her list of the most respected professions. I was
> the oldest, the only one in the family who was going
> to get a college education.[57]

Along with his mother's adherence to a strict hierarchical ordering of lofty occupations, this passage is also interesting for another reason. Other autobiographies, oral testimonies, and sociological observations dating from this period also show that Italian-American parents placed no great emphasis on what the young person himself really desired.[58] Further, the only reason higher education was warranted at all was because it was perceived as a form of apprenticeship leading to established occupational categories. Accordingly, Jerre's mother was uneasy over such an amorphous undertaking as "writing," which did not, in itself, contain unique qualities. It was only special characteristics which could be sold in the marketplace.

The parents of Manhattan's Harry Roskolenko worried about their son too. There was, however, a dramatic difference in the sort of worrying taking place. Even though the Roskolenko family in the early 1920s were East side "wage slaves" who had fled the Russian pogroms over a decade before, even though Harry and his brother Herschel early on were compelled by necessity to work as riveters at the Hog Island Shipyards, and even though their father was "still seating over a pressing iron," Harry's memoirs reflect a parental advocacy of intellectual creativity not evident in the autobiographies of a Covello, Mangione, or Di Donato.[59] Just as importantly, Harry's parents, despite their pressing poverty, never called upon their children to normalize alienation and the rigor of the timeclock as a way of coping. When Harry's mother became anxious over her son's reading habits, it was because they seemed to be taking him away from Judaism as a religion. But to spend one's spare time transcending the workplace was quite another thing. In time, parental approval of intellectual abstractions and explorations translated into social mobility for the young Jews of Harry's Cherry Street. One of Harry's friends

> ...became a professor of English literature and a specialist on Henry James; a second became a scientist, specializing in mathematical values; a third, a social historian; a fourth,...a famous editor....[60]

The effort of these young Jewish workers, which culminated in movement out of the ghetto, stood in stark contrast to the lives of their Italian neighbors. It is appropriate to consider why this was so. We must therefore turn to the Italian-American definition of success through the postwar period.

The "New" Image of Success

Just as in the period before 1920, submission to authority, an acceptance of alienation as natural, localism, and perceptions of discrimination all emerge mid-century when Italian-Americans wrote about their vision of "success."[61] Their often unique interpretation of that concept stood in contrast to the blazing confidence of Anglo-American bourgeois parents who taught their children that material and emotional gratification was a birthright secured through hard work designed to achieve specific goals, that upward mobility equaled geographical instability, and that prejudice was not applicable to a young person with big dreams. Further, Anglo-American young people were told to think beyond pre-ordained occupations and bureaucratic practices. In a prelude to what Norman Vincent Peale would later term "positive thinking," John Dewey delivered a 1931 Inglis Lecture at Harvard in which he urged teachers to encourage adolescents to think for themselves.

> Does not the presentation in doses and chunks of a ready-made subject matter inevitably conduce to passivity? The mentally active scholar will acknowledge, I think, that his mind roams far and wide. All is grist that comes to his mill, and he does not limit his supply of grain to any one fenced-off field. Yet the mind does not merely roam abroad. It returns with what is found, and there is constant exercise of judgment to detect relations, relevancies, bearing upon the central theme. The outcome is a continuously growing intellectual integration. There is absorption; but it is eager and willing, not reluctant and forced. There is digestion, assimilation, not merely the carrying of a load by memory, a load to be cast off as soon as the day comes when it is safe to throw it off. Within the limits set by capacity and experience this kind of seeking and using, of amassing and organizing, is the process of learning everywhere and at any age.[62]

Dewey expressed in a lecture on educational theory the process of middle-class parenting. His emphasis on growth implied both a disintegration of extended family ties and a geographic mobility which leads to cosmopolitanism. In effect, Dewey embodied the bourgeois view that constant supervision of one kind or another is an inappropriate way to raise young people.

The Italian-American family, however, endorsed the idea of direct supervision. Even as this gave way to modified practices, such as new forms of chaperonage, the emphasis remained on direct supervision of some sort throughout the adolescent period. One of the primary consequences of this practice was the development of a personality well-suited to accept as natural the dictates of authority in the workplace. Anglo-American middle class youth, however, began to learn at an early age that authority, if it was present at all, was a distant source which did not supervise them on a daily, routinized basis. They would thus have to make judgments on their own. Maybe more importantly, they soon realized that they would have few resources at hand to help them reach those judgments. Having made decisions on their own without the help of others above them, they were forced to accept the consequences of those plans as theirs alone. To triumph was to gain social dignity and an immense amount of self-respect. To fail was to be completely alone, for there was no one to blame when there was no advice forthcoming.

Direct supervision, modified or not, required geographical closeness. This issue of geographic mobility was the one faced by young Mangione when he "broke the news that [he] was going to an out-of-town university—Syracuse...."[63] His "relatives," we are told, "were plainly horrified." Mangione explained.

> Could it be that I was becoming a calloused American? The idea that I could bear to leave them behind offended some of them. They began to regard me as a heretic. A good Sicilian son stuck near his family; the only time he left it was to marry, and even then he lived close by so that he could see his relatives often. Life, after all, was being with each other. You never left your flesh and blood of your own free will. You left only when it was impossible to earn a living near them, or when you died.[64]

A study of demographic trends among Italian-Americans in cities such as Newark reveals just how effective the parental advocacy of stable residences were, and how that reflected a rejection of employment or educational opportunities which took young people away for extended periods of time. As early as 1910, Newark Italian-Americans resided primarily in four ward areas.[65] In 1975 Robert Corbo, a geographer who studied the Newark area, gave graphic representation to the trends outlined in Newark city records and federal census tracts.[66] Each of the areas studied by Corbo revealed that Italian-Americans were remaining in the same neighborhoods as their parents and grandparents. The core centers of 1910 remained the same in 1940, though they were obviously larger in size.

A surface consideration of the increasing number of Italian-American lawyers and teachers graduating from institutions like the University of Newark might lead one to argue that second and third generation Italian-Americans in the lower middle class were on their way to becoming full-fledged members of the bourgeoisie. Without looking at the housing patterns noted above, this is a tempting interpretation. But it is one which ignores the group's definition of success. For this demographic trend elsewhere included the ideal of a trade practiced in the area of one's birth. Despite an easing of language problems by 1945, along with other surface modifications of peasant customs, the older peasant practice of viewing neighborhoods as regions populated by *"paesano"* still held true.[67] Parents conveyed to their children the emotional importance of the local area, an emphasis rooted in the continuity of ritual and fixed guidelines for the establishment of social status. Pride was felt in the neighborhood's bustling shops and rows of brownstones and modest lawns owned by the descendants of landless peasants. When Leonard Covello was working for a master's degree at Columbia, he was one of the young professionals forced to decide where his profession should be practiced. His reaction was revealing:

> ...openings to teach French occurred at Wesleyan and Syracuse Universities. Here was an opportunity to realize my goal—a professorship. Yet the pay was such that I could not possibly afford to take either of these jobs. To do so would have meant leaving New

York....[68]

The possibility of practicing his craft in the area of his birth meant as much to Covello as the realities of finances and the increased prestige of a professorship. Covello had been taught by his parents that it was only by rising upward within the confines of his native region that success could be attained. What would be the use of traveling upward if neighbors and family could not see it on a daily basis? The pharmaceutical field was a clear example of this tendency. Between 1927 and 1946, 183 Italian-Americans received degrees in pharmacy from Rutgers University.[69] With most Italian-American communities located in northern New Jersey, it is not surprising that 86% of these graduates practiced in northern counties, as shown below.[70]

NUMBER AND PERCENTAGE OF
ITALIAN-AMERICAN PHARMACISTS
IN NORTHERN NEW JERSEY COUNTIES,
1927–1946

COUNTY	NUMBER	%
Essex	81	44.2
Hudson	47	25.6
Passaic	16	8.7
Bergen	13	7.1
TOTALS	157	85.7

Rooting success in one's neighborhood meant a suspicious attitude towards any form of cosmopolitanism for two reasons. Recall that the perception of cosmopolitanism undermined the goal of a localistic moral consensus. The potential introduction of new forms of social organization was threatening to the emergent lower middle class precisely because it could disrupt the local hierarchy which now legitimized a rise upward from the working class. Old peasant conceptions of distinct class levels thus combined with New World opportunities to reinforce an old and familiar conservatism. Any potential disruption of the class hierarchy was equated with a dreaded social disorder. Let us return momentarily to our group of New Jersey pharmacists. In October, 1936, Italian-American pharmacists in Newark met at Mike D'Allegro's pharmacy.[71] They formed an organization initially called "The Italian-American Pharmacists Association of New Jersey." Eventually, the name was changed to the "Pharmacist Guild of New Jersey." Along with organizing scholarship funds for Italian-American students at Rutgers, the Association sponsored numerous community activities. In a 1961 pamphlet entitled *A Brief History of the Pharmacist Guild of New Jersey*, Rocco Misurell wrote

> How brilliant, how successful, how active have Guild Members been in their chosen profession? This can be answered by giving the names of those who have reached the greatest height, membership on the State Board of Pharmacy. We see such men as Adolf Palumbo, Joe De Rosa, Emil Martini, Anthony De Rosa, and today we have Mike Vitale, Commissioner and Secretary to the Board. This is indeed a tremendous achievement. Here is an American minority group whose parents were immigrants from Italy and yet they have added their culture, their wealth of experience to the betterment of our democratic way of life. In this, the Pharmacist Guild of New Jersey is proud and happy to serve, work, play and live in the great land of America.

Italian-American pharmacists were far more than just a group of Horatio Algers. In the ethnic enclaves of cities such as Newark, their upward mobility tended to preserve the traditional sense of social hierarchy. While some historians tend to view any class mobility as evidence of community disintegration, groups such as those which formed at D'Allegro's drugstore provided a new form of old leadership which perpetuated the existence of a "*paese*" grounded in a rigid social hierarchy. Just as the *Mezzogiorno* artisans were distinguished from unskilled laborers by the relative independence and the status attached to that lifestyle, so too were Italian-American pharmacists whose public respect translated into public leadership.[72]

But that leadership did not, nor could it, transcend the boundaries of the ward for the great majority of pharmacists, physicians, attorneys, engineers, or teachers—because that leadership, which was largely the result of the prestige attached to an independent lifestyle and the ownership of property, was rooted in the local area.[73] Further, this was not a leadership which generally fostered community goodwill, for its cornerstone rested on the conscious cultivation of envy among the unskilled workers. This had been a prominent feature of the *Mezzogiorno* village, and it was replicated in the Italian-American wards of New Jersey and New York.[74] Being economically dependent on this group with respect to such matters as credit and placement in jobs requiring local endorsement, the workers were generally reluctant to openly castigate this New World elite.[75] The new elite had therefore taken over the roles filled by the *galantuomini* in southern Italy. It was a conservative system of reciprocal relations clothed in the garment of liberal mobility, and it thrived in what appeared to be an essentially closed world. Any introduction of outside ideas would only serve to weaken that perception. In her autobiography, Connie Rose Marie Franconero (whose stage name was Connie Francis) later remembered, as a young woman in one of Newark's "Little Italys" on Walnut Street in the mid-1940s, how

> In my neighborhood if you weren't Italian, not only were you a foreigner, but worse yet, you were American. (It's comical, but even today many Italian people still think this way. One can be anything—Polish, Greek, Spanish—but anybody non-Italian is considered American.)[76]

Success as the cultivation of local prestige and the rejection of outside influences led to an acceptance of authority not usually visible in the Anglo-American families of this area. Obviously, the authority which could most easily be challenged was that which was confronted daily—family and local elites. Cosmopolitanism, again through the introduction of new ideas, was viewed as undermining these two very conservative forces. Adolescents were accordingly supervised either directly or through a series of indirect measures that I have already suggested. This supervision tended to produce an outlook for both the lower middle and the working classes which reinforced the legitimacy of domination. One was free to disagree with the authority of a parent, but only to a degree determined beforehand for a given situation. Thus despite an appearance which left the impression that family matters were private, local elites relied heavily on the values cultivated by parents in the "privacy" of their homes.

The habits of subordination instilled at home and reinforced in the workplace helped local elites by circumscribing the scope of what appeared on the surface to be individual impulses and decisions. The normalization of exploitation, via such practices as the parental appropriation of wages, worked to render young people emotionally incapable of fulfilling the liberal expectation of individual rationality. The result was a confusing matrix of emotional levels in which children fought their parents in some cases and emulated them in others. But the eventual acceptance of local elites was secured in the same way that the parents' legitimacy was secured—by perceiving these forces as anything but arbitrary. This might begin to account for the political indifference characterizing many of the area's Italian-Americans. Success thus remained securely anchored in a relatively unchanged faith in the naturalness of the local order, for the most that one could realistically do was rise within it, but not away from it. One was expected to quarrel with superiors through a process of personal adaptation, but adaptation always meant acceptance and not transcendence in the final account. We therefore have the emotional adjustment of an Italian-American woman on the one hand, and, on the other, of a young physician described by novelist Guido D'Agostino in 1940.

> As a child and teen-ager this daughter (my aunt) was exceptionally headstrong and insubordinate. I remember my grandmother years later telling of her concern with her daughter's behavior. My aunt perceived my grandmother's attempt to cultivate in her the ideal of womanliness as an effort to impose a female-as-house-plant life upon her. She began to rebel as a child. Despite my grandmother's attempts to repress it, the resulting conflict reached a climax during my aunt's teen-age years. Although she was punished and even beaten, the girl's spirit remained unbreakable.[77]

A fatal rupture between this young woman and her family seemed to be brewing. But it was not as crucial as it initially appeared. In the end, the woman's rebellion served to produce another stitch in the tightly woven social fabric.

> My grandmother faced a dilemma. She was proud of her daughter's tough willfulness. She did not want to break the girl's spirit. She saw in her courage and determination—great material out of which to shape una buona femmina. To crush the girl's élan would turn her into a dullish functionary instead of a vital woman of the tradition. The contadini did not like washed-out womanhood any more than wayward women. My grandmother set herself the task of channeling her daughter's rebelliousness rather than erasing it. But she confessed that she was uncertain of her success until years later when she saw my aunt a grown woman, settled and worldly wise—sistemata e scoltra.[78]

In the case of this daughter, the social effect was the production of a young worker shrewd enough to deal with an assorted variety of neighbors, relatives, and factory supervisors. This shrewdness, as previously suggested, seldom took the final form of revolutionary defiance except among a very small minority of communists and anarchists. Even there, as in the case of activist Angela Bambace, it was tempered by a distinctly different home life. In any case, the young woman described in these passages grew up to readily accept the social relations of rent capitalism which were merely new forms of *Mezzogiorno* feudalism and its intricate network of reciprocal relationships. The young physician Emilio Gardella initially fought against those traditional social relations as well, even as his mother Giustina basked in the glory of her son, a member of the elite on "Wop-Roost":

> ...as Giustina stood by the window in the thickening night...Her lips pressed into a thin smile. She watched the illuminated sign out front as it slanted in the cold January wind. For the thousandth time since the sign had been placed there, almost a year

back, she spelled out the glittering gold letters:
Emilio Gardella, M.D.[79]

Emilio's mother has always insisted that public dignity and respect will come to her son if only he would practice within the confines of Wop-Roost. Emilio disagrees.

> If only I could get in good with Stone and the crowd he runs around with I'd be sitting on top of the world. But these things don't just grow out of the air. Sure Stone thinks I'm a good doctor. But he's seen me around town a couple of times with Hazel Lambertson. And don't you believe that doesn't help.[80]

But Emilio's sister Elena reminded the good doctor that a local worker, Giuseppe, waited unsuccessfully for medical attention while Emilio cultivated the favor of Stone. "You can't neglect those who depend on you," Elena told him, "just because you want to work yourself into the social set in town. The poor people need doctors too." With this, Emilio was beside himself with anger. He

> ...threw down his napkin. He looked at the ceiling and drummed his fingers on the table. "Listen to her. Jesus Christ, ten years' hard study and work just to be doctor to a bunch of dumb wops! Not me. Damned if I will...." "Ever since I set up my shingle the only patients I've had are those goddamn Italians up on the hill and a few other poverty-stricken families around. The hell with that."[81]

Arguments such as these intensified in the Gardella family as time wore on. This was especially true in light of Emilio's love affairs with both Angelina, the young worker, and Hazel, the social debutante. But when Emilio, ignorant of Anglo-American bourgeois manners, innocently offends Stone and his colleagues, he is told that you've killed yourself for a long time in this town.[82] The little bit of prestige that Emilio had managed to cultivate outside of Wop-Roost was thus arbitrarily destroyed. Emilio came to realize that the warnings of his family and neighbors had merit—prestige conferred outside of the ethnic neighborhood was fleeting at best. Only among his own people that Emilio could achieve a sustained public respect integral to the meaning of success. After telling Stone that he was weary of being a "half-assed wop at your mercy," Emilio returned to Wop-Roost to marry Angelina.

> They saw Emilio's car backing, plowing into the snow to turn around and the Italians from the other shacks gathered in curiosity. They stopped, watched the car straighten and come toward them and moved off to one side to let it pass. Then they saw Emilio, the fixed expression on his face, and Angela at his side, huddled low, clinging to his arm. Emilio didn't bother to look up at them, but Angela smiled, breathless, triumphant, and the car passed on its way down to the village.[83]

Emilio had, by the end of D'Agostino's account, accepted the definition of success imposed upon him by relatives and the community at large. There was, admittedly, a period of rebellion. But in the end, he accepted his position in the local hierarchy to no less of an extent than the young female worker in conflict with her grandmother. In other words, both had, from their own hierarchical vantage point, surrendered their individualism in a fashion dramatically different than what was in evidence in the culture of the dominant. Not surprisingly, Emilio tended to also accept as "natural" a practice of medicine which was not intellectually challenging. Emilio had been taught as a young man to accept with grace the reality of a working world in which there was little qualitative difference, in terms of emotional satisfaction, between being a physician and doing any other kind of work. And while we find that this attitude of detachment was preached to Emilio the physician, it is certainly not surprising that it was taught to unskilled laborers, people who needed to adapt themselves most of all to the most deadening of routines.[84]

This pervasive feature of working class life was intensified during the Great Depression, when increased housing shortages, unemployment, and declining wages only served to worsen the emotional effect of daily estrangement.[85] The oral testimonies of the Italian-Americans quoted below, who lived through the bitter decade of the 1930s in Newark, attests to the emotional effect of the Depression on numerous lives:

> We were eleven people living in three and a half rooms. No one ever had his own bed. I remember going to Hill's bakery for day old bread. We used to go to the firehouse to get our wood for heat. We rarely ate meat. We ate beans and macaroni, and banana sandwiches.

A young man at the time, Alphonse Miele recalled in an interview that

> My three aunts and grandmother worked in a coat factory. My grandmother took work home. The housing, the hunger, it was all bad. I remember the banks closing. And those bread lines and apple sellers were all real. People just existed.[86]

A tailor, Alessio Vitagliano, who stood by helplessly while his wages dipped from a high of $36.00 per week before 1929 to $14.00 per week by 1931, remembered that

> There was no hope. That was the life in those days. The Depression was twenty times, fifty times worse than when I first came to America. I remember on Commerce Street, every week one or two people would jump fifteen floors out of the buildings.[87]

Mary S. Vitagliano told of the situation in her parents' tenement.

> The tenants in the building would say they were going to jump out of the window or put their heads in the ovens if they were told they were going to be put out. They couldn't pay the rent, but my mother couldn't put them out. They had small children. One time, my mother went to collect the rent from this one family. They had eight children. She almost fell when she went into the apartment. The floorboards and baseboards were torn up. When she asked the man what happened, he told her they needed the wood because they couldn't afford coal to cook their macaroni.[88]

Finally, Ralph Fasano painted one of the most wretched scenes of all.

> If the grocer threw out a box, people would run for
> it. People would look in garbage cans for food.
> People would go to the dump and pick up wood
> and use it for heat. And women had no escape.
> Wives wouldn't burden their husbands with their
> problems of paying the rent, food, and clothes,
> because they knew their husbands had to worry
> about keeping their jobs. Mothers had a hard time.
> They had to worry how they were going to pay the
> rent, gas, and electric. The man made the money
> and the wife made the dollar stretch.[89]

Amidst such circumstances two older perceptions of "success" were reinforced as parents instructed their children. On the one hand, the Depression experience hardly encouraged parents to teach young people that work which was not emotionally satisfying should be avoided.[90] In the daily struggle for existence spoken of by workers such as Fasano, such a luxury was just not appropriate. Secondly, the acceptance of work as a means of physical survival reinforced older notions that when time did permit it, work, as an inherently unpleasant experience, should be avoided. There was not a perpetual search for happiness in labor; a search which characterized the dominant's representation of work. Even the lofty crafts did not provide the sort of fulfillment spoken of repeatedly in the literature of the dominant. Indeed, in the ethnic ghettos of Newark, professions did not even guarantee a financial reward, as the experience of a young law school graduate reveals.

> John Cervase graduated from law school in May
> 1929. The crash came in October 1929. He worked
> as a law clerk during the early years of the Depres-
> sion for $5.00 a week. He remembered that some-
> times people could not pay for his services at that
> time, so they would bake a cake or do something to
> show their gratitude.[91]

In his case, area residents were reminded that the "hard work" so emphasized in mainstream American culture had little to do with "success" as defined by that same culture.[92]

In conclusion, therefore, the evidence seems to reveal an image of Italian-American success which was, in the final analysis, an intricate socio-psychological process designed to allow for a scope of ambition within the severe constraints of a traditional social hierarchy run by local elites. Ambitions were formulated through the prism of a local culture which placed little emphasis on work as an inherently fulfilling experience in and of itself. Instead, occupational categories were important only as a way of securing local positions of political and economic leadership which were viewed as important in their own right. But even this level of ambition was tempered by an awareness that movement into "lofty crafts" did not necessarily translate into positions of power. This realization brought even the "successful" in the community back to the very frame of mind that they so struggled to escape from—that forces beyond the control of the individual often stymied a spontaneous desire to do a good job, to engage in the cherished dream of upward mobility. A high school student in New York City discussed the disappointment in his family when the American way proved fruitless.

> Both my parents are bitterly disappointed over my oldest brother. They thought that if Joe went through high school, he surely would become a politician or a highly paid official. Now they often say that Joe's years in high school were wasted. He could have had a junking business of his own without having cost my parents at least $1200...they figure if Joe had worked instead of going to school he would have given my parents this amount of money.[93]

And through the postwar period, more and more young people, along with their parents, abandoned even the quest for a locally-based success, and reverted with a vengeance to what Pietro Di Donato described in such works as the 1958 publication of *This Woman*. Here young Italian-Americans are forced to rely on shrewdness, their options limited by economic realities on the one hand and an unintelligible dominant culture on the other:

Behind was West Hoboken, and beyond it the setting sun reddened the meadowed sea of the Jersey swamps…. The Hoboken roofs were a level of dry tar fretted in unison with parapets, kiosks, and tired chimneys leaning souther. The factories were naked grimy clay-and-steel laborers who never went home, the river an unwashed white woman and the ships on her brackish belly were her industrious bastards. On the east shoulder of the river was the monumented plain of Shinar, the towering pyramiding tombs of Babel.[94]

CHAPTER FIVE NOTES

1. Concistre, "Adult Education in a Local Area: A Study of a Decade in the Life and Education of the Adult Italian Immigrant in East Harlem, New York City" (Ph.D. dissertation, New York University, 1943).
2. Refer to the broad overviews of Italian-American family structure in Paul J. Campisi's "Ethnic Family Patterns: The Italian Family in the United States," *American Journal of Sociology*, 53, 1948, pp. 443–449; Francis A.J. Ianni, "Italo-American Teen-Ager," *Annals of the American Academy of Political and Social Science*, 338, 1961, pp. 70–78; Andrew Rolle, "La Famiglia: Defending the Wold Ways," and "La Famiglia: Reaching Out," in *The Italian Americans: Troubled Roots* (New York, 1980), pp. 110–139; Donna R. Gabaccia, "The Nuclear Family and American Individualism," and "A Family Social Cycle," in *From Sicily to Elizabeth Street: Housing and Social Change Among Italian Immigrants, 1880–1930* (Albany, 1984), pp. 100–108; Kathryn E. Serota, "A Comparative Study of 100 Italian Children at the Six-Year Level," *Psychological Clinic*, October 1927, pp. 216–231; Eloise R. Griffith, "A Social Worker Looks at Italians," *Journal of Education Sociology*, 5, 1931, pp. 172–177; Marjorie Roberts, "Italian Girls on American Soil," *Mental Hygiene*, 13, 1929, pp. 757–768; B. J. Palisi, "Ethnic Generation and Family Structure," *Journal of Marriage and Family*, 28, 1966, pp. 49–50; Virginia Yans-McLaughlin, *Family and Community: Italian Immigrants in Buffalo, 1880–1930* (Ithaca, 1977); Anna Zaloha, "A Study of the Persistence of Italian Customs Among 143 Families of Italian Descent" (M.A. thesis, Northwestern University, 1937); Phyllis H. Williams, "Marriage and the Family," in *South Italian Folkways in Europe and America: A Handbook for Social Workers, Visiting Nurses, School Teachers, and Physicians* (New York, 1938), pp. 73–106; and Dennis Starr, "The Immigrant Family," in *The Italians of New Jersey: A Historical Introduction and Bibliography* (Newark, 1985), pp. 27–30.
3. See especially the work of Joseph F. Kett, "The Era of Adolescence, 1900—Present," in *Rites of Passage: Adolescence in America, 1790 to the Present* (New York, 1977), pp. 215–246; and Paula S. Fass, *The Damned and the Beautiful: American Youth in the 1920's* (New York, 1979).
4. Look at northern New Jersey for example. In an unpublished report

written by Lyndhurst High School principal Reeves P. Batten shortly
before World War Two, we are told that

> In 1900 we had 444 pupils enrolled in the high school
> grades in the whole county. There were about four
> high schools in the county and some of those were not
> four year high schools. Last year we had 12,532 pupils
> enrolled in the four year high school grades. This does
> not include junior high school pupils except those in
> the ninth year grade.
>
> We now have twenty senior high schools and
> thirteen approved junior high schools. As present we
> have three or four high schools in the County whose
> enrollment in each building is more than twice the
> enrollment of the total number of high school pupils in
> the entire County thirty years ago. In fact nearly every
> senior high school has an enrollment almost equal to or
> greater than that of the whole County thirty years ago.

In Batten, "Bergen County Schools," located in the Education file,
Bergen County Historical Society Archives, Hackensack Public Library,
New Jersey, pp. 5–6.

5. One social worker in 1929 observed that

> The Italian girl, as she comes through her school work
> and her employment into contact with girls of other
> nationalities and standards, begins to compare her
> home and her life with theirs, and resents the differ-
> ence. She meets here a certain intolerance and misun-
> derstanding of her race; its members are called "wops"
> and "dagoes" and are spoken of as "our criminal
> class." She begins to feel ashamed of her heritage and
> incurs the bewildered anger of her parents by refusing
> to speak Italian even at home and by insisting on
> adopting American customs...I shall never forget the
> pained indignation of one father when he learned that
> he daughter, instead of enrolling herself at her place of
> employment under her own unmistakably Italian name
> of Augusta Solamoni, had called herself Gussie Solo-
> mon.

See Marjorie Roberts, "Italian Girls on American Soil," *Mental Hygiene*, 13, 1929, p. 763.

6. Lynd, "School 'Life'," in *Middletown: A Study in Modern American Culture* (New York, 1929), pp. 211–222.

7. Batten, "Bergen County Schools," p. 6.

8. In her consideration of the growth of college football in the 1920s, Fass could just as easily have been describing varsity members on the high school level.

> When athletics and especially football are viewed as symbols of community spirit and group identity, it is easier to understand why varsity team members were unquestionably the "big men" on campus. They represented in the extreme the demonstration of peer loyalty and the subsuming of the individual to group expression that was basic to the campus code. Most school papers repeatedly urged varsity team members to wear their letters so that they might be recognized by all and be given the honor which was their due. They would also serve to remind students of the personal success that came from school spirit and loyalty. The injunction was, however, unnecessary, for everyone already knew who the big men were. Indeed, wearing the letter had become unfashionable. But the false modesty often attributed to those who failed to wear the insignia was not modesty at all, but an expression of that security which team members had of their campus prestige and prominence.

Fass, "Competition and Conformity in the Peer Culture," pp. 238–239.

9. "Foreword: History of the Junior College Movement," in *The Junior College of Bergen County: Catalog for Years 1936–37, 1937–38* (Teaneck, New Jersey), p. 14.

10. Dabney Park, Jr., and L. Steven Zwerling, "Curriculum Comprehensiveness and Tracking" *Community College Review*, Spring 1974, pp. 10–20.

11. *The Junior College of Bergen County*, p. 26.

12. Look, for instance, at Arthur Miller's depiction of Willy Loman in *Death of a Salesman*, not to mention Thornton Wilder's *Heaven's My Destination*.

13. *The Junior College of Bergen County*, p. 26.

14. Westervelt, ed., "Public Education" in *History of Bergen County, New Jersey, 1630–1923*, Volume I (New York, 1923), pp. 218–219.

15. In Covello, "The Prolongation of Social Infancy of the Italian Child in America," in *The Social Background of the Italo-American School Child: A Study of the Southern Italian Family Mores and Their Effect on the School Situation in Italy and America* (Totowa, New Jersey, 1972), p. 301. Also refer to Covello's *The Heart is the Teacher*, written with the assistance of Guido D'Agostino (New York, 1958).

16. In Covello, "The Shift of Conception of Social Maturity to Working-paper Age," p. 302. Writing years later about Italian-Americans in a different area, sociologist Herbert Gans was moved to comment that

> Indeed, academic skill is viewed as a kind of virtuosity, much like musical ability and is thought to be desirable—and attainable—only for the rare youngster who is intellectually gifted. Lower-class West Enders, on the other hand, retain some of the traditional hostility toward the high school and consider it as keeping the child from going to work at the earliest opportunity.

Gans, "The Outside World," in *The Urban Villagers: Group and Class in the Life of Italian-Americans* (New York, 1965), pp. 131–132.

17. Covello, "The Shift of Conception of Social Maturity to Working-paper Age," pp. 302–303.

18. Concistre, "On Planning for the Children's Future," p. 351.

19. Attendant to this was a repudiation of the very cornerstone of Italian-American parenting—supervision of one form or another. Harry Stack Sullivan told his readers that

> Contrary to a prevalent belief, the mother who offers little supervision of her adolescent daughter is the one who does the minimum of harm. Not only is this the case when it results from a satisfactory solution of her own difficulties, but also it is the case with all situations of apparent indifference. When permitted to exercise her own judgment, the girl has but to learn the ways of the social group in which she moves, and is freed of the necessity of making her life compatible

with the added complications resulting from too close supervision.

Sullivan, "Notes on Female Adolescence," in *Personal Psychopathology: Early Formulations* (New York, 1972), p. 248. This book was written between 1929 and 1933 while Sullivan, a medical doctor, worked at the Sheppard and Enoch Pratt Hospital in Towson, Maryland.

20. "Educational Research and Statistics: A Comparative Study of the Mental Capacity of Sixth Grade Jewish and Italian Children," *School and Society*, October 31, 1925, pp. 564–568.

21. Taken from the statistical compilations of John J. D'Alesandre, *Occupational Trends of Italians in New York City* (New York, 1935), n.p. This publication was produced under the auspices of the Casa Italiana Educational Bureau, and it appeared as Bulletin Number 8.

22. See Covello's discussion, "The Shift of Conception of Social Maturity to Working-paper Age," in *The Social Background of the Italo-American School Child*, pp. 301–311.

23. In Covello, p. 308.

24. Ibid.

25. The best introductory summary of the *Mezzogiorno* conception of the student is found in Covello, "The Southern Italian Concept of the Role of the Student," in *The Social Background of the Italo-American School Child*, pp. 326–327. Also refer to Alastair Davidson's *Antonio Gramsci: Towards an Intellectual Biography* (London, 1977), for an examination of what southern Italian society demanded of a young student via a consideration of Gramsci.

26. In Covello, "Recreational Education of the School as a Source of Complaint," in *The Social Background of the Italo-American School Child*, p. 326.

27. In 1922 John H. Mariano, in a discussion of organized athletics among New York City Italian-Americans, observed that:

> The older folks do not understand the modern American sports and recreation and frequently oppose them. Never having had any "play" themselves they believe that their children are growing up improperly and become lazy thru overplay. Much of this aversion to American games is due also to the strenuousness

involved and the consequent fear that injury will follow.

Mariano, "Relation and Effect to Community," in *The Italian Contribution to American Democracy* (Boston, 1922), p. 147.

28. Works Progress Administration, "Great Educators," in *The Italians of New York: A Survey* (New York, 1938), p. 121.

29. Ibid.

30. He asked if it "isn't cruel to force active, growing bodies to sit still in the same place for hours?" Going on, expressed his astonishment over parents asking that their youngsters "sit still when their arms and legs and backs cry out for exercise." In conclusion, he challenged Italian-American parents with this appeal:

> ...Modernize your idea of discipline. The only real discipline is self-discipline.

In "The Old School and the New," *School and Home* (New York, 1925), p. 219.

31. Ibid., p. 220.

32. Ibid.

33. See Mariano's discussion of Italian-Americans who could not accept the sort of individual freedom espoused by someone like Patri in "The Trade or Business Type (A Dogmatic-Emotional Type)", pp. 97–102; and "Report of Supervisor of Attendance," *Combined Sixty-Seventh, Sixty-Eighth and Sixty-Ninth Annual Report of the Board of Education of Newark, N.J.*, p. 255. Refer to this section in its entirety for larger statistical trends, pp. 254–279. Also refer to MacCall's "Bureau of Attendance, Child Welfare and School Census," in the *Combined 70th and 71st Report of the Board of Education, City of Newark, N.J.*, pp. 207–224.

34. See, for example, the *Annual Report of the Paterson Board of Education for the Year Ending June 30, 1920*, n.p. This report, along with others, is located at the Main Branch of the Paterson, New Jersey Public Library.

35. Ibid. Also consult John R. Mamone, "Italians in Paterson: Strife and Strike," in "Italian and Puerto Rican Male Social Bonds in School, Factory, and Community" (Ed.D. dissertation, Rutgers University,

1978), p. 79.

36. Kett, "The Age of Adolescence," p. 263. A conceptually related piece is Rosalind H. Williams, "The Dream World of Consumption: Its Emergence in French Thought, 1880–1914" (Ph.D. dissertation, University of Massachusetts, 1978).

37. This was the perspective of Newark's Superintendent of Schools. In David B. Corson's advocacy of a project called "The Platoon School" we are told that

> It is a well-known fact that the platoon school is founded upon a theory of education somewhat differ-ent from that of the traditional school. The new educa-tional theory recognizes and emphasizes social needs and social ideals, due primarily to the change and constantly changing conditions of modern society and to the increasing complexity of modern life. It cannot ignore and does not seek to minimize the subjective needs of the individual, but it does make clear that he must lie with his fellows and must learn to adapt himself to them...[we now] have seventeen platoon schools in Newark.

Corson, "Report of Superintendent of Schools," in the *Combined 70th and 71st Report of the Board of Education, City of Newark, N.J.*, p. 78.

38. Concistre, "On Choosing a Mate," p. 345.

39. Concistre, "The Italian Community," pp. 186–187.

40. Concistre, "On Family Government," p. 349.

41. See Rose Green's "George Cuomo," in *The Italian-American novel: A Document of the Interaction of Two Cultures* (New York, 1973), pp. 295–296.

42. *Bright Day, Dark Runner* (Garden City, New York, 1964); and *Among Thieves* (Garden City, New York, 1968).

43. The most recent additions to this literature are Harold J. Abramson's "Persisting Ethnicity: The Extent of Endogamy," in *Ethnic Diversity in Catholic America* (New York, 1973), pp. 52–56; and Jill Quadagno, "Endogamy: The Italian-American Family," in Robert W. Habenstein and Charles H. Mindel, eds., *Ethnic Families in America: Patterns and Variations*, 2nd Edition (New York, 1982), pp. 71–72.

44. Winsey, "A Study of the Effect of Transplantation Upon Attitudes Toward the United States of Southern Italians in New York City as Revealed by Survivors" (Ph.D. dissertation, New York University, 1966), p. 123.
45. Winsey, Table XVI, p. 162.
46. Winsey, "Interview with Mr. G. S.," pp. 245–246.
47. See Covello, "Intellectual Interests of the Contadino in Relation to High School Education," p. 319.
48. Winsey, interview with "Mr. D. B." pp. 292–296.
49. Charles W. Churchill, "The Italians of Newark: A Community Study" (Ph.D. dissertation, New York University, 1942), p. 158.
50. Complied from figures provided by Churchill and verified in the records of the John Cotton Dana Library, Rutgers University, Newark.
51. "The Italians of Newark: A Community Study," p. 154.
52. In Covello, "The Shift of Conception of Social Maturity to Working-paper Age," pp. 309–310.
53. Mangione, "American Pattern," in *Mount Allegro: A Memoir of Italian American Life* (New York, 1981), p. 219.
54. "American Pattern," p. 220.
55. Mangione, "Growing Up Sicilian," in *An Ethnic at Large: A Memoir of America in the Thirties and Forties* (Philadelphia, 1983), p. 32.
56. "New Bread, Old Wine," pp. 225–226.
57. Ibid.
58. Rolle has provided insightful analysis in this regard.

> The struggle to make it in America was first played out within a self-contained setting. The immigrant's home was his sanctuary, his retreat from the harshness of life. Ideally, family and work should remain divided. Inside the household there existed a protective coloration, indeed flocking behavior. This quasi-animalistic unity called for loyalty to parenti (a large number of extended kin), as well as to father and mother. The rule of the parents, especially the father, was law.

Rolle, "La Famiglia: Defending the Old Ways," pp. 110–111. My reading of Mangione's autobiography—along with others in this book— has been facilitated through such works as Elizabeth W. Bruss,

Autobiographical Acts: The Changing Situation of a Literary Genre (Baltimore, 1976); Eugenio Donator's "The Ruins of Memory: Archeological Fragments and Textual Artifacts," *MLN*, 93, 1978, pp. 575–596; William C. Spengemann, *The Forms of Autobiography* (New Haven, 1980); and James Olney, *Metaphors of the Self: The Meaning of Autobiography* (Princeton, 1972).

59. Roskolenko, "America, the Thief: A Jewish Search for Freedom," in *The Immigrant Experience: The Anguish of Becoming American* (New York, 1971), pp. 151–178.

60. Ibid., p. 173.

61. Italian-Americans throughout this period were constantly confronted with a daily manifestation of Anglo-American hatred which is revealed time and again in local sources. While newspapers in Newark and Paterson clearly expressed such sentiments, we should not overlook the attitudes of social workers as well. In their observations, one can detect either condescension or outright hostility. In 1931 the former was represented by Eloise R. Griffith, a social worker in Nutley, New Jersey:

> It was not difficult to like them, for they were always polite and usually cooperative, since I came always as a friend sent by the school or the hospital to help them out of trouble. They began to understand that "social service" meant helping them to solve their problems in what was to them a strange, complicated environment full of snares and pitfalls unless they were wary. They never could say Griffith. The nearest they ever got to that name of many consonants was "Mista Grifta."

Now look at a representation of hostility on the part of Harriet T. Cooke, of the Woman's Patriotic Committee of Orange, New Jersey:

> The Italian element in Orange—about one-seventh of the whole population—has its own little settlement which we have always rather taken for granted as a necessary eyesore, dirty, ill-kept and ill-smelling. "Wops and dagoes," they have been to us—our "hewers of wood and drawers of water," our street cleaners, garbage collectors, gardeners, fruit venders—beyond

their usefulness in these directions, of no particular
interest to us.

Griffith, "A Social Worker Looks at Italians," *Journal of Educational Sociology*, November 1931, p. 172; and Cooke, "An Italian Colony," *The Survey*, 20 November 1920, p. 277. It is interesting to note that the wife of Thomas A. Edison is mentioned as a member of Cooke's group (p. 278).

62. Dewey, *The Way Out of Educational Confusion* (Cambridge, Massachusetts, 1931), pp. 34–35.
63. *Mount Allegro: A Memoir of Italian American Life*, p. 27.
64. Ibid.
65. I used a number of sources while studying these demographic trends. Among these were U.S., Department of Commerce, Bureau of the Census, *Thirteenth Census of the United States* (Washington, D.C., 1910); U.S., Department of Commerce, Bureau of the Census, *Sixteenth Census of the United States* (Washington, D.C., 1940); Ironbound Council, *Foreign Nationalities in the Ironbound* (Newark, 1931); and the collection of city maps int he New Jersey Reference Room of the Newark Public Library. Also see Paul V. Flynn, "First Italian Mission in Newark," in *History of St. John's Church, Newark: A Memorial of the Golden Jubilee of Its Consecration, in the Eighty-Second Year of the Founding of the Parish, with a Retrospect of the Progress of Catholicity* (Newark, 1908), pp. 216–217; Samuel H. Popper, "Newark, N.J., 1870–1910: Chapters in the Evolution of an American Metropolis" (Ph.D. dissertation, New York University, 1952), pp. 218–219; and Carl D. Hinrichsen, "The history of the Diocese of Newark, 1873–1901" (Ph.D. dissertation, Catholic University of America, 1962), p. 312 passim.
66. Corbo, "Italian Settlement in Newark, New Jersey" (M.A. thesis, East Carolina University, 1975), n.p.
67. In 1938 Phyllis Williams summarized the popular origins of this intra-Italian animosity, later written about by such scholars and diarists as Samuel Baily, Rudolf Vecoli, and Vincent Panella, to name but a few.

> ...Italian folk sayings derogatory of other districts furnish a sharp contrast to the American's lumping together of all Italians. Benevento in Campania, for

example, was said to be the home of the witches. They assembled there every night at a famous nut tree and then flew from it over the countryside.... The following rhyme popularly repeated regarding the people of Scafati described them in no uncertain terms: The people of Scafati smell to the skies; They are worth no more than the grass underfoot. The Neapolitans accuse the Calabrians of having teste dure (thick heads). The saying, "Non c'e sole nel Castellamare"...may merely arise from the existence there of a large state prison. The inhabitants of Girgenti (Agrigentum on the south coast of Sicily) were reported to be so quarrelsome and treacherous that they would eat bread with a man and then stab him in the back afterwards on the street. Regardless of the origin of these sayings, their currency intensifies the contrast between the American's notion of himself with the culture of a specific state and especially of a single village or commune.

Williams, "The Homeland," pp. 13–14. Also refer to the maps provided by Robert Park and Herbert A. Miller in *Old World Traits Transplanted* (New York, 1921), pp. 147 and 242. Also see treatments of geographic stability among Italian-Americans in the 1970s and 1980s. The best of these are Colleen L. Johnson's *Growing Up and Growing Old in Italian-American Families* (New Brunswick, New Jersey, 1985); and Anthony L. LaRuffa's *Monte Carmelo: An Italian-American Community in the Bronx* (New York, 1988).

68. Covello and D'Agostino, *The Heart is the Teacher*, pp. 89–90.
69. Roy A. Bowers and John L. Colaizzi, "Italian Americans in New Jersey Pharmacy," in *Italian Americans in the Professions: Proceedings of the Twelfth Annual Conference of the American Italian Historical Association*, ed. Remigio V. Pane (Staten Island, New York, 1983), p. 215.
70. Compiled from the figures offered by Bowers and Colaizzi, p. 215.
71. Ibid., p. 217.
72. The portrayal of Gerald R. Manfro in *The Italian Tribune* in 1941 is illustrative. A member of the Newark Board of Health and the "First Ward section's representative," he was born in Newark in 1904 to two Italian immigrants. Graduating from the Rutgers College of Pharmacy in 1923, he went on to numerous positions of local leadership. His

later acquisition of an M.D. degree only served to increase his opportunities for political appointment. See "Gerald R. Manfro, M.D., Another Appointment of High Calibre by Public Works Director Pearce R. Franklin," *Italian Tribune*, 2 May 1941, n.p.

73. But there was something else in the local area which kept its leaders there, and it is not as easy to initially spot as the ownership of property or work habits. That intangible, which is repeatedly played out in such sources as the *Italian Tribune*, is what can be called an arena of morality. That is to say that the leadership function of the New World *prominenti* evolved within the institutional context of a locally-based morality which was intertwined with the process of interaction between leaders and led. That context only made sense in the First Ward; it was not transferable to another part of the city with different patterns of leadership styles. The needs of the led, be they economic, psychological, aesthetic, etc. were formed on the basis of local conditions—and could only be responded to by leaders fully cognizant of these desires. Hence, the legitimacy of the local leader was dependent upon the ability to provide choices within a pre-existing framework of accepted alternatives. A relevant book in this regard is Jerome Krase and Charles La Cerra, *Ethnicity and Machine Politics* (Lanham, Maryland, 1992).

74. This desire to possess what someone else has worked to both undermine and reinforce liberalism at the same time. On the one hand, it sometimes induced a variation of the Anglo-American work ethic which had as its goal not moral perfection, but rather, the simple acquisition of goods in order to increase public prestige. On the other hand, it undermined the twentieth century consumption ethic because people were wary about letting jealous neighbors know just exactly how much they had. In some instances, sources suggest that physical beauty itself should not be enhanced, as it could inspire the sort of black magic that I will deal with at length in a subsequent section. Look, for example, at the passage below:

> When my cousin Rosina went crazy, there was so
> much grief among my relatives that some of them
> forgot their disdain for superstitions and began to say
> that Rosina's madness was undoubtedly brought about

by a fattura. How else, they argued, could so healthy and normal a human being become insane?

A fattura was far more deliberate and insidious than the evil eye, for it presupposed the services of a witch with a professional knowledge of black magic. Rosina was more loved and admired than any other Sicilian woman in the neighborhood; she was as generous and kind as she was beautiful. "How could anyone dislike her so much as to hire a witch to put a curse on her?" my mother asked, the tears gathering in her eyes.

Rosina's mother and Mr. Michelangelo had a ready answer to questions like that. The person they blamed for the tragedy was the middle-aged spinster who lived next door to Rosina. They explained that this jaded virgin had become envious of Rosina's beauty and her three young sons that she had gone to a witch and asked her to place a fattura on her. Envy, they pointed out, was at the root of most evil.

Mangione, "Evil Eye," in *Mount Allegro: A Memoir of Italian American Life*, pp. 104–105. Also refer to Norman Douglas' summary of envy in the *Mezzogiorno* in "Reposing at Castrovillari" and "Old Morano," *Old Calabria* (London, 1915), pp. 126–127; and 129.

75. And for this they were often castigated by radical leaders in such newspapers as Paterson's *La Questione Sociale* and *L'Era Nuova* at the beginning of the twentieth century. This tradition continued into the 1920s as *Giustizia* became increasingly militant and supportive of the Bolshevik revolution. Ironically, the very fury directed against the *prominenti* by the radicals for supporting a local, rigid hierarchy (and from their point of view, "duping" the workers in the process), was eventually to fuel the bitter attacks of Luigi Antonini. A case in point is the summer of 1923. Antonini, General Secretary of the Italian Dress and Waistmakers' Union, wrote a series of letters to Benjamin Lipshitz, an Executive Secretary of the Workers' Party of America. The issue was ostensibly Antonini's support of the *N.Y. Call*. But for our purposes, it is indeed fascinating that Antonini's polemic against the Workers' party leadership was founded upon the very same conception of individual liberty tempered by community constraints that guided

other Italian-American radical attacks against the *prominenti*.   In Antonini's rhetoric we can already detect the embryonic shape of what would later become the basis for Italian-American Republicanism, which was really the continuation of an older variation of conservatism which never ceased to be the creed of the Italian-American working and lower middle classes.

See the series of articles and letters beginning with "Perche' Sono Uscito Dal 'Workers' Party'," *Giustizia*, 18 October 1924, p. 6 passim, especially pp. 7–8.   Useful background reading on the *promenenti* is Alberto Giovannetti's "The Little Italys," in *The Italians of America* (New York, 1979), pp. 108–120.

76. *Who's Sorry Now?* (New York, 1984), p. 9.
77. Richard Gambino, "La Serieta—The Ideal of Womanliness," in *Blood of My Blood: The Dilemma of the Italian-Americans* (Garden City, New York, 1974), p. 174.
78. Ibid., p. 175.
79. Guido D'Agostino, *Olives on the Apple Tree* (New York, 1940), pp. 1–2.
80. Ibid., p. 5.
81. Ibid., pp. 5–6.
82. ibid., p. 289.
83. Ibid., p. 300.
84. Accordingly, in the early 1930s Caroline Ware observed that:

> ...the Italian group recognized little social advantage in one job over another and showed slight interest in steering their children into any particular line of work. Respect for craftsmanship had been reduced by 1930 to a gauge of security—a man with a trade might function anywhere, whereas one whose occupation depended upon particular local conditions would be less flexible.... As one mother expressed it to her son who was working as a mechanic and delivering for a bootlegger at the same time, 'Stick to your trade. You could be a mechanic in China, but where else could you be a bootlegger?' Even this much respect for the skilled trade was waning. It was the observation of social workers that whereas ten years before Italian families tried to send their boys to a trade school, in 1930 a few

tried to have them learn stenography, while most left
them to drift into any occupation whatever.

Ware, "Business and Work," in *Greenwich Village, 1920–1930: A Comment on American Civilization in the Post-War Years*, ed. Caroline Ware (New York, 1965), pp. 68–69.

85. See the unpublished compilation of oral interviews conducted by Donna DiMartino, located in the Newark Public Library. It is entitled "The Italians of Newark, New Jersey: The Impact of the Depression on Their Lives."

86. Ibid., interview of Frank Vignola, p. 20.

87. Ibid.

88. Ibid., pp. 21–22.

89. Ibid., p. 22.

90. Within this context, DiMartino commented that

> Hardships were reality. Their life was a struggle.
> They worked and made just enough to sustain them-
> selves. There were no luxuries...They were used to
> being a low class...Their needs were not fulfilled as
> they should have been in Newark...Wages were low,
> families worked hard just to get by, and housing was
> poor. Also, about 25% of the persons receiving relief
> were Italians.

"The Italians of Newark, New Jersey: The Impact of the Depression on Their Lives," p. 12.

91. Ibid., p. 21.

92. For those in the neighborhood who had a measure of economic security, it was also evident that the hard work which had proved valid for them was not a universal law; that the economic system did not always reward the deserving. In this regard, Mrs. Vitagliano recalled the relief labor of herself and her friends:

> We would pick up day old bread at the Dugan bakery
> on 4th Street and we would go to Mulberry Street and
> they would give us escarole and celery. Then we
> would go, a group of us, Mrs. Toma, Mrs. Santora,
> Mrs. Mango, to Frelinghuysen Avenue to the slaughter-

house, and they would give us liver, tripe, and lung. We would distribute it to those less fortunate than we were. We would get shoes from shops on Central Avenue to give to families. We would pay electric and gas bills for the elderly if they were going to be shut off.

Di Martino, "The Italians of Newark, New Jersey: The Impact of the Depression on Their Lives," p. 26.

93. In Covello's "Retention of Parental Concepts Among High School Students," p. 354.

94. Also see Jerry Della Femina, *An Italian Grows in Brooklyn* (Boston, 1978), Jonathan Rieder, *Canarsie: The Jews and Italians of Brooklyn Against Liberalism* (Cambridge, Massachusetts, 1985); David K. Shipler, "The White Niggers of Newark," *Harpers*, August 1972, pp. 77–83; Jo Pagano, *The Condemned* (New York, 1947); Antonia Pola, *Who Can But the Stars?* (New York, 1957); and Lucas Longo, *The Family on Vendetta Street* (New York, 1968).

III.

RELIGION
AND THE STRUGGLE
AGAINST DOMINATION

6

RELIGION IN THE *MEZZOGIORNO* IN 1880

Even the priests are indifferent
as they mumble out prayers of which
not a word is understood nor even heard....
  Luigi Villari, in *Italian Life
  in Town and Country*

Introduction

The importance of Roman Catholicism among southern Italian peasants was founded upon the perception that it was a force against arbitrary domination. As we saw earlier, that domination was perceived in one of two ways. It was, on the one hand, the result of the natural environment. Conversely, domination was perceived as a quality of those in power; influential people used their authority in a capricious fashion. Accordingly, the Catholicism of the peasants was more than a simple retreat into the privacy of the heart. It was, instead, an indication of the active social role which a subordinate class engages in. Peasants might have generally been politically passive in a formal sense, but that behavior never flowed into their religion. The central qualities of their religious world remained one of their own making. In the process, it was used to assert class dignity.[1]

The Catholicism of Italian peasants offered a diverse assortment of rites and public ceremonies. It made no pretense of being theologically rigorous, and rejected most attempts on the part of the Catholic hierarchy to systematize beliefs. Indeed, many peasant rituals continued to be grounded in ancient customs predating Catholicism. Religion thrived as a spontaneous force invoking the supernatural against forces of arbitrary domination. In Giovanni Verga's 1880 publication of "The She-Wolf," we are given a fictional illustration of how Christian customs combined with pre-Christian beliefs to ward off evil:

> In the village they called her the She-wolf, because she never had enough—of anything. The women made the sign of the cross when they saw her pass, alone as a wild bitch, prowling about suspiciously like a famished wolf; with her red lips she sucked the blood of their sons and husbands in a flash, and pulled them behind her skirt with a single glance of those devilish eyes, even if they were before the altar of Saint Agrippina. Fortunately, the She-wolf never went to church, not at Easter, not at Christmas, not to hear Mass, not for confession. Father Angiolino of Saint Mary of Jesus, a true servant of God, had lost his soul on account of her.[2]

The Christian rites which Verga described were, in reality, manifestations of pre-Christian beliefs. The sign of the cross, for example, was not utilized as a means of expressing reverence. Instead, it was a defensive strategy designed to ward off the She-wolf's evil. The priest too was not given his proper place in the Christian social order. An ordained minister of the sacraments whose primary responsibility was the care of souls, Verga's account informs us that peasants saw the priest himself as unable to retain his own soul—not to speak of the souls of others. Such views point to the profound gap between the Church's version of Christianity and that of the peasantry. The Church was seen not as a representative of God's kingdom, but rather, as merely another tool in the peasant's arsenal; a repertoire of strategic devices whose sole purpose was to counter arbitrary dominance. Church leaders were perceived as part of that manipulative array which served to make the peasant's life a hard one. As a result, the gulf between Church leaders and the local populace was not easily bridged. Priests on the local level understood this better than their superiors. This helps to account for peasant apathy, an apathy which such commentators as Luigi Villari noted.

The Church and the People

Rural Italian class relations were as clear in the church as in society at large. The unification of Italy by 1871 only served to change the peasant's relation to the church—but only sporadically. Before unification, the hierarchy of the church, including that of the priests, was comprised almost entirely of members of the elite. This collection of titled nobles, courtiers, and university-trained intellectuals did not attempt to appeal to the peasantry in their own terms. The very language of the Mass—Latin—was one peasants did not usually comprehend. The rigidity of official Catholicism stood in stark contrast to the amalgam of Catholic and pre-Christian religion which we shall examine shortly. The Catholicism of the privileged was one which solidified culturally the class distance between itself and the peasantry.

This social distance was also widened by inequities in the control of communal property. In the years before unification, material benefits distributed within the framework of a traditional society lessened peasant suspicion of elite culture. In traditional society, the Church played a leading role as a benefactor to the poor. Roman law still dictated, until 1861, that Church lands were also public lands and as such were subject to the legal authority of local municipalities.[3] Municipal officials were thus obliged by law to uphold the distinction between public land traditionally held by the Church and administered by the municipality on the one hand and, on the other hand, the domains of the princes and their rights to private land.[4]

In effect, the Church was part of a legal tradition which extended back to at least the second century. Central to this tradition was the principle of *"usufruct,"* a crucial benefit in the daily life of the peasant. Alan Watson has succinctly defined this principle as "the right to use and enjoy the fruits of another's property but not to alter its character fundamentally or destroy it." The elite, through the institution of the Church, lived up to its conservative role as social leader by providing the peasant access to public land. Here the peasant was able, for example, to hunt and forage for wood. But it should also be remembered that the peasant never forgot that this "right" was a privilege which could be revoked.[5] Indeed, as one scholar notes, "the Church never asked permission or the endorsement of the peasant whenever it chose to build a new convent or a monastery."[6] Such structures served to limit the amount of acreage available to the peasant. Their access to public lands, while beneficial, nevertheless drove home the constant presence of a personal vulnerability rooted in a clearly subordinate social position.

In the years after unification, land reform hit the Church particularly hard in the south. The newly constituted central government enacted a series of land reforms that, by 1880, resulted in the privatization of at least one million acres.[7] A major source of wealth was rapidly slipping away from the Church. Peasants who had traditionally relied upon public lands suddenly found themselves illegally trespassing on private lands owned by barons and a rising middle class.[8]

This had a profound effect on the peasant perception of the Church. The alien culture of priests with elite backgrounds had been tolerated because of access to public land. With these benefits now lost, the bonds between the Church and the peasantry slackened. As the Church rapidly became impoverished, so too did its ranks of priests. Not surprisingly, during the first two decades after the completion of Italian unification, the privileged departed from the priesthood in unprecedented numbers, though they still remained in the higher echelons of the Church hierarchy.[9] Priests recruited from the lower social classes, e.g. the artisans and the peasantry, were rapidly replacing them.[10] But instead of bringing the church closer to its parishioners it had, surprisingly, just the opposite effect. Peasants had deferred to the priest who was a member of the elite. The control which those priests exercised over public lands reinforced deference. Impoverished priests, however, exercised no such authority over lands that were in any event private. Both Church and peasantry grew increasingly poor. Poor priests and monks, who still retained the stigma of lower class origins, were forced to go through the village as beggars. Benefactors had become little more than street urchins. What deference remained by the later nineteenth century was based as much as anything else, on personal factors such as fear of the priest's curse. One immigrant from the village of Ventimiglia in Calabria recalled that

> There were three churches with three priests. Besides there was a duomo (cathedral) that was connected with a monastery on the outskirts of the town. Some of the one hundred or so monks performed duties as priests or as teachers in the local school. The majority of them did begging, going from village to village and from house to house. People hated these parasites but were afraid to refuse them a donation because these holy men could curse one's crop or bring about some other misfortune.[11]

Thus before the land reforms of the 1860s, the gap between the Church and the peasantry was of a traditionally conservative nature which rested on a system of reciprocity between elites and the lower classes. With the coming of the poor priest recruited from the peasant and artisan classes, the gap between the Church and the peasant widened as the clergy came to be viewed as a hindrance instead of a benefactor. Deference came to be the product of fear rather than a respect born of material benefits. Beyond that emotional boundary, deference to the Church did not exist. Just as in the period before unification, the basis for the perspective lay in the distance between official Church dogma and the religion of the peasantry.

The Role of the Pre-Christian

The myriad of rituals and beliefs which composed the peasant's religious world did not have Christianity as its exclusive basis. Their religious outlook began with a dualistic appraisal of reality which was characterized by what was visible and what was not. Events in the natural world were conceived of as visible; "natural" and "visible" in such instances pointed to ordinary perceptions of the senses. One could see, smell, or touch disease, for example, and recognize its reality and the threat it posed. Its origins, however, lay in a murky, invisible world of curses and spells typically classified under the rubric of "il mal occhio"—"the evil eye." The evil eye, whose origins can be traced to the ancient Greeks who colonized southern Italy, was only one of numerous invisible foes embedded in the Catholicism of the peasantry. Curses and spells devoid of the evil eye stare also abounded in the south. One Sicilian, for instance, told the following story.

> A member of our family wished the death of a neighbor. So she went to a maga [witch]. The witch made a figure of a woman from clay and then told my relative to stick a needle three times into the heart of the clay figure, repeating after the witch a certain magic spell. A few weeks later the person died.[12]

In this instance, reality was composed of two interrelated parts. There was, on the one hand, the visible quality of the neighbor's death. It was at that point that the invisible world was invoked as a means of explanation. The rituals used as defenses in such cases were pre-Christian in nature. Even when dressed in Christian garb, the rationales for action were still based on ancient beliefs predating the Church. With this in mind, look at the understanding of puddles and springs of water.

In ancient Greece, puddles and springs were viewed as the surface eyes of subterranean monsters.[13] This perception lasted even in the language of southern Italian peasants in the early 1970s, where the puddles and springs were called "*occhi*," or "eyes."[14] Peasants spoke warily of the powers beneath these waters, where it was usually suspected that the monster was a "*drago*" (dragon), a direct conceptual descendant of the Hellenic "drakon." Two peasants spoke of their view of puddles.

> Certain ponds in Apulia were dangerous for swimmers unless a bunch of flowers or some shiny object was thrown before into the water.

The next peasant tells us that

> In Basilicata, around Matera, people abstained from
> loud talking while passing certain caves less the
> sdrago be angry.[15]

The dragon spoken of by the last peasant lurked in the caves; the puddles
nearby serving as a view on the world.

The evil which emanated from surface water could be fought through
the use of what appeared to be, on the surface, Catholic rituals. Thus the
introduction of a host of saints whose sole purpose was protection. These
saints were especially useful when one sought to counteract the onslaught
of the evil eye. Like the belief in monsters and puddles, the evil eye had
its roots in the pre-Christian era. Early on, Christian saints were appropriated by the peasantry in order to, among other functions, ward off the
threats posed by dragons and evil eyes. Protection was also extended to the
use of various amulets worn around the neck. These had clear origins in
the ancient world.[16] In her discussions with southern Italian immigrants,
Phyllis Williams discovered that the saints and amulets were used to defend
specifically against what was described below.

> The Evil Eye...[is] a power inborn in certain men
> and women, who by a mere glance could cause
> physical injury, business reverses, sickness, and even
> death. The possessors of this mystic force acquired
> it unknowingly. It was found in the child whose
> mother during pregnancy turned around in church
> at the elevation of the Host; it occurred in the unfor-
> tunate being born on Christmas Eve and in certain of
> those who committed any of the numerous possible
> infractions of the social and religious codes.

Williams went on, explaining that workers with the evil eye

> ...were in all other respects ordinary human beings,
> who married and had children and lived otherwise
> uneventful lives. No benefit was reaped from the
> fatal gift; on the contrary, those possessing it were
> feared and, where possible, avoided.... A person

> possessing the "eyes"…could generally be recognized
> by certain signs, the most typical of which were
> eyebrows joined in an unbroken line.…[17]

The Church frowned upon these relics of the pre-Christian era. Priests and parishioners engaged in ideological battles over the legitimacy of their respective views. The infusion of the lower classes into the ranks of the priesthood did nothing to soften this struggle. Church officials continued to insist on a theology in which God was the center of the universe. Peasants, however, were not impressed with the alleged power of an almighty male God. Instead, there had developed by the last quarter of the nineteenth century an even wider array of Christian saints who had their origins in the polytheism of the ancient world. These saints, created by the peasants and appropriated by the Church as a means of boosting attendance, were linked in numerous ceremonies to outright pre-Christian worship. Francesco Perri tells us of cows adorned with ribbons who were offered as sacrifices to St. Mary.[18] In Vincenzo Balzano's *Abruzzi e Malise*, we are given passages which reveal peasant sacrifices to Catholic saints. "A statue of Adriadne on the banks of a stream near Monteleone in Southern Italy," he says, "is used today as Saint Venere."[20]

It was the panoply of saints which drew the devotion of the peasantry. Not only was God ignored as an object of veneration, but in addition, the Church made little headway with Jesus as well. Each saint had a specific duty to perform. Thus San Vito protected one against dog bites, while San Pantaleone looked over the fortunes of gamblers. Santa Barbara sheltered peasants from the onslaught of lightning. Every conceivable danger was provided for, as the saints stood guard against the attacks of the invisible world. But only one saint stood as an omnipresent force; as a divinity able to defend her worshippers against all of the misfortunes induced by the mysterious forces of the invisible universe. Leonard Covello summarized the historical origin and social significance of what some have termed the "Madonna cult."

> The worship of the Madonna seems to have grown
> from the fondness of the Greeks for the worship of
> female deities. The goddess Cybele was especially
> venerated in the south of the Italian peninsula. She
> was worshipped as the giver of life and the Queen of

> Heaven.... From this probably developed the con-
> cept of a universal Madonna...who in the south of
> Italy, had entirely eclipsed the worship of her son
> Jesus.[21]

The elevation of Mary to a saint of the highest order stood as the
clearest theological repudiation of official church religion.   Church
historians who have focused on the history of sainthood have noted that the
Church typically conferred sainthood on men. Evidence suggests that this
was a policy designed to undermine the ancient emphasis on female deities.
In effect, the Church's institutionalization of Mary as a high-ranking saint
was a concession to the popular demand for female gods in the Hellenic
tradition. Popular depictions always went far beyond church teachings,
however. Never did the church relegate Jesus and God to a subordinate
position vis-a-vis Mary.[22]

Mary assumed such grandiose proportions because she was a clear
embodiment of the peasant's ideal family. At the center of that idealized
picture we find the mother. Men stood as representatives to the harsh
world outside, but they did not play a central emotional role in the daily
activities of the family. Accordingly, Norman Douglas observed that "if the
Mother of God had not existed, the group [the Holy Trinity] would have
been deemed incomplete; a family without a mother is to them like a tree
without roots—a thing which cannot be." Douglas was astounded to find
that the Trinity of Calabrian peasants differed from the Church's father
(God), son (Jesus), and Holy Ghost triad. He pointed out that

> ...their Trinity is not ours; it consists of the Mother
> [St. Mary], the Father (Saint Joseph), and the Child
> [Jesus]—with Saint Anne looming in the background
> (the grandmother is an important personage in the
> patriarchal family). The Creator of all things and the
> Holy Ghost have evaporated; they are too intangible
> and non-human.[23]

"Too intangible and non-human." Douglas isolated a key difference
between Italian people's religion and that of the Church. The deities
worshipped by the peasants had a profoundly pragmatic quality which had
nothing to do with the formal intellectual systems of Church theology.

Saints were expected to produce tangible benefits for the peasantry. If a saint was perceived as powerless to stop a drought, for example, then he or she was exiled and replaced with another saint of the people's choosing. Within this mindset, the vague conception of an almighty God was irrelevant. "He is too remote from themselves and the ordinary activities of their daily lives…" Douglas observed.[24] The deities were responsible for their respective spheres, and God reigned over too undefinable a realm to be of much help. James Frazer, in *The Golden Bough*, told how Sicilian villagers reacted to a drought in 1893. In this scenario, God the almighty was totally absent:

> Even the great St. Francis of Paolo himself, who annually performs the miracle or rain and is carried every spring through the market gardens, either could not or would not help. Masses, vespers, concerts, illuminations, fireworks—nothing could move him. At last the peasants began to lose patience. Most of the saints were banished.

Frazer then went on to describe this fascinating spectacle in more detail.

> At Palermo they dumped St. Joseph in a garden to see the state of things for himself, and they swore to leave him there in the sun till rain fell. Other saints were turned, like naughty children with their faces to the wall. Others again, stripped of their beautiful robes, were exiled far from their parishes, threatened, grossly insulted, dunked in horseponds. At Caltanisetta the golden wings of St. Michael the Archangel were torn from his shoulder and replaced with wings of paste board…. At Licata the patron saint, St. Angelo, fared even worse for he was left without any garments at all; he was reviled, he was put in irons, he was threatened with drowning or hanging.[25]

Frazer went on to conclude that the villagers screamed in the face of St. Angelo, warning him that it would either be "rain or the rope." This emphasis on pragmatic theology explains the relegation of Jesus to a secondary position. Church depictions of Jesus as a moral philosopher, especially in lessons which emphasized the Sermon on the Mount, remained too idealistic—not to say irrelevant—from the peasants' perspective. Jesus as an adult seemed too unreal. He was not married, nor did he father children. He did not enter the trade of his father—nor did he ever develop one of his own. A poor wanderer without close family relations, he was not the kind of man who inspired respect in a society which so prized visible signs of honor.[26] Instead, the Jesus loved by the peasants was the baby Jesus. This too has pre-Christian origins, as Georg Wissowa has pointed out.[27] He saw the "bambino cult" as a continuation of the Roman Lares, young family protectors who merited gifts on certain days of the year.

But even the cult of the infant Jesus did not place St. Mary in the background. Tales of the baby and adolescent Jesus were usually told from the perspective of a mother's concerns; a point of view which dwelt on a Jesus who disobeyed his wise mother and hence, was in need of constant supervision and sometimes violent punishment. The St. Mary of these stories was also the divine healer. A mother to Jesus personally and to her followers through veneration, she was invoked to intercede in a variety of situations.[28]

None of this is said to suggest that the Church was completely rejected. Rather, the cults of the saints and the Madonna, whose roots predated Christianity, was injected into the rituals of the official Church. The Church housed these cults, providing a public place for worshipping the deities. Thus attendance at Church was important. For the females of the village, it was absolutely imperative.[29] Because attendance at Mass was induced by the desire to invoke saintly intervention, the more Catholic aspects of the ritual were ignored. Church attendance did not equal Catholic devotion, as some priests sadly noted.[30] Mass was a gathering of villagers who interspersed their devotions to the saints with a variety of activities which had nothing to do with what the priest wanted. An immigrant from the Sicilian village of Altavilla consequently remembered a typical Sunday mass:

> Throughout the mass one heard a constant drone
> produced by whispers, pious Amens, giggles, sneez-
> es and coughs of the people.... The majority ambled
> around or tried to stay motionless. It was a restless

> crowd, paying little attention to the service, especial-
> ly when Latin was used. Some slept.... It was a
> merry crowd.[31]

While the Church unintentionally provided a public forum for pre-Christian concerns, the sponsorship of religious festivals was quite another matter. The Church openly sponsored public homages to Catholic saints while knowing full well that the rationales for peasant worship predated Catholic teachings.[32] A primary motivation on the Church's part was the relatively large amount of wealth laid at the saint's feet.[33] These festivals were noted by observers for their lavish processions, frenzied dancing, rich eating, and public trances induced by mass chanting to the saint being honored.[34] Feasts sometimes lasted for days, and for peasants, they provided a welcome relief from the weary routine of agricultural labor. Whole villages were temporarily transformed, their dull and monotonous architecture decked with banners and flags of assorted colors and shapes. "To such customs," Phyllis Williams observed, "the little town of Polizzi Generosa in Sicily added the lowering into the street of children dressed as angels, supported by ropes from the balconies, as the statue was borne past."[35]

Not only did such extravagant displays periodically enliven the peasant's life, but furthermore, they stood as stark testimonies to the peasant's refusal to be totally subordinated to elite groups. While the formal political system and its institutions were largely looked upon apathetically, the production of cultural forms remained one area of life in which the peasantry insisted on some autonomy. When Church officials attempted to impose a systematized, formal theological system which had at its core a centralized institution founded upon a belief in one almighty God, they were met with a resistance which was not overcome. Feasts, for example, functioned as a public celebration of the subordinate onslaught against Church standardization. While peasants accepted their status as human tools in the political and economic realms, they resisted, nonetheless, any effort to rationalize their intellectual and cultural life. Theirs was a culture of decentralization, and that decentralization became manifest in the array of saints they worshipped.

Insistence on the autonomy of culture production within the realm of theology undermined the Church's drive to make the peasantry passive in all respects.[36]   Church religion allowed little scope for imagination and creativity in the way that a constantly evolving, decentralized people's religion did.   Peasants detected quite accurately that Church leaders felt uneasy about independence from Church culture.[37] Images of authority in the form of God and Jesus could be easily manipulated into images of social authority outside of the realm of religion. It was much harder to manipulate dozens of deities which predated the Church itself.

So while the Catholic hierarchy welcomed attendance at Mass and the revenue accrued from festivals, it still expressed an uneasiness over the rationales which induced participation on the part of the peasantry. But as contemporary writers pointed out, Church officials were willing to accept a peasant parishioner who engaged in the form of Catholicism in lieu of one driven out of the Church entirely. "The fact is that the whole fabric of Latin Catholicism is far too delicately constructed," Richard Bagot wrote as late as 1913, "to admit of the taking away of a single one of the supporting stones of dogma."[38] He went on to add in the clearest of terms that

> The vast majority of Italians, and among them very many priests, hold their tongues. A small proportion of these do so out of loyalty to the Church, and also because they are sensible enough to realize that Catholicism contains only two ways—its own, and the way out.[39]

Bagot, like other commentators, was struck by the unwillingness of the Church to press too hard on the matter of pre-Christian beliefs. In one passage he told his readers that

> As to the parish priest, frequently a peasant himself, he has to swim with the current and act in the general interests of the community. If he is fortunate enough to have in his church a miracle-working picture or statue, he very often does not believe in its powers himself, and if you possess his confidence he will probably hint as much to you.… Were he to be honest, and tell his people that their sacred statue or picture had no supernatural powers, but was merely to be reverenced as a symbol of the personage it represented, his honesty would speedily be checked

by an intimation that he was damaging the pecuni-
ary interests and the reputation of the *paese*, and
that he must either play the game or the place would
be made too hot to hold him.

What Bagot did not see, however, was that the struggle for cultural
hegemony within the Church brought forth more than a simple series of
tactical retreats on the part of Church officials. The incorporation of ancient
beliefs within the Church created an expanding web of newly created needs
which the peasantry had not anticipated. To see ancient deities clothed in
Catholic garb, and to see priests back down on issues of religion, was to
achieve an air of dignity not usually seen in peasant life. Hence, the
Church unwittingly contributed to the legitimization of the counter-
discursive by housing it within the confines of a powerful institution.

Conversely, this process undermined the development of a theology
rooted in the worth and power of the individual. The Church's uninten-
tional institutionalization of pre-Christian rites strengthened a theological
system which depicted the individual as fundamentally passive. Active
engagement with one's environment was always a defensive strategy.
Saints, for example, were gods capable of intervening on behalf of relatively
weak and powerless people. Theirs was not a religion which emphasized
a disciplined, systematic, and devout path to heaven. Indeed, lacking a
conception of heaven, there was nothing in their religion to point the way
toward salvation. Salvation was a "priest's tale" which had nothing to do
with a self-defense grounded in a defense of the entire village against both
natural and human marauders. Peasants in southern Italy, like peasants
elsewhere, could never afford the luxury of an immersion in the self which
would render them insensitive to their very real social condition.

Unlike the Church hierarchy in Italy—not to mention the one staffed
largely by Irish-American priests which greeted these peasants in New
Jersey and New York—Italian people's religion nowhere lent itself to an
autonomous individual who, through the exercise of initiative, could
embrace a success which was both material and spiritual. The writings of
the Catholic spokesman Paul V. Flynn are instructive in this regard. In his
description of Catholic education in Newark at the end of the nineteenth
century, he depicted a link between self-initiative and spiritual devotion
that differed little from the Protestant work ethic of the era.[40] Poor Irish

children, he argued, had risen to places of prominence in Newark because of their hard work and spiritual immersion in Catholic dogma. Like other Christians of that era, Flynn's Catholics combined the initiative of economic man with an attack upon the baser side of human nature.

Southern Italian peasants, both before and after arrival in America, never quite understood this tension between Christian ethics and the imperatives of a marketplace. Their religion did not endorse the proliferation of subjective and, at least ideally, autonomous moral demands. Instead, their array of intervening saints spoke to a clearly developed theory of religion grounded in the need of the individual for effective protection against capricious and arbitrary enemies. Within such a framework subjective guides to behavior had no place. Religion for southern Italian peasants was fundamentally conservative—the history of the individual was a series of tactical defensive maneuvers. Spiritual devotion never led to a better world, either on earth or beyond. This perspective was brought to New Jersey and New York, where it clashed not only with the liberalism of Protestantism, but additionally, with the systematic and hopeful optimism of the Catholic Church.

CHAPTER SIX NOTES

1. Fascinating introductions to the religious system of the peasantry include J. J. Blunt, *Vestiges of Ancient Manners and Customs, Discoverable in Modern Italy and Sicily* (London, 1908); Norman Douglas, *Old Calabria* (London, 1915); Anne MacDonnell, "Religion in the Abruzzi," *In The Abruzzi* (London, 1908), pp. 70–95; Alberto Giovannetti, "The Basement Catholics," in *The Italians of America* (New York, 1979), pp. 229–272; Richard Bagot, "The Italian Peasant" and "Church and State," in *The Italians of Today* (Chicago, 1913), pp. 42–49, and 95–117; Luigi Villari, *Italian Life in Town and Country* (New York, 1095); and Rudolph J. Vecoli's "Prelates and Peasants: Italian Immigrants and the Catholic Church," *Journal of Social History*, Spring 1969, pp. 217–268.

2. "The She-Wolf," in *The She-Wolf and Other Stories* (Berkeley, 1962), p. 3.

3. See the analysis of Alan Watson for an elaboration of this conception in *Roman Private Law Around 200 B.C.* (Edinburgh, 1971). For a discussion of Church lands in this regard, consult Leonard Covello, "The Church as an Economic and Educational Force," in *The Social Background of the Italo-American School Child: A Study of Southern Italian Family Mores and Their Effect on the School Situation in Italy and America* (Totowa, New Jersey, 1972), pp. 136–140.

4. Ibid. Also see the analysis of Dennis M. Smith, *Italy: A Modern History* (Ann Arbor, 1959), pp. 87–88; and Martin Cleark's *Modern Italy, 1871–1982* (New York, 1990).

5. In this regard, the peasants interviewed by Bagot were characterized as having "the most cynical scepticism…" (p. 45).

6. Covello, "The Church as an Economic and Educational Force," p. 137.

7. Mack Smith, p. 87.

8. See Manlio Rossi-Doria, *Dieci Anni di Politica Agraria nel Mezzogiorno* (Bari, 1958); Leopoldo Franchetti, *La Sicilia nel 1876: Condizioni Politiche e Amministrative* (Firenze, 1925); and Sidney Sonnino's *La Sicilia nel 1876: I Contadini* (Firenze, 1925).

9. Covello, "The Role of the Priest," pp. 137–139.

10. Ibid.

11. In Covello, p. 139.

12. In Covello, "The Basic Religious Beliefs," p. 106.

13. Covello, "Anthropomorphic Elements," pp. 108–109; Richard Gambino, "Religion, Magic and the Church," in *Blood of My Blood: The Dilemma of the Italian-Americans* (Garden City, New York, 1974), p. 214; and Douglas, who wrote that

> The dragon has grown into a subterranean monster, who peers up from his dark abode wherever he can—out of fountains or caverns whence fountains issue. It stands to reason that he is sleepless; all dragons are "sleepless;" their eyes are eternally open, for the luminous sparkle of living waters never waxes dim. And bold adventurers may well be devoured by dragons when they fall into these watery rents, never to appear again.

"Dragons," in *Old Calabria*, p. 102.
14. Gambino, p. 214.
15. Quoted in Covello, p. 109. Douglas spoke of this connection with Hellenic culture:

> What is a dragon? An animal, one might say, which looks or regards (Greek drakon); so called, presumably, from its terrible eyes. Homer has passages which bear out this interpretation.

Douglas went on to add this interesting passage:

> It may well be that the Homeric writer was acquainted with the Uromastix lizard that occurs in Asia Minor, and whoever has watched this beast, as I have done, cannot fail to have been impressed by its contemplative gestures, as if it were gazing intently (drakon) at something.

Douglas, pp. 100–101.
16. Phyllis H. Williams has provided a fascinating photograph entitled "Amulets to Avert the Evil Eye." In it we see a hand making horns, along with scissors, a hunchback, a horn, a tooth, and a fish. See this in "Religion and Superstition," *South Italian Folkways in Europe and America: A Handbook for Social Workers, Visiting Nurses, School Teachers,*

and Physicians (New York, 1969), insertion after p. 142. Also consult Lawrence DiStasi's *Mal Occhio, The Underside of Vision* (San Francisco, 1981).

17. "Religion and Superstition," p. 142.
18. Perri, *Enough of Dreams* (New York, 1929), p. 249.
19. Balzano, *Abruzzi e Malise* (Turin, 1927).
20. Quoted in Covello, "The Church and Popular Superstitions," p. 20. MacDonnell also observed this trend. She noted that

> One of the most interesting features of the Talami, and one that is invariably present, is the distinct proof of their pagan origin, hardly concealed at all. The festa may be that of Our Lady of Refuge, or Our Lady of the Rosary; but in reality Mary here is but the heiress of Ceres.

"Religion in the Abruzzi," p. 90.

21. "The Church and Popular Superstitions," p. 118. Douglas too observed that

> Of the Madonna no mention occurs in the songs of Bishop Paulinus (fourth century); no monument exists in the Neapolitan catacombs. Thereafter her cult begins to dominate.
>   She supplied the natives with what Orthodox Christianity did not give them, but what they had possessed from early times—a female element in religion. Those Greek settlers had their nymphs, their Venus, and so forth; the Mother of God absorbed and continued their functions.

"Southern Saintliness," p. 247. Also refer to John Bossy's *Christianity in the West, 1400–1700* (New York, 1985).

22. In her discussion of the "difficulties with a patriarchal tradition," the theologian Elisabeth Moltmann-Wendel summarized the Church's position on Mary and other leading women in the Bible:

> A long accepted view of the Bible, which is mostly hostile to women, has given form to a history of the

tradition which has made a deep mark on human
consciousness. Women are associated with sexuality
and sin (Mary Magdalene), cooking and housekeeping
(Martha), and motherhood (Mary).

The Women Around Jesus (New York, 1982), p. 8. For a wider consideration of how the patriarchal God was institutionalized in numerous
ways, refer to Hans Kung, *Structures of the Church* (New York, 1982).

23. "Southern Saintliness," p. 250.
24. Ibid., p. 248.
25. Quoted in Covello, "The Cult of the Saints," pp. 126–127. Also useful
    is John B. Vickney, *The Literary Impact of The Golden Bough* (Princeton,
    1973).
26. An excellent discussion of honor is offered by Jane Schneider, "Of
    Vigilance and Virgins: Honor, Shame and Access to Resources in
    Mediterranean Societies," *Ethnology*, January 1971, pp. 1–24.
27. Refer to the summary of his views in Covello, "The Madonna Cult," p.
    120. Douglas went even further, and summarized the peasants'
    conception of Jesus in this way:

> Three tangibly-human aspects of Christ's life figure
> here: the bambino-cult, which not only appeals to the
> people's love of babyhood but also carries on the old
> traditions of the Lar Familiaris and of Horus; next, the
> youthful Jesus, beloved of local female mystics; and
> lastly the Crucified—that grim and gloomy image of
> suffering which was imported, or at least furiously
> fostered, by the Spaniards.

"Southern Saintliness," p. 248.
28. We again turn to Douglas, who described how this was possible.

> This saints have fixed legendary attributes and histo-
> ries, and as culture advances it becomes increasingly
> difficult to manufacture new saints with fresh and
> original characters...Madonna, on the other hand, can
> subdivide with the ease of an amoeba, and yet never
> lose her identity or credibility; moreover, thanks to her
> divine character, anything can be accredited to her...the

traditions concerning her are so conveniently vague
that they actually foster the mythopoetic faculty.

"Southern Saintliness," pp. 249–250.

29. Giovannetti, for example, wrote that the "Italian men were usually the type who sent their views and children to confession and Mass while they set foot in the Church only on Christmas and Easter, and then they stood as close to the door as possible" (p. 252). Covello remarked that for men, church attendance was optional, but that "among women—old and young—attendance was imperative" (p. 120). Robert Orsi's research also reveals that peasant immigrants carried this tradition to Harlem. See "Women and the Devotion to the Madonna of 115th Street," in *The Madonna of 115th Street: Faith and Community in Italian Harlem, 1880–1950* (New Haven, 1985), especially pp. 204–207.

30. Many priests thus eventually surrendered to a situation perceived as hopeless. Covello, for instance, wrote that

> It is true that a priest would often officially admonish
> a peasant for pagan beliefs, but would add, "Come
> prete non vi posso aiutare ma da me..." (As a priest I
> cannot do it but, personally, I shall not hinder you (p.
> 115).

Catholic clergy at the end of the nineteenth century noted how easily Italian immigrants could be driven to disrupt Mass when the hierarchy pursued Church religion too rigidly. Thus in the personal correspondence of Bishop Wigger of the Newark Diocese, we find a description of a near riot during Mass at Holy Rosary Church in Jersey City on October 31, 1896. This was the result of the priest's announcement that confirmation could only be conducted on adolescents who had undergone religious instruction—rather than on infants, as had been the practice in some southern Italian villages. See Wigger's letter, presented in Carl D. Hinrichsen's "The History of the Diocese of Newark, 1873–1901" (Ph.D. dissertation, Catholic University of America, 1962), p. 323.

31. Quoted in Covello, "Church Attendance," p. 130.

32. Refer to the summaries of Lawrence Cunningham, "The Bureaucratization of Sanctity," in *The Meaning of the Saints: Its Rise and Function in*

Latin Christianity (Chicago, 1981). Also see Ninian Smart, *The Phenomenon of Christianity* (London, 1979).

33. Thus in the Sicilian colony of East 69th Street and Avenue A studied
by Robert E. Park and Herbert A. Miller in 1921, "feasts...[were] not
approved by the priest," yet, "offerings [were] made during the most
important of these feasts...[amounting to] four to six thousand dollars."
Miller and Park discovered that this practice of exorbitant spending
was common in the village of Cinisi, and that it was a standard feature
of Sicilian Catholicism. An examination of the financial statements of
Our Lady of Assumption Church in Bayonne, New Jersey between 1907
and 1925 also reveals that income derived from "Holy Day Collections"
formed a considerable percentage. In 1907, for example, income from
feast day offerings amounted to 56.7% of the Church's total income.
The closest source of income next to this, "Monthly Collections,"
amounted to a mere 12.7%.

See Robert E. Park and Herbert A. Miller, "The Italians," in *Old
World Traits Transplanted* (New York, 1921), p. 155; and The Parish
Reports of Our Lady of the Assumption Church, located at the
University Archives of Seton Hall University in South Orange, New
Jersey.

34. An interesting example of this lavishness is found in Douglas, "A
Mountain Festival," pp. 151–159. MacDonnell too offers a graphic
description in "Religion in the Abruzzi." In 1853 George S. Hillard
wrote that

> The peasantry near Rome, both male and female, are
> fond of showy costumes, and have a native taste for
> the disposition of colors, and the appropriate use of
> ornaments of gold and silver. On all festival and
> holiday occasions, when they appear in their best attire,
> the general effect produced is very fine and forms a
> strong attraction to artists, who learn here the differ-
> ence between costume and dress.

See "Personal Appearance," in *Six Months in Italy* (New York, 1853), p.
430.

35. "Religion and Superstition," p. 140. Also consult Barbara C. Pope,
"The Origins of Southern Italian Good Friday Processions," in *Italian*

Americans Celebrate Life: The Arts and Popular Culture, eds. Paola A. Sensi and Anthony J. Tamurri (West Lafayette, Indiana, 1990), pp. 155–168. G. Cammarei's *La Settimana nel Trapunese Possato e Presente* (Traponi, 1988), is also useful.

36. In 1917 Antonio Mangano outlined just how forceful the Church was in matters of theology. I present below some of the points which Mangano made about the Church's dictatorial nature:

> 1. There is no salvation outside of the Church of Rome.
>
> 2. Forgiveness of sin is dependent upon confession to a priest and the performance of the penance which he may impose in granting absolution.
>
> 3. Partaking of the communion, attendance upon mass, performing pious works, and advancing the interests of the church are all means whereby merit is acquired which may be applied to satisfy God for the sins one commits.
>
> 4. Priests are the only channel of divine grace to men, regardless of the moral and private life of the priest.
>
> 5. The Bible is a pious book, but the church is superior to it, because the church produced the Bible.
>
> 6. The pope alone is infallible when he decides what all Christians must believe and practice.
>
> 7. Out of the (Holy Catholic) Church no one can be saved, because she alone was founded by Christ to save men.
>
> 8. Give thanks to God that you are a member of the Catholic Church. If you live as a good Catholic you will also die as such and go to heaven. If not, you will be punished in hell more severely than the pagans.

In Mangano, "Religious Backgrounds," *Sons of Italy: A Social and*

Religious Study of the Italians in America (New York, 1917), pp. 82–83.

37. See Mangano's discussion, pp. 94–95.

38. "Church and State," p. 101.

39. "The Italian Peasant," p. 46. Also see Mangano, "Parallels With Heathen Customs," pp. 75–78; MacDonnell, *In The Abruzzi*; and Douglas, *Old Calabria*.

40. Flynn, *History of St. John's Church, Newark: A Memorial of the Golden Jubilee of Its Consecration, in the Eighty-Second Year of the Founding of the Parish, With a Retrospect of the Progress of Catholicity* (Newark, 1908). Also refer to Daniel T. Rodgers, *The Work Ethic in Industrial America, 1850–1920* (Chicago, 1978), for a good overview of Protestant liberalism and its preoccupation with spiritual perfection through the act of labor.

7

ITALIAN-AMERICANS AND THE AMERICAN CHURCH

We all looked at the priest.
He was a man in his late forties,
resolute, aggressive....

        a laborer, Giuseppe Cautela,
        in 1928

The gap between the Roman Catholic Church and southern Italians continued to widen in New Jersey and New York at the end of the nineteenth century. The American church, dominated by an educated and nationalistic Irish-American clergy, wielded a power that was not seriously challenged through 1980.[1] To the Irish-American churchman, the Catholic church was his. It was a church with strong political roots in the resistance against British imperialism in Ireland.[2] It had sustained Irish immigrants in a hostile Protestant America, serving as a central institution in the forging of a strong group identity devoid of the regionalism so prevalent among Italians. Along with the sheer numerical dominance of the Irish, there was again the issue of theological doctrine. Just as in Italy, the church in America engaged in a constant battle with popular religious forms. But the Irish-American hierarchy had no experience with the popular Catholicism unique to Italian peasants. And they were not about to accept it into their church.

Thus in comparison to Italian peasant theology, Irish Catholicism's systematic and rigid qualities appeared even more pronounced. With an emphasis upon the supremacy of God and focus upon Jesus as the primary object of worship, there was no place for the myriad of deities which abounded in the Italian religious construct. Irish priests were horrified that the religion of Italian immigrants relegated God and Jesus to a secondary position. "Unlike their Irish Catholic neighbors," a Rochester Italian-American remarked, "[Italians] had almost no fear of God and felt as much at home with him as they did with each other."[3] Such perspectives were interpreted by Irish-American clergy as paganism at best and as religious apathy at worst. A writer in the *Ecclesiastical Review*, commenting on Italian immigrants, argued that "religious indifference is a ravaging contagion among them...."[4] Father Reilly of New York's Nativity Church added that

> ...the Italians are not a sensitive people like our own. When they are told that they are about the worst Catholics that ever came to this country, they don't resent it or deny it. If they were a little more sensitive to such remarks they would improve faster. The Italians are callous as regards religion.[5]

Another writer, Paul V. Flynn, sadly lamented that "it is unfortunate...that so many of the men are so lukewarm, indifferent to the practices of their religion." He then brought up a familiar point. The men, he was astonished to observe, "are seemingly contented to have their wives and daughters do all the praying."[6]

From the Irish point of view, Italian immigrants posed a clear theological threat. Their system of saints was incomprehensible to a clergy and lay people steeped in the absolute authority of God and Jesus. So too was the institutionalization of theology among southern Italians, which featured informal Masses, feasts with dubious Christian links, strict separation between the public religious duties of men and women, and, what appeared to be most threatening of all, the tendency of Italian-Americans to dismiss priests who insisted upon a strict interpretation of Catholic theology. We again return to Flynn for an appropriate comment.

> ...some seem to think that they may at will discharge
> the Priest whom the Bishop has sent to them and
> supplant him with another of their own selection.
> Shortly after the Mission was opened, no less than
> three Italian priests were invited by their countrymen
> to come to Newark. These people would like to own
> a church edifice, to do with it as they please....[7]

Not surprisingly, antipathy quickly became the dominant feature of Irish-Italian relations in the church. Irish clergy, and their followers, commented bitterly on the "heathen" quality of *Mezzogiorno* worship. They were continuously stunned by what they perceived as disrespect for both the Church and God himself. An Irish-American in Harlem commented that

> These Italians were strange people, very strange to
> us...that they were dressed in a manner unaccus-
> tomed among us, that their language was nothing
> like what had been told us about the sonority of
> Italian speech, that they were noisy and ill mannered
> mattered little.... We even had pity for them. But,
> for God's sake, when they began to come to our
> church and made a market place of it, we were sure
> that they were the people whom the Lord chased
> from the temple. In those days we were quite sure,
> and even today I don't see how they have the nerve
> to call themselves Christians when they are not.[8]

As a result of such appraisals, Italian-Americans became what writer Alberto Giovannetti called "basement Catholics." In 1886, one immigrant remembered that "we Italians were allowed to worship only in the basement part of the Church" at East 115th Street in East Harlem.[9] Other documents of the period, such as the *Souvenir History of Transfiguration Parish-Mott Street, New York, 1827–1897*, reveal the sharp distinction between the "upper" and "lower" Catholic church.

> While all that we have spoken of refers to the upper
> church, let it not be forgotten that we have three
> Masses in the basement for the Italians of the parish,
> and that Father Ferretti, under Father McLoughlin's

direction, does very efficient work for that portion of
his flock.[10]

Theological differences which led to this sort of discrimination
intensified the conflict between Italian immigrants and the Irish-American
church in an unexpected way. A small but vocal number of immigrants
began to break completely with Catholicism. Irish clergy had not cultivated
the spirit of theological conciliation evident in southern Italian villages,
where the Church viewed Catholic form as better than no Catholicism at all.
Continued insistence on using Irish priests in Italian neighborhoods, along
with a refusal to recognize the legitimacy of pre-Christian rites, drove some
immigrants to desperate measures.   In their case, complete secession
appeared to be the only option.

In 1914 "The Independent National Roman Catholic Church of St.
Anthony of Padua" was formed in Hackensack, New Jersey. In a privately
published history written in 1962, Father Joseph Anastasi tells of the Italian-
Americans who were denied a church of their own by the Irish-dominated
hierarchy in Newark.[11] "They petitioned the Bishop of the Roman Catholic
Diocese of Newark to send them an Italian priest to organize an Italian
parish," Anastasi explained, "but their request was not granted." He added
that "a petition was repeated time and again, and each time it was met with
the same denial by the Roman Hierarchy; St. Mary's Church was good
enough."[12]

After months of fruitless petitioning to the Bishop, a young priest at
Our Lady of Mount Carmel in Newark, Father Antonio Giulio Lenza,
entered the strife. An assistant pastor frustrated by his lack of responsibility at Mount Carmel, and disturbed by the Irish hierarchy's treatment of
Italian-Americans, Lenza was also a political populist. He began to travel
frequently to Hackensack in an effort to persuade "the people to organize
their own Italian parish in spite of the Bishop's refusal." He was confident
that "such action would force the Bishop's hand and, if necessary, the case
could be presented to the Apostolic Delegate in Washington and to the
Holy Father in Rome." We are told that the "whole colony rallied to him."
Thus during the Christmas season of 1914, St. Anthony of Padua was
"incorporated under the State Law."[13]

The reaction of the Church in Newark and Washington was swift and
sure. Anastasi recalls that

> ...the Roman Bishop of Newark was not to take all
> of this with a smile. The adventurer priest was "ipso
> facto" suspended and another priest was dispatched
> to Hackensack to organize a bona fide Roman parish
> among the Italians of the First Ward. A letter from
> the Apostolic Delegate in Washington, denouncing
> the suspended priest as an imposter, was freely
> circulated and all the Italians were urged to support
> the priest sent to them by the Bishop and to have
> nothing to do with Father Lenza.[14]

After struggling for years with debts and the "hate and antagonism" of local Catholics who remained loyal to the Church, St. Anthony's was eventually reorganized under the auspices of the Episcopal church. Unlike the Catholic church in Hackensack, the Episcopalians made numerous concessions to the popular religious rites of Italians immigrants. Interested only in "our Lord's 'lost sheep,'" the Episcopalians undertook such an array of accommodations that "the people of St. Anthony's were fully convinced of the Catholicity of the Episcopal Church and of the validity of her Sacraments."[15]

The spirit of independence evident among Italian Catholics which, in this case, propelled them into the clutches of Episcopalians, was a concern among some of the lesser Irish clergy from the early 1880s on. Unlike their superiors who had far less contact with Italian immigrants, these clergymen were concerned about the Italian propensity for independence. They thus mounted a campaign with the hierarchy which called for compromises with popular religion.[16] Incidents like the one in Hackensack were occurring with alarming regularity. The intransigence of the Irish hierarchy continued to be met with Italian rebellion throughout the New York metropolitan area. A letter from a local pastor to Bishop Wigger in Newark is indicative of the warnings emanating from the local level.

> The contagious fever of building private chapels...by
> the Italians in Hoboken is on the increase. Another
> son (T. Damelio), a good man taken by this kind of
> spirit, is building another chapel on his own proper-
> ty, and at his own private expense.[17]

This outbreak of rebelliousness, along with the conversion of a minority of Italian-Americans to evangelical religions, eventually convinced the Irish hierarchy that some compromises were called for.[18] What we see, then is an eventual adoption of the attitude visible in the Roman Catholic Church of Italy—the outward form of Catholicism is better than no Catholicism at all. Even a Catholicism replete with pre-Christian rites was superior to the spectacle of Italian immigrants wandering into such institutions as the Broome Street Tabernacle or the Brooklyn City Mission. Evangelical preachers were increasingly capitalizing on the alienation and anger felt by Italian-Americans towards the Catholic church. Working on a daily basis in working class communities, ministers were able to see what local Irish priests were warning about. In Albany, the Reverend Creighton R. Story of the First Baptist Church noted that

> We have made some gratifying discoveries, some of which might be mentioned. First of all, the Italians are not such loyal Romanists as we supposed. Some of them are, but the majority have nothing but indifference or aversion for the whole extortionate and oppressive system.... They are most susceptible to sympathy; they do not desire alms, but Christian friendliness.[19]

Irish clergy thus began mounting a counterattack on the intrusion of evangelicals through a concerted accommodation with the southern Italian religion. As early as 1899 such churches as Our Lady of Mount Carmel in Newark were known for their "Italian ways and traditions, such as the celebration of certain Italian patron saint's feast days." "Diocesan authorities acquiesced here," we are told, "as they had at St. Peter and Paul in Hoboken."[20] Acquiescence translated into a reluctant toleration of pre-Christian rites which the Irish hierarchy continued to openly disdain.[21] That toleration, however, was fundamentally different from the kind evident in Italy. In New Jersey and New York, Irish-American church leaders insisted on a clear theological division between popular forms and Catholic doctrine. Irish priests continued to advocate the rigid and impersonal theology of the Church while ignoring such manifestations of southern Italian theology as the feast. Italian communities were eventually allowed to construct their own churches—but they were generally churches staffed by Irish-American or northern Italian priests.[22] Parishioners continued to complain of this policy, but they tempered their resentment with a realization that the Church was making compromises. However, few knew just what some of "their" Italian priests thought of them. In 1903 Father Gideon de Vincentiis wrote to the Pope from New Jersey.

> Your Holiness, we earnestly beg you to save us that shame which more than any other causes us Italian priests to blush. This terrible and glaring ignorance of our people makes us the butt of sarcasm and depreciation. It is our real cross in America.[23]

Italian-American workers, typically ignorant of what their spiritual leaders really thought, were satisfied with the concessions won by the beginning of the twentieth century. They went out happily to live those victories, triumphs which, they were convinced, made them no less Catholic than their Irish superiors.

Rural Italian Catholicism in the United States

The first signs of victory for those popular rites (not yet tolerated within the confines of the American Catholic Church) were apparent in the 1880s. Numerous observers noted the initiative taken by immigrants in fostering their traditions without benefit of the Church's approval.[24] "Nominally they are all Roman Catholics," a writer in *The Cosmopolitan* discovered, "but as a class they are very little attached to that organization." Accordingly, Italian immigrants "often [have] superstitious, though not reverential, awe of the religious observances to which they are accustomed...."[25] Writers such as the famed Jacob A. Riis, who in 1899 observed the worship of saints among immigrants from the village of Auletta, were astonished to see the lengths to which immigrants went in order to worship any of a number of deities. Having discovered "that some Italian village saint was having his day celebrated," Riis and a friend set out to observe what was going on.

> It led us to a ramshackle old house in Elizabeth street, and halted there in front of a saloon.... We followed the women, the children, and the scraggy

> ones through a gap in the brick wall that passed for
> an alley to the back yard, and there came upon the
> village of Auletta feasting its patron saint.
>
> It was a yard no longer, but a temple. All the
> sheets of the tenement had been stretched so as to
> cover the ugly sheds and outhouses. Against the
> dark rear tenement the shrine of the saint had been
> erected, shutting it altogether out of sight....[26]

Riis saw one of numerous pre-Christian rites brought to America. Along with the worship of saints, there were the offsetting powers of evil invested in the workings of those who had the evil eye.[27] As in southern Italy, saints were invoked to protect loved ones against the transgressions of *il mal occhio*. In fact, the role of saints in this regard became intensified in New Jersey and New York, as, not surprisingly, Irish-American priests refused to intercede against the intrusions of the evil eye.[28] On those occasions when saints were proven to be ineffectual, another rural Italian custom—that of wearing protective amulets—was employed. In Rochester, for example, the

> best way of protecting yourself from the Devil was
> to carry a pointed amulet, preferably a horn, so that
> you could grasp it when someone with the evil eye
> looked at you. If you did not have the amulet, then
> the next best thing you could do was to form your
> hand in the shape of two horns.[29]

The same menacing evil emanating from the evil eye also emerged from the witches of New Jersey and New York. Disease and personal misfortunes were typically blamed on the workings of a *"strega,"* or witch, a practice which did not die with the immigrant generation.[30] Witches were seen as sheer repositories of creative evil, people who devoted their lives to the acquisition and practice of terror. A *"fattura,"* or the curse of a witch, was "far more deliberate and insidious than the evil eye, for it presupposed the services of a witch with a professional knowledge of black magic."[31] "Professional" was not a random choice of words. Some immigrants believed that witches received specialized training in the southern Italian town of Benevento.[32] The social worker Phyllis Williams writes that after "the witches received their instructions there, they went around the villages seeking to do harm either because they had a grudge against someone or 'just for the devil of it.'"[33] Williams' observation, though important, misses a key element in the perception of witches—their professional status in the eyes of many southern Italian immigrants. Witches earned a living through the collection of fees for their services, thereby receiving a grudging respect as independent practitioners. They were available to anyone who wanted to settle an old score—and were willing to pay money for that pleasure.

Look at the case of a woman named Rosina in turn of the century Rochester. A solid laborer who "was more loved and admired than any other Sicilian woman in the neighborhood," she was mysteriously stricken with mental illness and eventually committed to an asylum. Friends and relatives, unable to understand why "cousin Rosina went crazy," turned angrily to one of their neighbors, who was suspected of having placed a curse on Rosina. "How could anyone dislike her so much as to hire a witch to put a curse on her?" one woman asked, "tears gathering in her eyes."[34]

The suspected neighbor was a middle-aged spinster who had been disappointed years earlier by a lover who never married her. It was thought that she envied the beautiful and vibrant Rosina and her three little boys. Neighbors recalled that the spinster had recently filed a complaint which charged that Rosina was not taking care of her children properly. Because she was the sister of a Rochester alderman, city officials simply assumed the complaint to be true and visited Rosina. They warned her that if such complaints continued, local authorities would take the boys from her and place them in foster homes.[35]

Rosina and her family, already pressed financially and emotionally due to husband Vincenzo's heavy drinking, was now confronted with a new burden—the peering eyes of local social workers. Rosina, pregnant with her fourth child, became increasingly beset with anxiety as the world seemingly caved in on her. We are told that

> She began to see ugly faces peering in through the
> windows; she heard voices outside the kitchen door
> telling each other what a bad mother she was, and
> when she found window rods and chairs in her
> home mysteriously broken, she was sure that some-
> one was plotting against her.[36]

As her condition worsened, her relatives, "certain by this time that Rosina was the victim of a fattura," persuaded Vincenzo that the only remedy was to hire a "good" witch. Such witches, who were of both sexes, "did not always work evil." "They healed diseases," Williams discovered, "mended broken hearts, dissolved spells, and even caused [old] men to pine away and die."[37]

Accordingly, Rosina's relatives contacted a male witch named Cristo in Buffalo. Throughout the early decades of the twentieth century, he enjoyed "a wide reputation in upstate New York for fighting the Devil successfully." Anyone who was as capable as that was surely a good choice to dispel a mere curse in Rochester. Before agreeing to meet Rosina, his relatives had to promise to bring a large fee in the form of food and drink. The family subsequently left for Buffalo.[38]

Upon arrival "they were ushered into the inner sanctum of Cristo." Seating Rosina, Cristo "began to mutter incantations over her" while pouring oil down her back. "The experience had a healthy effect on Rosina for a while," we are told. Vincenzo and his relatives "began to believe that perhaps Cristo had actually succeeded in curing Rosina." But their conclusion was premature. Several days later Rosina had her worst attack to date. Confined to a psychiatric hospital, her visits home became fewer as her illness deepened. Eventually, she did not return home at all.

Rosina, a laborer overwhelmed with problems, was able to make herself heard without being able to make those around her understand that what had really caused her breakdown was fear. It was a fear rooted in real causes—primary among these were the economic uncertainties of proletarian life and the added burden of threatening city officials. The remedy of Cristo was merely another manifestation of what can be called a religion of fear; one which called for a continuous set of protective measures through the use of ritual. Rosina and those around her were essentially powerless, and they knew it. A semblance of personal control was thus reached through religious rituals. The rituals of witches became objective truth because they enjoyed a legitimacy constructed through common consent.

And there were other rituals beside those of saints and witches. Rites conducted during the feasts of St. John the Baptist at Manhattan's Baxter Street Church and Hoboken's Santa Maria Church are a good example of how people's religion was used in an attempt to gain some personal control. These feasts, which took place annually on June 24, featured attempts to glimpse at a young girl's future marriage. On the evening before the feast, Italian-American girls placed an egg in a glass of water. Sign readers the following morning interpreted the girl's future marriage through a study of the shapes taken by the eggs and through a consideration of the configuration of the water bubbles in the glass. This custom was reported to work only during the time of *festa*. Attempts to utilize it at other times were futile.[39]

Rituals such as this bring us to another aspect of Italian people's religion. While fear of the seemingly unmanageable world provided a central rationale for a theology of tactical defense, the pragmatic thrust of a theology designed to meet immediate needs also legitimized the social organizations within which workers lived. For instance, egg readings legitimized the maintenance of a known and accepted social universe. The outer boundaries of social reality, i.e., the limits binding one within an exploitative web of capitalist social relations, were already beyond the individual's capacity for immediate change. But the construction of institutions such as weddings was clearly within the province of the worker's control. Rituals such as egg reading reinforced this perception, and lent an air of optimism to an otherwise fatalistic culture.

There was even a discernible division of labor within the context of theological practice. Witches with various specialties and sign readers specializing in eggs served the function of normalizing a society administered by experts. Egg readers did not compete with witches, for they occupied different provinces. One learned within the ethnic enclave that skilled experts had control over a specific portion of the social landscape. Just as in southern Italy, such rituals strengthened traditional ways of looking at the world. Initiative could be carried only so far. Rituals which exuded habitualization limited the range of possible human action. We are thus confronted with the spectacle of workers who often question a Roman Catholic Church that seemingly infringed upon conservative tradition.

With such perceptions paramount in the lives of Italian workers, a Catholic doctrine which emphasized an unworkable set of absolute Christian ethics appeared, at best, irrelevant. It was precisely those high-minded values which Irish-Catholicism stressed. One young Irish-American in the late nineteenth century recalled how he dreaded the frightening priest, whose "sermons in Lent scared me into a nervous misery although I was not in the least a sensitive child. You can find how he talked about hell and purgatory in Joyce's first novel."[40] Irish Catholicism closely resembled the Protestantism of the nineteenth century in its doctrinal intolerance.[41] This attitude was rooted in the particular Catholicism of Ireland, where rituals such as the Mass were conducted with a reverence unheard of in rural Italy.[42] It was most clearly embodied in a formal and unyielding theological system that lacked the fluidity and ethical relevance of Italian rural religion.[43] Represented in the very architecture of the Irish-American church, this system gave use to ornamentation which "represents the light of faith which the Dominicans carried in their combat with heresy."[44] Integral to Irish Catholicism was Irish nationalism, a nationalism which proudly featured Irish saints who were there to be revered rather than used as intermediaries in a harsh world. At St. John's Church in Newark, there were "two side towers recalling the ancient Round Towers of Ireland—all recessed and interlaced most delicately and standing as a monument to the mind that conceived the modeling...." St. John's also featured statues of saints who occupied "positions of honor [which] are wisely assigned to the great Patron and Patroness of the Irish race."[45]

The clear national pride of the Irish church—which did little on that level alone to make the Italian-American feel comfortable— matched a theology of serous moral purpose on the local level. Differing little in intent or appearance from Anglo-American reform groups of the Progressive era, the "parochial societies" of the Irish-American Church worked to protest "profanity, blasphemy, and immorality." Holding demonstrations in Elizabeth, Paterson, and Jersey City, such groups as the Holy Name Society worked to forcibly impress upon immigrants the importance of accepting a Christianity replete with a moral zeal unknown in Italian churches. In Newark, Protestant officials lay aside doctrinal differences with Irish Catholics in order to pursue a Christianity that was morally absolute. For example, a description from 1907 reads:

> A few Protestant gentlemen took part in the procession in this city, including Police Justice David T. Howell. Individual members of the Holy Name Society have another duty to perform besides taking

> part in parades, approaching the Sacraments at
> stated times and refraining from blasphemy and
> profanity—when walking along the highways and
> byways or employed at their daily labors, let them
> uncover their heads whenever they hear the Name of
> God taken in vain or the Holy Name blasphemed,
> raise their hearts to Heaven and say, "Blessed be the
> Name of God," or "Blessed be the Name of Jesus
> ...."[46]

Irish Catholicism's moral purpose was undoubtedly bourgeois in its cultural implications. Confident moral zeal indicated a belief in the relevance of planning for a future which would be qualitatively better than the present. To cite an obvious example, heaven was something in preparation for which to discipline oneself; an avoidance of "profanity, blasphemy, and immorality" constituted progress towards that end. It was a theological strategy of positive construction, one that differed dramatically from the defensive thrust of rural Italian theology. Irish Catholicism, like its Anglo-Protestant counterpart, was pragmatic only in order to serve higher moral purposes. The advice of Bishop Wigger of Newark that Irish Catholics utilize a specific method in order to avoid blasphemy illustrates how moral earnestness gave rise to seemingly pragmatic attitudes.

> Say to him that every time he swears or blasphemes
> let him fine himself—take ten cents out of one
> pocket, put it into another and give the money to the
> poor. Let him do this and he will soon break himself
> of the habit, for there is nothing which appeals to the
> heart and conscience of some men and tends to
> refresh the memory like touching the pocketbook.[47]

Pragmatism in Italian-American Catholicism had nothing to do with the moral absolutism advocated by Wigger and other officials of the American Catholic church. Because this was a central religious difference with both Irish Catholicism and Anglo-American Protestantism, it merits an elaboration.

Pragmatic Catholicism

The emphasis on a pragmatism devoid of higher ideals had its basis in the Hellenic conception of "pragmatikos." This pre-Christian idea of value had, as it foundation, the concern that something had worth because it worked in the social context of daily life.[48] Such a vantage point did not easily lend itself to more abstract notions of good and evil. Workers consequently determined the worth of a religious belief by its apparent ability to produce desired ends. Italian rural theology thus "employed" and "fired" saints with dizzying regularity. The philosophical absolutes of Catholic doctrine became irrelevant in such a system. People could avoid evil and misfortune through any of a number of devices—anything went so long as it seemed to produce desired results. In the case of saints, we know that Italian peasants openly discarded holy relics when they did not do what they were supposed to do. This tradition continued in New Jersey and New York well into the twentieth century.

Thus in Rochester, Luigi, a dissenting Sicilian worker castigated his relatives for spending money to placate saints:

> This extravagance is part of the bribery you extend
> to your saints…. You try to get on their good side
> because you are afraid of them, and so you spend
> your hard-earned dollars in this fabulous way.

Luigi went on to add that these "Christian" practices were Catholic in a very dubious way:

> In the old days, before anyone knew about dollars,
> they used to kill people to make the gods happy.
> Now you run out and buy a chicken and kill that.
> The principle is really the same.[49]

Placation did not always work, however. Rochester residents thus spoke of Italian-Americans who burst into church with the intention of destroying a saint's statue and replacing it with another who hopefully fulfilled the purpose assigned to it.[50] This was evident in the New York metropolitan area as well through the 1940s.[51] Such behavior horrified an Irish-American clergy steeped in a theology which emphasized unquestioning piety and devotion to Catholic ideals.[52]

The conditional reverence exhibited towards saints, Jesus, and God was, form the perspective of Church officials, bad enough. Other aspects of Catholic life among the men, and the amount of money contributed to Catholic causes, further irritated Irish-American clergy. Julian Miranda, whose grandfather had emigrated from the Sicilian village of Castelbuono in 1907 recalled that "Southern Italian men were not so church scrupulous as the women although they were Catholic." Another commentator remarks that "among Italians...religion was strictly for women, and, as in Italy, generally even those men considered devout absented themselves from services with a studied and uniform regularity."[53] Scholars have pointed to the preponderance of women in church devotions, while novelists such as Garibaldi M. Lapolla have focused on the primary importance of women in Italian-American religious rituals.[54] That importance rested in a belief in the female's ability to be more readily understood by the saint to whom she prayed. Women embodied suffering; a suffering intensified by childbirth, thus making women physically akin to the powerful Madonna.[55] When Carmela lay agonizing during labor in Lapolla's *The Grand Gennaro*, it was an old woman who was brought in to pray.

> Oh, Virgin Mary...she broke into a clear loud cry...
> thou who hast had the agony of a suffering child,
> thou wilt understand when we pray thee to be
> merciful, to go before thy glorious Son and tell Him
> to be kind to our Carmela.[56]

As important as their similarity to the Madonna was the cultural centrality of women, who generally exercised control over the home in a way not apparent in the dominant American culture through the mid-twentieth century.[57] That power made them a logical emissary to the world of supernatural deities, who were thought to respond most favorably to those who merited respect. Rural Italian society had long emphasized the dominant position of the wife and mother; they could not be replaced as easily as fathers and husbands.[58] Devotion to the Madonna who, as a woman, soared above men in terms of everyday practical importance, expressed this central cultural motif. Historian Robert Orsi provides an illustration of this importance:

> Rose Marello Tiano immigrated to East Kingston,
> New York, from Calabria in 1906. By the time of her
> death in 1939 at the age of one hundred and two,
> Rose Tiano was presiding over a huge domus, a
> "prolific tribe," in the words of one of her grandchil-
> dren, which included some three hundred members
> spanning four generations. Rose's authority over this
> domus was total. She never learned how to speak
> English and insisted that all her grandchildren and
> great-grandchildren be taught the Calabrian dialect,
> which they were, out of respect and fear of Rose.
> No family decision could be taken without her
> participation.[59]

Irish Catholicism did not emphasize a strict division between the
religious importance of men and women. Nor did Anglo-American
Protestantism. In both of these theological systems, men and women
subscribed to a set of rigid moral standards in which the practicality of
those standards was a secondary consideration in the pursuit of moral
absolutes.[60] The Italian religious system accorded women a primary role in
devotional service precisely because the sole objective was to get practical
results, and the cultural primacy of the female, along with her physical
kinship with the Madonna, made her a logical choice. Practicality was
never a route to spiritual fulfillment; it was always the end objective.[61]

Italian theology thus embraced the world in a different way than did
Irish Catholicism. Designed as a defensive strategy to cope with the status
quo, it did not seek to move beyond in hopes of building a better world.
Its religious ethics were eclectic at best, and they were always modified to
meet the situation at hand. Its only coherent philosophy was one of
immediacy and defense against a hostile world not subject to change.
Italian Catholics did not exhibit the rational consistency of either Irish
Catholicism or Anglo-American Protestantism, a consistency always
synthesized in some kind of higher order exuding moral absolutes. They
viewed reality as hostile, arbitrary, and irrational, and their defensive
theological categories were designed accordingly.

Workers' theology became apparent in the elaborate public displays of Italian-American feasts, during which religious rituals expressed defensive strategies founded on fear. In most feasts, the length of the celebration was irrelevant—they could be days or weeks long, depending on the perceived success of warding off evil for another year.[62] Guided by spontaneous behavior, these rituals lacked the rigid and temporally disciplined quality of Irish Catholic services, as Orsi has suggested:

> Italian Harlem slept little during the days of the festa. Children played with their cousins from New Haven and Boston and then fell asleep in the laps of the adults, who stayed up all night talking and eating. People went into the crowded streets at two or three in the morning to go to confession or to attend a special mass at the church that had been offered to la Madonna for the health of their mother or in the hope of finding a job.[63]

Any emphasis on a disciplined religious ritual equated with "worship" as such was relegated to an obscure position during the festa. Throughout, the concern was a public and unpremeditated defense against the onslaught of misfortune. As Lapolla remarked in 1935, the society of Saint Elena was formed, "as the gaudy pink banner of heavy fringed silk proclaimed to the world, for the purpose of mutual protection against disease and mishaps."[64]

Rather than seeking higher moral ideals through disciplined worship, participants in the feast achieved some semblance of safety in the world through devotion to caring saints and the purchase of charms. Devotion to saints often reached intense heights of self-inflicted pain. Thus Riis wrote in 1899 that a woman carries a mighty candle on her bare shoulder, walking barefoot on the hot asphalt." He went on. "Some march barefoot the six miles and over from Mulberry Street, choosing the roughest pavements and kneeling on the sharpest stones…lest there should be none sharp enough, the most devout carry flints in their pockets to put under their knees."[65] This intensity did not wane with the immigrant generation. Thirty-six years later Lapolla observed that at the feast of Saint Elena in Harlem "dozens of …men and women both, would…get on their knees and cry aloud or mutter wild, incoherent prayers, beating their breasts, raising their hands with fingers widespread."[66]

Purchasing charms was the other public way of warding off danger for another year. Booths were set up along the sidewalk, offering an assortment of horns, hunchbacks, and wax body parts.[67] These charms were then proudly displayed in the numerous parades featured during the feasts. Statues of the saints to be worshipped were carried in these processions. The faithful rushed out to pin money on the saint as another form of devotion. In 1938 the *Italian Tribune* in Newark told how "Newarkers Observe Our Lady of Mt. Carmel Day:"

> The observance of the traditional religious feast of Our Lady of Mt. Carmel took place in the Italian churches with more than 50,000 Roman Catholic parishioners participating....
> On Saturday afternoon, to herald the opening of the feast, a forty piece band marched through the streets of the Ironbound section.[68]

Another important part of the feast was the enormous outlay of foods present at every turn. Neighbors and visitors alike gathered for dinners that went on for hours. Snacks were offered continuously between meals and they could be found in both private homes and in booths on the street. Just as Riis had spoken of the "cry of the chestnut-vender" and "pink lemonade...hawked along the curb," Lapolla later on tells us that the "sidewalks were lined with booths, each booth strung with dried nuts and laden with masses of tinted cakes and torroni."[69] The turn of the century reformer, Anna Ruddy, wrote that

> Booths lined the streets on every side, where one might buy Italian dainties of every description. Impromptu restaurants were ready to serve delicious macaroni at tables on the sidewalks, and street vendors cried their wares as the procession passed: tempting pies filled with tomato, red pepper and garlic; Italian beans boiled in oil and red pepper; hot waffles, boiled corn, ice-cream, sliced watermelon, and a dozen cooling beverages.[70]

All three aspects of the ceremony—devotions to the saints, charms, and food—attempted to ward off misfortune or, especially in the case of food, to affirm a momentary sense of personal safety.[71] The threat of hunger was a lingering fear of both the immigrants and their descendants through the middle of the twentieth century.[72] Accordingly, an elaborate and abundant display of food symbolized a momentary harmony with the world in a vivid, physical sense. As Ruddy wrote, Italian workers at *la festa della Madonna di Monte Carmine* noticed a "pale and pinched" child's face. A "feast of good things to eat that day" would alleviate the boy's hunger pangs temporarily.[73]

The need to ease anxieties intensified in an urban and industrialized environment. Italian-American workers clung to the festive abundance of food as a public symbol of temporary order and serenity. Festival booths attempted to convey the yearning for social rhythm and personal order—both strong emotional components of personal safety and security. The offering of traditional foodstuff in large amounts underscored the cultural ideals of familiarity and consistency. Food booths at the feast managed to temporarily subdue one of the workers' greatest fears—impending hunger. This was a reassuring notion in a culture steeped in distrust and fear. "A feeling of security," dietary scholars tell us, "is associated with orderliness or a lack of anxiety and tension over whether food will be forthcoming. Certain foods foster [emotional] security more than others, even apart from their ability to satisfy hunger."[74]

So again we find ourselves in an essentially defensive struggle. The individual worker has a self-image of powerlessness rooted in the reality of the worker's place in the social hierarchy of both rural Italy and New Jersey and New York. There was not room in this system for an individual to aspire to a higher moral plane through worship. The individual worker was effectively crushed by both the dominant American culture and the oppressive conservatism of Italo-American views of the world. No wonder, then, that the efforts of Italian religious reformers generally fell on deaf ears.

The Irrelevance of an Independent Path to Salvation

From the 1880s on, a small minority of Italian-American Protestants attempted to exploit dissatisfaction with the Irish Catholic church, and turn that dissatisfaction into new Protestants. In 1887 the Mt. Pleasant Baptist

Church was organized in Newark. In 1894 the Buffalo Baptist Union "turned towards the large and growing settlements of Italians, with a deepening conviction that effort should be made to evangelize them." The First Italian Mission began in 1897, and in 1900 was joined by another Brooklyn evangelical effort, the Ainslie Street Baptist Church. Other areas of New Jersey and New York, among them Mt. Vernon, Troy, Albany, Rochester, and Passaic, saw organized and zealous efforts designed to draw Italian-Americans away from Catholicism.[75]

The most prominent of the Italian Protestant reformers was Angelo di Domenica. A prolific writer and pamphleteer, he authored such works as *Siete Stato Battezzato?* (Have you been Baptized?); *Chi Sono I Pentecostali?* (Who are the Pentecostals?); *America Is Good To Me*; *Is the Pope the Representative of Christ on Earth, or the Successor of Peter?*; and *Protestant Witness of a New American*. The son of poor peasants from the village of Schiavi d' Abruzzo, di Domenica first became acquainted with evangelical preachers through his older brother, who had been converted through the effort of an Italian preacher at the Five Points Mission House in Manhattan. In *Protestant Witness*, di Domenica recalled that

> Before my conversion, I was addicted to card playing
> and other gambling devices…. One Sunday morning
> I began to play cards about nine o'clock; and the
> game continued until after twelve. My keen anxiety
> to win made me forget to go home for dinner….
> After dinner was over, my elder brother learned
> what I had been doing. Thereupon, he reproached
> me so severely that I would have preferred a good
> whipping instead.

di Domenica then went on to explain how his brother's angry indictment had filled him with guilt and foreboding about his future. This culminated in his conversion.

> I was desperate; I did no know what to do; I could
> not rest. Every morning and evening I prayed that
> God would give me victory. Gradually I became
> more interested in reading the Bible, and I listened to
> the preaching of the gospel by my brothers. After
> three months, I gave my heart to Jesus Christ who

> gave me peace and rest. Ever since that time I have never handled cards.[76]

di Domenica did indeed turn his attention from gambling. He spent the next several years engaged in evangelical work. He held open-air services in Newark. He traveled to the North Orange Baptist Church in Orange, New Jersey to preach to Italian workers on Sundays. Finally, he became involved in the Home Mission Society of Buffalo. He spoke optimistically of the goal of the Buffalo Baptist Union in 1894:

> The Buffalo Baptist Union, in its survey of the needy fields of that city, turned toward the large and growing settlements of Italians, with a deepening conviction that efforts should be made to evangelize them.... The mission was attended from the outset with success.... The "feast of the first fruits" was held in the Prospect Avenue Baptist Church, when 26 Italians, nearly all of them adults, made profession of their faith and were baptized...the work was progressing on all sides, as the gospel of salvation was preached to those who had been kept in darkness and in the shadow of unbelief.[77]

Despite di Domenica's unending optimism, the actual rate of conversion to Protestantism among Italian-Americans remained low. The absolute number of Italian-American Protestants remained low in New Jersey and New York between the late nineteenth century and the middle of the 1930s, as the research of historian Silvano Tomasi reveals.[78] By 1917 the absolute numbers of Italian-American Protestants in the New Jersey/New York area had not risen dramatically. The Protestant theologian, Antonio Mangano, complied statistics in 1917. They illustrate that no more than 1.8% of all Italian-American had been converted to Protestantism.[79] In two New York boroughs—Brooklyn and Queens—only 0.4% of all Italian-Americans were Protestant by 1935. Their dispersion among different demoninations is shown below:[80]

ITALIAN-AMERICAN PROTESTANTS IN
BROOKLYN AND QUEENS IN 1935

	Brooklyn		Queens	
Denominations	Churches	Members	Churches	Members
Baptist	5	753	0	0
Congregational	1	30	0	0
Lutheran	1	40	0	0
Episcopal Methodist	0	0	2	926
Presbyterian	5	816	0	0
United Presbyterian	1	152	0	0
7th Day Adventists	1	90	0	0
Church of the Brethren	1	85	0	0
Pentecostal	5	550	0	0

Thus the earlier optimism of a missionary such as di Domenica proved to be unfounded. Italian immigrants and their descendants did not flock to Protestantism, despite their differences with the Irish hierarchy of the Catholic church. An examination of di Domenica's writings helps to explain why this was so. Like Irish Catholic spokesman Paul Flynn, di Domenica stresses the individual's responsibility for salvation. Salvation, as an absolute moral ideal, was itself a problem within the Italian theological sphere. That issue aside, di Domenica's conversion experience was highly personal, centered in the control of the soul. In di Domenica's accounts, little distinguishes the self-discipline which allegedly adds up to material wealth from the salvation attained through prayer. Both goals placed at the forefront the qualities of thrift and industry.

However, di Domenica failed to comprehend that he was advocating another form of the dominant's work ethic—a conception already being redefined within the context of working class life. Replacing material poverty with spiritual poverty, di Domenica proposed that the latter resulted from "popery." Empty rituals, poor church attendance, and the outlay of scarce resources on feasts all added up to the presence of a "laziness" and "lack of thrift" which yielded spiritual poverty. di Domenica worked his way "up" from employment as a laborer in a shoe factory—and thereby entered into God's graces—only when he shunned the "moral and spiritual condition of the Italian people" in a highly personal way:

> I went into my bedroom, knelt before a chair and placing my hand on the Bible, promised the Lord that I would never handle cards again. I prayed fervently to God that he would give me strength to resist all temptations.[81]

Thus the Protestant road to moral purity was a lonely one. According to Italian American workers, Protestantism lacked the comforting reassurances earned in an essentially hostile world. Commenting on Presbyterian missionaries in 1918, Enrico C. Sartorio noted that there was "a chasm between the mentality of simple Italian women and that of the American lady parish visitor...[who enforces here] views without much consideration for the views and traditions of the other race."[82] Alberto Pecorini, whose observations of Italian-American laborers are recorded in numerous essays, said that Protestants "did not make proselytes among Italian immigrants, as they might have expected to do in the case of other races since Italians lacked that individual evolved conscience that Protestantism presupposes."[83] Pecorini understood that the Protestant way to salvation, like the Irish Catholic way, presumed the Christian's adherence to an individualistic creed. That creed never figured centrally in rural Italian culture at large—not to mention its religious component. Accordingly, even if one assumed there was a road to salvation, it was necessarily a group road, one in which like-minded workers comforted each other along the way.

Numerous workers commented that Protestantism's emphasis on the lone individual was not soothing in the same way as a group's relationship with a saint.[84] Nor did the whole enterprise of striving for salvation, a process inherently optimistic, fit in with the defensive thrust of Italian theology. Italian-American conceptions of God always emphasized the notion of fate. "I always offer all my suffering to God: May it be his will," one female worker wrote to the Madonna in 1947.[85] Such a perspective did not induce a turn towards an individual initiative designed to achieve pure goodness.

Indeed, the idea of human perfectibility was not accepted. Italian theology through the first half of the twentieth century typically remained an arena in which bargains with powerful saints were struck, saints who would hopefully provide protection against misfortune. Optimistic individualism could never transcend the assumption of fate. Little changed through 1980, as the theology of defensive struggle continued unabated.

CHAPTER SEVEN NOTES

1. See Silvano Tomasi, *Piety and Power: the Role of Italian Parishes in the New York Metropolitan Area, 1880–1930* (New York, 1975); Leonard Bacigalupo, "Some Religious Aspects Involving the Interaction of the Italians and the Irish," in *Italians and Irish in America*, ed. Francis X. Femminella (New York, 1985), pp. 115–129; Carmine A. Loffredo, "A History of the Roman Catholic School System in the Archdiocese of Newark, New Jersey, 1900–1965" (Ed.D. dissertation, Rutgers University, 1967); and Dennis J. Starr, "Roman Catholic Church," in *The Italians of New Jersey: A Historical Introduction and Bibliography* (Newark, 1985), especially p. 36. Also refer to Raymond J. Kupke's *Living Stones: A History of the Catholic Church in the Diocese of Paterson* (Clifton, New Jersey, 1987).

2. Edward Wakin, "Catholic Like No One Else," in *Enter the Irish-American* (New York, 1976), p. 86.

3. In Jerre Mangione, "God and the Sicilians," *Mount Allegro: A Memoir of Italian-American Life* (New York, 1981), p. 68.

4. W. H. Agnew, "Pastoral Care of Italian Children in America: Some Plain Facts about the Condition of our Italian Children," *Ecclesiastical Review*, March 1913, p. 258.

5. Quoted in Tomasi, "American Views of Italian Newcomers," p. 45.

6. Flynn, "First Italian Mission in Newark," in *History of St. John's Church, Newark: A Memorial of the Golden Jubilee of Its Consecration, in the Eighty-Second Year of the Founding of the Parish, with a Retrospect of the Progress of Catholicity* (Newark, 1908), p. 217.

7. Ibid., p. 216.

8. Quoted in Leonard Covello, "Cultural Dissimilarity of Italian Contadino As a Basis for Conflict in the United States," *The Social Background of the Italo-American School Child: A Study of the Southern Italian Family Mores and Their Effect on the School Situation in Italy and America* (Totowa, New Jersey, 1972), p. 278.

9. Ibid., p. 278.

10. *Souvenir History of Transfiguration Parish—Mott Street, New York, 1827–1897* (1897), p. 44.

11. Anastasi, *The History of The Church of St. Anthony of Padua, Hackensack,*

New Jersey (1962). This paper is housed in the Special Collections Room of the Archibald Stevens Alexander Library, Rutgers University.

12. Ibid., p. 5.
13. Ibid.
14. Ibid., pp. 5–6.
15. Ibid., p. 12.
16. See Loffredo's discussion of Our Lady of Mount Carmel church in Newark, in "A History of the Roman Catholic School System in the Archdiocese of Newark, New Jersey, 1900–1965," pp. 100–101.
17. Quoted in Tomasi, "The Emergence and Growth of the Italian American Parish," p. 95.
18. Refer to Tomasi's "Pluralism in the Church," pp. 177–185; and the letter of Father John B. Kayser, pastor of Our Lady of Victories church in Paterson, to Bishop Wigger, dated January 15, 1894, and reproduced in Carl D. Hinrichsen's "The History of the Diocese of Newark, 1873–1901" (Ph.D. dissertation, Catholic University of America, 1962), p. 318.
19. Quoted in E. E. Chivers, "Our Baptist Italian Mission Work," *The Baptist Home Mission Monthly*, May 1905, p. 198.
20. Loffredo, "A History of the Roman Catholic School System in the Archdiocese of Newark, New Jersey, 1900–1965," p. 101.
21. See, for example, Bishop Wigger's views on the southern Italian practice of confirming infants. Refer to Loffredo, p. 323.
22. In a 1906 article in *L'Opinione*, Pecorini wrote that

> Once they have arrived in New York...[the Italian priests] present themselves to the Archbishop, expecting to be sent to a parish. But they realize they are received with sweet-sour words, always discouraging. They can obtain only a temporary permit to say Mass for sixty days. The most fortunate are recommended to some Irish pastor, who allows the poor "dagoes" to meet in the basement of his church to say Mass on Sundays and the poor Italian priest is obliged to find himself in contact with someone who almost always despises him....

"L'attivita religiosa della italiani in America," *L'Opinione*, 29 March 1906, p. 1.

23. Quoted in Tomasi, "The Italian American Parish in Action," p. 161.

24. Anastasi, *The History of The Church of St. Anthony of Padua, Hackensack, New Jersey*; Geremia Bonomelli, *Lettera pastorale al clero e al popolo della sua diocesi* (Cremona, 1896); Grace Abbott, "Leo XIII and the Italian Catholics in the United States," *The American Ecclesiastical Review*, February 1889, pp. 41–45; J. G. Lognese, "Italian Catholic," *America*, 44, 1931, pp. 475–476; M. J. Hillenbrand, "Has the Immigrant kept the Faith?" *America*, 54, 1935, pp. 153–155; and Viola Roseboro, "The Italians of New York," *Cosmopolitan*, January 1888, especially p. 405. Also consult Henry J. Browne, "The 'Italian Problem' in the United States, 1880–1900," *U.S. Catholic Historical Society: Historical Records and Studies*, 35, 1946, pp. 46–72.

25. Roseboro, "The Italians of New York, " p. 405.

26. Riis, "Feast-Days in Little Italy," *Century Magazine*, August 1899, p. 491.

27. Two literary depictions of this belief are found in Jerre Mangione, "Evil Eye," in *Mount Allegro: A Memoir of Italian American Life* (New York, 1981), pp. 100–108; and Pietrero di Donato, *Three Circles of Light* (New York, 1960), pp. 157–160. Also refer to Phyllis Williams, "Religion and Superstition," in *South Italian Folkways in Europe and America: A Handbook for Social Workers, Visiting Nurses, School Teachers, and Physicians* (New York, 1969), pp. 141–145. Also see the interesting study of Edward S. Gifford, *The Evil Eye* (New York, 1958).

28. As Riis pointed out in "Feast-Days in Little Italy," the protecting saint belonged to the workers, not the church hierarchy.

> The Saint belonged to the people, not to the church.
> He was their home patron, and they were not going to
> give him up. (p. 493)

29. Mangione, "Evil Eye," pp. 101–102. Also see the fascinating photograph of numerous amulets in Williams, "Religion and Superstition," between pp. 142 and 143.

30. Jerry Della Femina, for example, speaks of seeing this as a young boy in the 1950s. See *An Italian Grows in Brooklyn* (Boston, 1978), pp. 75–76.

31. Mangione, "Evil Eye," p. 104.

32. See the discussion of Williams, "Religion and Superstition," p. 144.

33. Ibid.

34. Mangione, "Evil Eye," p. 104.
35. Ibid., p. 105.
36. Ibid.
37. Williams, "Religion and Superstition," p. 144.
38. Mangione, "Evil Eye," pp. 106–107.
39. See two newspaper articles devoted to this ritual in the *New York Times*, 13 June 1913, p. 30; and the *Corriere della Sera*, 24 June 1909, n.p.
40. Quoted in Wakin, "Catholic Like No One Else," pp. 97–98.
41. Look, for instance, at the remarks of Father Thomas J. McCluskey, a Catholic educator speaking at a New York City communion breakfast in 1908.

    > We do not experiment on the boy. We know what we intend to teach, and we teach it. We know our conclusions in Philosophy, and we have defended them before the world for three hundred years and upon our system has been placed the approval of the Church, "the pillar and the ground of truth."

    Quoted in Flynn, "A Most Remarkable Speech by Dr. Woodrow Wilson, President of Princeton University," p. 101.
42. For an example of it, we again return to Flynn, who quoted Bishop O'Connor.

    > Our churches are not meeting houses. The Catholic idea of a church is that it is the House of God, the dwelling place of Christ in the Blessed Sacrament. This is why we respect and reverence it and why the devout are willing to sacrifice their worldly means to decorate and beautify it.

    "Congratulations by Bishop O'Connor," p. 14.
43. An interesting summary in this respect is found in Richard Gambino's "Religion, Magic, and the Church," in *Blood of My Blood: The Dilemma of the Italian-Americans* (Garden City, New York, 1974), pp. 235–239.
44. Flynn, "The Art of St. John's," p. 19.
45. Ibid., pp. 19–20. Also see John Bossy, *Christianity in the West, 1400–1700* (New York, 1985), p. 12.

46. Flynn, "The Parochial Societies," p. 79.

47. Ibid., p. 81.

48. This is what Norman Douglas meant by religious "realism." Look at his depiction of the legend of St. Peter among the peasantry in "Tillers of the Soil," *Old Calabria* (London, 1983), p. 60.

49. Quoted in Mangione, "God and the Sicilians," p. 93.

50. Ibid., pp. 69–70.

51. Anger was also periodically directed against the Madonna herself, as a woman quoted in *Il Progresso Italo-Americano* made clear in a July 17, 1949 article (n.p.).

52. An Italian-American priest in East Harlem spoke of the Irish clergy's views of the festa:

> They thought we were Africans, that there was some-
> thing weird. They didn't accept it at all.... We were
> always looked upon as though we were doing some-
> thing wrong...and I knew from my own experience...-
> [that] they looked down on us.

Quoted in Robert Orsi, "Devotion to Mount Carmel in Italian Harlem," *The Madonna of 115th Street: Faith and Community in Italian Harlem, 1880–1950* (New Haven, 1985), p. 56.

53. Refer to the summary of church attendance in Hinrichsen, "The History of the Diocese in Newark, 1873–1901," pp. 317–318; and the oral interview of Julian Miranda, in *The Immigrants Speak: Italian Americans Tell Their Story* (New York, 1979), especially pp. 131–132.

54. *The Grand Gennaro* (New York, 1935).

55. Orsi, in *The Madonna of 115th Street*, speaks of this closeness in East Harlem.

56. Lapolla, *The Grand Gennaro*, p. 344.

57. As feminists such as Betty Friedan argued, middle class women were expected to be mere domestic fixtures, rather than active agents in their homes, families, and communities. Men had the authority to make ultimate decisions; their wives were mere recipients of orders. Novels about Italian-American life—not to mention the historical analysis of such scholars as Donna Gabaccia—reveal an Italian woman who is a local community leader; one to whom the husband turns respectfully

towards as a central matriarchal figure.

58. In the Sicilian district of Caltanissetta the law read that

> Any property that belongs to a wife may be disposed
> of by her without the husband's consent.... Either her
> dowry or gifts made to her by her children are outside
> the jurisdiction of the husband.

In Messina, Sicily, the legal code revealed that

> In case of separation, the wife retains the dowry no
> matter after how many years of married life it occurs.

An Italian-American laborer from the Ragusa district of Sicily was
quoted as saying that

> If we obeyed our father, it was so because we were
> afraid of him. We had no fear of our mother; but we
> obeyed and respected her because she was first a
> mother and secondly because she was an elderly
> woman.... Once in a while we made fun at some old
> man, but nobody would dare to do that to an old
> woman.

Finally, a popular expression from Catanzaro in Calabria:

> If father is dead, the family suffers; if mother dies, the
> family cannot exist.

Consult Covello, "Matriarchal Survivals," pp. 207–210; "Dominance of
Women in the House," pp. 210–217; and "Some Aspects of Father's
Inferior Position in the Home," pp. 217–220.

59. "Conflicts in the Domus," p. 131.

60. The writings of Flynn are instructive in this respect.

61. In the Irish-American church, moral absolutes always took precedence
over the development of a religious system which was flexible enough
to meet immediate practical demands. Indeed, some Irish clergy
preferred an empty church to one which compromised on theological
matters in order to attract parishioners. In Greenwich Village during

the 1920s, Caroline Ware observed that

> The Irish churches largely ignored the trends and changes of the time and, with a firm sense of their age-old foundation and the assumption that the essentials of human character are unchangeable, stood firm, shaping as far as possible their people to their mould. For the Irish churches, the measure of their weakness or their strength was thus the success or failure with which they kept their following within the pattern which they had drawn and maintained. For the Italian churches, by contrast, their measure of success or failure was the success with which they caught the key to the changing spirit of their people and so adjusted themselves to it as to pass with them through a process of change.

"Irish Catholic Conservatism," in *Greenwich Village, 1920–1930: A Comment on American Civilization in the Post-War Years* (New York, 1965), p. 305.

62. Orsi quoted one man who spoke of the feast's indeterminate time period:

> ...people came from Paterson...there was a group of these people from our *paese* who lived there...they would eat and drink for four days, five days, going on....

"The Days and Nights of the Festa," p. 2.

63. Ibid.
64. *The Grand Gennaro*, p. 46.
65. "Feast-Days in Little Italy," p. 498. Other instances of religiously inspired self-mutilation are described by Mangione in *Mount Allegro*.
66. *The Grand Gennero*, p. 46.
67. See the numerous references compiled by Orsi. Also refer to the article of Riis.
68. "Newarkers Observe Our Lady of Mt. Carmel Day," *Italian Tribune*, 28 July 1938, p. 1.
69. *The Grand Gennaro*, 47.

70. *The Heart of the Stranger: A Story of Little Italy* (New York, 1908), p. 69.
71. The social role of food in this respect has been discussed in Miriam E. Lowenberg et al., *Food and Man*, 2nd ed. (New York, 1974); Stanley Regelson, "The Bagel: Symbol and Ritual at the Breakfast Table," in *The American Dimension*, eds., W. Arens and Susan P. Montaque (Sherman Oaks, California, 1981); and John C. Camp, "America Eats: Toward a Social Definition of American Foodways" (Ph.D. dissertation, University of Pennsylvania, 1978).
72. The most comprehensive medical survey of malnutrition among Italian-American workers in the New York metropolitan area was completed in 1924 under the auspices of the New York Association for Improving the Condition of the Poor. The Association concluded, subsequent to a medical survey of 3,507 Italian children, that

> ...family income in most cases is inadequate to supply a proper standard of living.... Thorough physical examinations of large numbers of these children have revealed serious physical defects. In early childhood rickets of a severe form is unusually prevalent. Nearly forty percent of the children are found on the doctor's diagnosis to be undernourished.

John C. Gebhart, *The Growth and Development of Italian Children in New York City*, Publication Number 132 of the New York Association for Improving the Condition of the Poor (New York, 1924), p. 18. Also consult Genoeffa Nizzardini's "Infant Mortality for Manhattan, Brooklyn and Bronx, 1916–1931," *Italy-America Monthly*, 25 May 1935, pp. 12–17.
73. *The Heart of the Stranger*, p. 68.
74. Lowenberg et al., "Food Habits and Foodways," p. 147.
75. See the summary of Chivers, "Our Baptist Italian Mission Work."
76. di Domenica, "My Conversion and Aspiration," in *Protestant Witness of a New American: Mission of a Lifetime* (Philadelphia, 1956), pp. 26–27.
77. "The Italian Baptist Association," pp. 37 and 44.
78. Taken from the table presented in Tomasi, "The Italian American Parish in Action," p. 155.
79. *Sons of Italy: A Social and Religious Study of the Italians in America* (New York, 1917).

80. Taken from a table complied by Tomasi, p. 158.

81. "My Conversion and Aspiration," p. 26.

82. *Social and Religious Life of Italians in America* (Boston, 1918), p. 123.

83. Quoted in Alberto Giovannetti, "The Basement Catholics," *The Italians of America* (New York, 1979), p. 270.

84. An interesting summary of these views is found in May C. Marsh, "The Life and Work of the Churches in an Interstitial Area" (Ph.D. dissertation, New York University, 1932).

85. Quoted in Orsi, "The Theology of the Streets," p. 227.

8

THE MATURING OF
ITALIAN CATHOLICISM
IN THE POSTWAR PERIOD

My home, which by no means was a retreat
for the devout, still had its share of
artifacts. We had saints all over the place,
here a statue, there a painting.
> Jerry Della Femina, *An Italian*
> *Grows in Brooklyn* (1979)

Italian-American Catholicism, surface modifications to the contrary, did not undergo radical changes in the second half of the twentieth century. The main thrust of this religious system—its use as a protective device by workers who perceived themselves as particularly vulnerable to the arbitrary wielding of power—continued uninterrupted. In order to facilitate the attainment of this protection, Italian-American workers continued to see saints as powerful representatives to a mysterious and vague world beyond. Attendant rituals continued to play an important role. Not surprisingly, Protestantism and Irish Catholicism were still looked upon as incomprehensible systems emphasizing a personal path to moral absolutism which did not meet the demands of the real world. Accordingly, the historic conflict with the Irish hierarchy continued. Irish and Italian Catholics by 1980 still looked suspiciously upon one another.

It was an apprehension grounded, on the one hand, in the Irish argument that Italian-American Catholicism was really peasant "paganism."[1] The Irish hierarchy had grown more subtle than in previous years, however. Mindful of the threat of Italian secession, the Irish hierarchy from the late 1930s on openly endorsed the formation of what were termed "national parishes." By 1953, eighty-eight new parishes had been formed in the Brooklyn diocese under the direct sponsorship of Bishop Molloy. We are told that of "these 88 new parishes it is notable that 80, including two for Negroes, were English-speaking, seven were Italian, and one was Polish."[2] A church spokesman in 1954 outlined the Church's "new" stance concerning ethnic parishes:

> In bygone days each new national and ethnic group upon its arrival had to contend with prejudice from those who had preceded them. This was illustrated in the advent of the Irish and of the Germans. Since them America has become conscious that its destiny and the source of its strength is to be an amalgam of many peoples—e pluribus unum.[3]

Lofty rhetoric aside, Bishop Molloy's efforts to establish an officially sanctioned diversity within the Church was probably guided not so much by adherence to the notion of pluralism as by a fear of Italian departure.[4] Just as importantly, the Church's definition of pluralism did not mean that cultural diversity was itself a goal. Rather, pluralism via the ethnic parish was viewed as a transitional stage on the way towards a monolithic Catholic Church guided by the dictates of Irish Catholic doctrine.

At the same time that dioceses such as the one in Brooklyn were moving ahead with plans to create ethnic churches with unprecedented local autonomy, the Church hierarchy of the New York metropolitan area was quietly forging plans to centralize broad policy decisions even more than had been the case in the past.[5] Local Italian churches, though staffed by a growing number of Italian-American priests, still remained unable to formulate truly independent policies without the approval of a hierarchy which remained hostile to Italian practices.[6] The Irish-dominated hierarchy was still able, despite the unprecedented creation of ethnic parishes, to have the last say on broad matters of policy. The place of Catholic education was one clear example of how local parishes, though able to retain traditional practices, were nonetheless unable to extend those traditions past the periodic public displays of feasts and the veneration of saints.

In 1959 the leadership of the Newark diocese created an Archdiocesan Office of Education. Ethnic parishes displaying an interest in building parochial schools were in need of both Church approval and Church funds. However, those funds were only forthcoming when the parish asking for them agreed to meet strict theological guidelines. Italian parishes in need of church funds thus had to open themselves to the possibility of exposing their children to doctrinal principles not of their own choosing. Archdiocesan officials insisted on the doctrinal "purity" of prospective teachers and school administrators. What this meant, in effect, was that the local parish had little influence in the recruitment and retention of educators.

Italian-American parishes in the Newark diocese were quick to react to this perceived intrusion.[7] There remained from the late 1930s on a continuous struggle for doctrinal hegemony within the parochial schools. It was a contest in which Italian-American parishes in need of money from a centralized authority remained at a distinct disadvantage. Nonetheless, the battle to incorporate southern Italian moral philosophy into the curriculum went on to the chagrin of Church officials. At St. John's grammar school in Trenton, parents insisted in the early 1960s that "Italian culture [be] taught within the structure of the regular social studies curriculum."[8] Sister Anna Pompei, principal of Our Lady of Mount Carmel School in Newark, talked in 1965 of how "Italian is still taught" in her school, "as are Italian customs...."[9] Sister Martha Marasculo, principal of Our Lady of Mount Carmel School in Orange, New Jersey, explained that the parents of her students demand an emphasis on *Mezzogiorno* theology, for the "parish has been traditionally all Italian."[10] Sister Mary Anne de Salvo of Newark's St. Rocco School, which opened in 1956, discussed the same perspective among the "people of Italian descent" which attended her school.[11] Another Catholic school official, Sister Grace Polizzotto of the St. Nicholas School in Palisades Park, New Jersey, described her institution:

> School was established in 1958...parish predominant-
> ly Italian-speaking. program started with grades K

> through second...a grade was added each year from
> 1959 to 1964 until a full Kindergarten through eighth
> grade program was established...Italian language,
> customs, traditions, patron saints days, holidays are
> all observed and celebrated.[12]

Local insistence that funding should be available for Italian parishes retaining traditional outlooks met with strong resistance from the Irish hierarchy. Mary Perkins Ryan captured the perspective of the Irish leadership in her 1963 publication of *Are Parochial Schools The Answer?* She answered her own question with a qualified yes. "Some of our most cherished institutions will no longer seem necessary," she argued, "since they developed in response to a past situation and in accordance with a mentality belonging to the past—they may now be a positive deterrent to carrying out today's urgent tasks."[13]

"Today's urgent tasks" did not include the perpetuation of the "Italian culture" spoken of by the numerous local school officials I quoted. Church leaders instead advocated the doctrines espoused by the Third Plenary Council of the American hierarchy, which had originally met at Baltimore in 1884.[14] The Council emphasized an application of official Catholic doctrine at every possible point in the curriculum. As a result, parents and teachers on the local level did not have the authority to question numerous doctrinal assertions.

While the struggle over religious doctrine waged on endlessly within the parochial school classroom, the context in other areas had already been decided in favor of Italian-American workers. Throughout the post-war period, *Mezzogiorno* Catholicism was practiced without any sustained resistance from the Irish-American leadership. As in earlier days, the veneration of the saints and the various rituals of the people's religion formed the core of this system. Both of these ceremonial routes were founded on the belief that individuals wee in need of protection from a hostile and arbitrary environment.

Accordingly, the worship of saints continued in full force. Local parishes worshipped their namesake as a protector, as an intermediary who provided assistance in the struggle against unemployment, mental illness, the evil eye, or any other conceivable misfortune which the lone worker could not possibly fight against. Mt. Carmel parish in Lyndhurst, New

Jersey is a case in point. In a songsheet which included verse in both English and Italian, workers in the late 1970s recited a "Prayer to Our Lady of Mount Carmel":

> Holy Virgin Mary, splendor of Carmel, you favor us who worthily wear the blessed scapular of Mt. Carmel with your maternal protection. Fortify our weakness with your power, inspire us with your wisdom, increase in each of us the virtues of Faith, Hope and Love.
>
> You highly favored daughter of God, Full of Grace, help us in material and spiritual needs; grant us your loving intercession as we now ask God to hear our prayers and petitions.... Help us to seek and accept God's will in our lives as you did; with courage, trust and christian resignation.[15]

This passage is revealing in a number of ways. There is, first of all, the focus on Mary. Mary is the target of the prayer, not God. God looms as a background presence who merely finalizes what Mary has already decided. It is Mary, not God, who provides love and protection. All of the other songs on the songsheet emphasize this position of Mary as well. Secondly, there is the passive stance of the person saying the prayer or singing the song. None of the entries on this sheet reflect optimism. Instead, only a defensive bout with life's woes are spoken of. From this perspective, look at a song entitled "Hail Queen of Heaven."

> Hail, Queen of heaven,
> the ocean star, Guide
> of the wand'rer here
> below! Thrown on life's
> surge we claim they care,
> Save us from peril and
> from woe. Mother of Christ,
> Star of the sea, Pray for
> the wanderer, pray for me.[16]

Thus the veneration of Mary underscored a central theological element in *Mezzogiorno* religion—the essentially impotent position of the individual.

This frame of reference was classically conservative in the most intense of ways, for it depicted the individual as dependent upon powerful people for favors and protection. Individual initiative had no place in this view. The only initiative to be taken was the cultivation of the powerful's favor in an attempt, as one song put it, of surviving "in questa misera."[17]

This contrasted sharply with the Irish Catholicism of the New York metropolitan area. In an essay entitled "Some Aspects of Recent Catholic Life," John K. Sharp spoke glowingly of how parishioners "go forth...to spread the glad tidings among strangers...." They had, he argued, dedicated "themselves to Christian perfection."[18] Church leaders spoke continuously of their belief in the perfectibility of human beings, a position clearly at odds with what was being propagated in such parishes as Mt. Carmel in Lyndhurst.[19] The Irish hierarchy, unable to effectively eliminate this basic theological thrust on the local level, was able, nonetheless, to keep it from reaching the higher levels of the Church. This was accomplished through the simple expedient of promoting only theologically safe Irish priests. In 1983, for example, none of the five New Jersey dioceses had an Italian-American bishop or archbishop.[20] *The Official Catholic Directory* of that year also revealed that on the diocesan administrative level, none of the vicars general were Italian-Americans.[21] In New York the same pattern was evident. It was not until 1968, for instance, that Francis J. Mugavero became the first Italian-American bishop in the city.[22] The hierarchy in New York continued to be devoid of Italian-American representation at the policy-making level through the 1970s.[23] One observer captured the fundamental difference between Irish and Italian Catholicism which gave rise to this.

> Both the rationalistic, Thomist-oriented elite among the Irish and the Irish majority who followed their own unique religious folkways found the Italian practices at best superstitious and alien and at worst pagan and sacrilegious.... The strong creedal orthodoxy, institutional loyalty, and pro clerical feelings of the Irish were jolted by the Italians' chaotic individualism about doctrinal matters.... Perhaps above all, the Italians' pragmatic attitude toward the church and all things sacred outraged the intense piety common to Irish Catholicism.[24]

The Maturing of Italian Catholicism in the Postwar Period 277

The "sacrilegious" practices spoken of in this passage were the ritualistic expressions of a theological fatalism differing sharply from that of the "Thomist-oriented elite." Along with the subordination of God in favor of saintly intermediaries, there was the presence of numerous rituals involving the evil eye.[25] Local parish priests grudgingly accepted this, knowing full well that attempts to eradicate these beliefs would only serve to alienate parishioners even more than they were from Catholicism at large. Writers who emerged from the Italian-American working class in the postwar period spoke of the evil eye; of fears which permeated the lives of people in their neighborhood.[26] Here one author described what was called an "overlook" in the 1950s:

> Let us say, hypothetically, that someone who wished my parents evil comes into our home…. The guest, with evil in his or her heart, might give me the "eye," or an "overlook." If I was "overlooked," a curse had been put on me and then, naturally, my parents had to exorcise it.

Accordingly, "a little ceremony to get rid of the evil eye" was in order. Certain women in his Brooklyn neighborhood had been designated as witches capable of exorcising the curse. The trick was to understand that a curse had been placed. The evil eye was perceived as a most subtle force. We are therefore informed that

> The tipoff to whether a person had been "overlooked" or not depended upon what the evil person said. Signal phrases such as "What a lovely child you have" from a particularly evil person meant that the overlook had to be removed and plenty fast.

On other occasions, a child complaining of a headache was enough to indicate the presence of a curse.[27]

Still present were the same remedies for the evil eye which novelists and social workers had spoken of seventy years before. Scissors, for instance, were used in the same way that Phyllis Williams had described. Little packets of garlic were draped around the afflicted person's neck. A woman recalled that when the evil eye struck, her family "went through the ritual of getting out the garlic, oil, and scissors."[28]

Unlike their parents and grandparents, the Italian-American workers of the postwar period tended to privatize this aspect of their religious system. Unlike the public veneration of the saints through the feast, beliefs in the evil eye, and the remedies designed to eradicate it, were put safely away within the confines of home and local community. They were not admitted to outside of this circle of like-minded people. In Trenton during the 1970s, for instance, thirty-one-year-old Lisa remarked "it's something private and humble."[29] Mary Ann, age twenty-nine, described her private religious practices; customs which permeated all of the domestic facets of her life in Trenton:

> I wear St. Joseph and St. Francis [religious medals].
> The Last Supper is in my kitchen. Crosses are in all
> the bedrooms. The house is blessed each year. The
> children wore medals as babies, it is a bad omen if
> they are lost.[30]

Oral testimonies such as these, along with the writings of such working class novelists as Frank Miceli, suggest that it became increasingly important to publicly deny the presence of traditional religious practices to the outside world. The rationale for this behavior was the third and fourth generation's perception that the dominant American culture ridiculed Italian-American working class culture in general.[31] Thus their presence, when it left the home, was confined to the community in which it was practiced. Local Italian-American newspapers consequently carried a fascinating array of advertisements for witches skilled in the craft of removing curses or putting them in place. In 1968 "Sister Bright" of Orange Street in Newark advertised herself as a "healer and advisor" in the *Italian Tribune*. Her qualifications read, in part, that

> There's no hope so fond or wish so great that she
> can't accomplish for you. She guarantees success
> where others fail. She can and will help you on ALL
> affairs of life such as love, courtship, marriage,
> divorce, business, lawsuits, speculations and transac-
> tions of all kinds. She never fails to reunite the
> separated, cause speedy, happy marriages, overcome

enemies, rivals, lovers quarrels, evil habits, stumbling
blocks and bad luck of all kinds.[32]

Other "advisors," such as Madam Costa on Lyons Avenue in Newark, Mrs.
Lawrence in Manhattan, or Sister Grace in Newark, all competed with each
other to convince their prospective clients that their methods will succeed
where others have failed.[33]

Witches such as Sister Bright emphasized that they were Christians
performing traditional services. Advertisements were adorned with the
symbolism of Christianity—especially the cross.[34] Other, more public
activities were also depicted as "Catholic" or "Christian." The most notable
of these was the feast. Along with the more famous—such as Manhattan's
San Gennaro—the New York/New Jersey region played host to hundreds
of small, local homages to patron saints.[35] As the feasts of years past, their
primary purpose was to pay public homage to a protective saint. As had
also been the case in the past, the most powerful of the saints was the
Virgin Mary—the Madonna.

The "Feast of Lights" was one example of local reverence to the
Madonna. Held for seventy-eight consecutive years at St. John's Church in
Trenton, both young and old through the early 1980s publicly displayed
their faith in the Madonna's protective powers. A thirty-two-year-old
laborer, Angelo, explained what the Madonna meant to him:

> As far as we're concerned in the community, we've
> placed her high on the scale of religious figures....
> For me, it's not just the indoctrination that did it, but
> it's something I concocted in my own mind to be a
> fact that she is high on the scale of people to ad-
> mire....[36]

Angelo's devotion to the Madonna was matched by his neighbors. The five
day feast, sponsored by both the church and the Italian Society of Trenton,
featured a statue of the Madonna paraded through the streets around the
church. This ritual, which began in the southern Italian village of
Casandrino, grew out of a peasant legend concerning the discovery of the
Madonna in a field.[37] Brought to Trenton in 1905 by a group of laborers
from Casandrino who were exuberant over their attainment of jobs at a
Trenton wire plant, these workers vowed to give public thanks to the saint

who made their success possible. The feast continued annually until the 1960s, when the church seemingly survived the tumultuous effects of rural Italy, *Mezzogiorno* immigration, and New Jersey. It exuded not change, but continuity; a security based on subservience to powerful lords, rather than a faith in the capacity of the individual to improve life's circumstances. The festival was rooted in an agrarian past, and it continued into an industrial future. The shift from feudal to capitalist social relations notwithstanding, the feast remained emotionally rooted in the hierarchical standards of conservatism. It was a vision of the future grounded in the events of the past, as a young worker who yearly witnessed the feast suggested:

> I think the respect we show the Madonna is really a
> spine-chilling kind of experience that I'm glad
> continues and I hope always will continue. It's an
> event that really comes out of our past and I would
> really like my son to see it, his children to see it, and
> I think it's just like live history....[40]

The public ritual of the feast served, a central legitimizing function. Younger generations needed to be convinced of the "rightness" of their community life. Indeed, they needed to learn where this rightness began. The enthusiasm and unyielding faith directed toward the Madonna objectified some of these answers in the most elaborate of ways. The formal institutional practices of Italian people's religion appeared as "self-evident" reality. The real world of the Madonna became so when it yearly became a venerated part of the community. Legitimation of the values it imparted—especially the feasibility of subordination to authority—were worked into the fabric of working class culture by their mere presence. Values from one generation to the next were fed intravenously through the rituals of the feast.

But mere symbolic presence is only one requirement on the road to legitimizing cultural values. Accordingly, the feast also offered a thoughtful and constantly changing inventory of popular moral maxims and proverbs which, while meeting the changing demands of a new generation served, nonetheless, to provide answers. Thus the Italian-American feast, in Trenton and elsewhere, featured a host of folk tales and legends. These folk tales and legends took new forms while explaining, and therefore legitimizing, the accepted way of doing things.[41] It was through the development of *festa* maxims that the workers achieved a theoretical self-consciousness in their life not usually evident elsewhere.[42]

The proverbs described in New York by folklorist Pauline N. Barese served to bring into focus the context within which the feast was situated. Myth and language were fused in the Italian-American feast, a fusion which produced in the mind of the *festa* participants a unity of the symbolic, the real, and the imaginary.[43] Hence, objective truth. Even the merging of subtle gesturing and dialect residuals served to form cultural points of reference, as David Efron suggested in the 1941 publication of *Gesture and Environment*:

> In general there is little difference between the gestural lexicon of the "traditional" Neopolitan in New York City and that of his ancestor in Europe one century ago....[44]

The proverbs of the feast stood on Catholic territory in opposition to Catholicism. Thus their oppositionist position legitimized, in the mind of the worker, the culture from which they sprang.[45] Legitimation of a cultural world view was facilitated by a series of short observations on how the world worked. The religion of the Italian-American laborer posed as an omnipresent force which seemingly explained the world in terms comprehensible to all. Italian-American religion, in the final analysis, achieved legitimacy because it did not appear constructed in the formal way that the Irish dominated church was. Its linguistic constructions, the powerful presence of the Madonna, indeed, the sensuous aroma of the different food which filled local streets, all gave the impression of a tradition beginning long ago and continuing into the indeterminate future. The feast celebrated the protective quality of a patron saint who was seemingly the product of nature itself. People merely facilitated the arrival of what was already there. The institution of the feast, unlike the institution of the Church, grew out of the creative power of workers. It was not imposed upon them.

Because it was viewed as a creative urge in tune with nature, the religion of Italian-American workers lacked the systematic quality of Irish Catholicism. A brief look at Irish Catholic doctrine reveals just how different it looked from the spontaneous and fluid religion of Italian-

American neighborhoods. Perhaps the most concise expression of the Irish hierarchy's view in the postwar period is found in the writings of Richard P. McBrien. In his two volumes of *Catholicism*, he explored in detail church doctrine on matters ranging from "human existence" through "Mary and the Church."[46] Acknowledging his debt to such people as Dermont Lane of the Irish Theological Association and Robert Wister of the Archdiocese of Newark, McBrien outlined a Catholicism in which the central tenets of Italian people's religion, e.g., the homage paid to the Madonna, were completely absent.

In the Church doctrine of "Marian maximalism," McBrien indicted any Catholicism which exaggerated the importance of either Mary or other saints. To place Christ behind them "demeans the instrumental causality of the humanity of Christ." In the following passage, McBrien elaborated on this argument, one which clearly denied a doctrinal place for southern Italian saints:

> It is always the inner transforming presence of God that ultimately counts, and not the sign and instrument of that presence. Therefore, it is not because Mary and the saints have the power of influence with God that they are objects of veneration and devotion. Rather it is because the grace of God has triumphed in them.[47]

From the perspective of the local Italian parish, this is a troubling passage. McBrien emphasizes the "transforming presence of God," a process overshadowing the pragmatic implications of Mary's power. Remember, however, that the viability of *Mezzogiorno* religion rested on the workers' perception that it was a belief system with measurable, practical results. A vague "transforming presence," which McBrien went on to identify as a brand of moral absolutism, had no place in this scheme. Christ and moral absolutes formed the core of Church doctrine by 1980, which McBrien stated in the clearest of terms.

> It is Christ's, not Mary's, achievement that we celebrate.... The Church is not just an institution...with Mary and the saints as "successful graduates" who have some measure of influence with "the adminis-

> tration." It is not comparable to a filling station,
> where automobiles replenish their supply of fuel.
> The Church is the People of God, the Body of Christ,
> and the Temple of the Holy Spirit.[48]

From commentary such as this, it is clear that official Church doctrine frowned upon the "marian maximalists" at work in the local Italian-American parish. McBrien's fiery condemnation of the "filling station" was a direct and open affront to the dominant characteristic of pragmatism motivating Italian-American workers to worship Mary and the other saints. McBrien emphasized unconditional devotion to God and Christ—and the Church which they established. One could not reject a saint because he or she did not appear to provide protection.[49] Just as importantly, McBrien argued that the moral absolutes propagated by the Church were unquestionable. Doctrinal authority flowed downward to the local parish, not upward from it.

McBrien's passionate plea for the ultimate doctrinal authority of the Church was an indication of the maturing which had taken place. With the obvious exception of parochial school education, the Irish hierarchy in New Jersey and New York had grudgingly come to the realization that they could not extend their polemic against Catholic deviationism past relatively obscure theological mediations. The history of local Italian parishes seceding from the Church over just such disputes sensitized the leadership to the dangers of pushing too hard. Accordingly, McBrien's definition of what was "characteristically Catholic" as a "sense of tradition, of doctrine" remained within the safe confines of a dense scholarly treatise.[50]

Conversely, Italian-American parishes throughout the second half of the twentieth century confidently pursued traditional practices within the Church. Unlike parishioners of numerous parishes at the turn of the century, there was no longer a felt imperative to bolt from the Church in an effort to maintain theological integrity. Confident enough by the 1950s to live in an uneasy theological peace with Irish-American officials, the local Italian parish was able to be Catholic in its own way. Its earlier pleas for doctrinal tolerance had been heeded, not out of respect for diversity or, of course, theological integrity, but rather out of the need for some semblance of church unity.[51] The position of the Italian-American parish was strengthened in some quarters by the infusion of another immigrant group in the late 1960s, the Portuguese. Their traditions closely resembled Italian rural religion in its deemphasis of individual initiative, its focus on saints, and the use of magic. The Portuguese became prominent church members in Newark and Greenwich Village.[52]

But the confident maturity attained within the Church did not, for Italian-Americans, extend outward toward the wider American culture. Third and fourth generation workers, while not denying the legitimacy of their beliefs, came to feel a self-consciousness about them that their forebears did not generally feel. In effect, the public expression of their religion was reduced to the elaborate spectacle of the feast, an event which workers were not reluctant to put on display. As for the rest—witches, the evil eye, and even the emotional subordination built into the veneration of protective deities—all of those remained within the safe confines of the working class community. Like the immigrants, there was still a reluctance to completely expose oneself to what was perceived as an essentially hostile and alien world.

CHAPTER EIGHT NOTES

1. This perspective was revealed in an assortment of privately circulated memoranda among the Irish hierarchy of northern New Jersey. Peter J. Wash and other scholars have catalogued these papers in c convenient volume entitled *Guide to Northern New Jersey Catholic Parish and Institutional Records* (South Orange, New Jersey, 1984). This volume was a useful guide in the location of scattered references contained i the collection of the New Jersey Catholic Historical Records Commission at Seton Hall University. See the correspondence of Bishops Thomas J. Walsh between 1928 and 1952; Thomas Boland between 1952 and 1974; and Peter Gerety, between 1974 and 1986.

2. John K. Sharp, "The New Parishes and the Old," in the *History of the Diocese of Brooklyn, 1853–1953*, Volume II (New York, 1954), p. 189.

3. Sharp, "The New Parishes and the Old," p. 188.

4. Although I do not have direct evidence to attribute this motive to Molloy, I have no reason to believe that his perspective differed sharply from that of Walsh, Boland, or Gerety in the Newark archdiocese.

5. Look at the case in Newark, for example. See Margaret A. Vance, "Archbishop Looks Back," *Newark Sunday News*, 30 May 1965, p. 18.

6. See the references in Note 1. An early and interesting polemic against Irish Catholic control is John Zarilli's *A Prayerful Appeal to the American Hierarchy in Behalf of the Italian Catholic Cause in the United States* (Two Harbors, Minnesota, 1924).

7. Consult the local parish records of Our Lady of Mount Carmel Church in Orange, New Jersey; and the Diocese of Newark archives at Seton Hall University, which houses the relevant material for approximately thirty Italian-American parishes in the Newark area.

8. The study of this culture also included a study of the Italian language between grades kindergarten and eight. Refer to Concetta A. Chiacchio, "Current Patterns of Socialization and Adaptation in an Italian American Community" (Ed.D. dissertation, Rutgers University, 1985), p. 162.

9. Personal correspondence presented in Carmine A. Loffredo's Appendix, "A History of the Roman Catholic School System in the Archdiocese of Newark, New Jersey, 1900–1965" (Ed.D. dissertation, Rutgers Universi-

ty, 1967), entry #31; p. 465.

10. Ibid., entry #74, p. 483.
11. Ibid., entry #102, p. 493.
12. Ibid., entry #111, p. 496.
13. *Are Parochial Schools the Answer?* (New York, 1963), p. 71.
14. See Alice and Peter Rossi, "Some Effects of Parochial School Education in America," *Daedalus*, 90, 1961, pp. 300–328.
15. Untitled song and prayer sheet, Mt. Carmel Church, Lyndhurst, New Jersey (1980), n.p.
16. Ibid.
17. Ibid., song #10, "Mira Il Tuo Popolo" (Aim of Your People).
18. In *History of the Diocese of Brooklyn, p. 256.* It also differed dramatically from the Protestantism of the New York metropolitan area. Look, for example, at the optimistic appraisal of a perfectible world in "The Church of the Epiphany Episcopal and The Highlands United Presbyterian Church Celebration of Worship," 11 January 1976; and Wilma Supik's "Of Such is the Kingdom," *Week-End Magazine*, 6 November 1954, n.p. (a discussion of the Church of the Epiphany in Allendale, New Jersey). Both of these documents are located in the archives of the Bergen County Historical Society, Hackensack Public Library, Hackensack, New Jersey.
19. I discussed this issue with a retired Newark garment worker, Marie Pulsinelle, who also was a parishioner of Mt. Carmel's (Summer, 1985).
20. Dennis J. Starr, "Roman Catholic Church," in *The Italians of New Jersey: A Historical Introduction and Bibliography* (Newark, 1985), p. 36.
21. Ibid.
22. Patrick Gallo, "The Saints Are Older Relatives and Friends," in *Old Bread, New Wine: A Portrait of the Italian-Americans* (Chicago, 1981), p. 195.
23. Ibid.
24. Richard Gambino, "Religion, Magic, and the Church," in *Blood of My Blood: The Dilemma of the Italian-Americans* (Garden City, New York, 1974), p. 235.
25. See the descriptions in Jerry Della Femina's autobiography, *An Italian Grows in Brooklyn* (Boston, 1978), pp. 75–76.
26. Along with Della Femina and Gambino, there were the first-hand

observations of the folklorist Pauline N. Barese. Writing in 1965 that Italian-American workers in New York City were people "with very few ideas altered or weakened by the currents of life around them," she went on to describe the Evil Eye:

> There are still those who believe in the Evil Eye or Mal'occhio. If someone suffers persistently from headaches, the ailment is blamed on contact with this evil. To remove this spell, they would place a small saucer of water upon the victim's head and then proceed to mumble words to drive away the bad spirit.... To this day, some Sicilians who also believe in the Evil Eye [like descendants of immigrants from Calabria] try not to forget to put their first stocking on the left leg, in order to ensure a day of good luck.

"Southern Italian Folklore in New York City," *New York Folklore Quarterly*, September 1965, pp. 185–186.

27. *An Italian Grows in Brooklyn*, p. 75.
28. Ibid., p. 76. Also see Anthony L. LaRuffa's "Mario's Family," in *Monte Carmelo: An Italian-American Community in the Bronx* (New York, 1988), especially page 73.
29. Quoted in Chiacchio, "Current Patterns of Socialization and Adaptation in an Italian Community," p. 126.
30. Ibid., p. 125.
31. This perspective was summed up by the Newark community activist Steve Adubato in 1972. He was quoted as saying that

> The liberals are so good at understanding every other group, why don't they want to understand us? Our mothers work in factories—we're the white pigs.

Quoted in David K. Shipler, "The White Niggers of Newark," *Harpers*, August 1972, p. 82.

32. "Sister Bright: Spiritual Reader, Healer and Advisor," *Italian Tribune*, 1 March 1968, p. 6.
33. "Madam Costa," *Italian Tribune*, 9 February 1968, p. 10; "Mrs. Lawrence, Gifted Reader and Advisor," *Italian Tribune*, 21 July 1967, p. 6; and "Sister Grace," *Italian Tribune*, 21 July 1967, p. 5. The newspaper

Il Progresso also carried regular advertisements for witches through the early 1980s. One, for example:

> Specializzata in rita spiritici per l'annullamento di: *Malocchio* (my emphasis added).

See "Angelica E Rosanna: Spiritualista Europea," *Il Progresso Italo Americano*, 20 July 1984, p. 23. *Il Progresso* was published in Emerson, New Jersey.

34. See Sister Bright's advertisement cited in note 32.
35. Consult such descriptions as Rose Ann Di Popolo, "An Italian Feast: Saint Gerard Maiella," *New Jersey Folklore*, Spring 1984, pp. 23–25; Barrese, "Southern Italian Folklore in New York City;" Janet Bukovinsky, "The Best-Fed People in New Jersey: They Mangia in a Small Section of Trenton called the Burg," *New Jersey Monthly*, August 1981, especially page 74; Alan A. Siegel, *Out of Our Past: A History of Irvington, New Jersey* (Irvington, New Jersey, 1974); Della Femina, *An Italian Grows in Brooklyn*, pp. 151–153; John Lewis, "Belmont remains an Italian Oasis," *New York Daily News*, 14 March 1982, p. 3; and LaRuffa, *Monte Carmelo: An Italian-American Community in the Bronx*.
36. Quoted in Chiacchio, "Religious Beliefs and Activity," pp. 125–126.
37. "The Festival of Our Lady of Casandrino," *The Trentonian*, 6 September 1984, n.p.
38. Bukovinsky tells us that the "pastor of St. Joachim's Catholic Church 'discontinued' the celebration in 1962 because he felt it was becoming too much like a carnival, too pagan." Due to popular pressure, it was reinstated, however (p. 74).
39. Quoted in Chiacchio, "The Feast of Lights," p. 130.
40. Ibid., p. 132.
41. Barrese, in "Southern Italian Folklore in New York City," tells of other popular tales, especially proverbs, which provided guidelines for living. See pages 184–185.
42. See, for example, the "Program of the Feast of St. Joseph," (Lodi, New Jersey, 1967), p. 2.
43. Della Femina's accounts of Italian-American life in Brooklyn suggest this, as does the research of di Popolo and Barese. Also, consult Paolo Vivante, "On Myth and Action in Pindar," *Arethusa*, Fall 1971, pp.

119–135; and Albert Cook, *Myth and Language* (Bloomington, Indiana, 1980).

44. *Gesture and Environment* (New York, 1941). Also refer to Michal La Sorte's "Itaglish: The Immigrant Idiom," in *La Merica: Images of Italian Greenhorn Experience* (Philadelphia, 1985), especially page 174.

45. An interesting approach to the process of legitimation is found in Peter L. Berger and Thomas Luckmann, *The Social Construction of Reality: A Treatise in the Sociology of Knowledge* (Garden City, New York, 1967). Also refer to Jack Zipes, *Breaking the Magic Spell: Radical Theories of Folk and Fairy Tales* (London, 1979).

46. *Catholicism*, Volumes I and II (Minneapolis, 1980).

47. "Marian Devotions: Theological Criteria," p. 891.

48. Ibid.

49. Jerry Mangione, in *Mount Allegro*, provides the most compelling discussion of how Italian-American workers rejected saints who did not provide "protection."

50. "The Roman Catholic Church," p. 722.

51. According to Loffredo, this was a chief rationale for the centralization movement in the Newark diocese in the late 1950s.

52. Donald Tricarico has outlined this process in his sociological field study of "the neighborhood parish" in the 1970s, entitled *The Italians of Greenwich Village: The Social Structure and Transformation of an Ethnic Community* (New York, 1984).

Conclusion

THE REALITY OF THE COUNTER-DISCOURSE AND THE ISSUE OF CONTINUITY

Entering and exiting. These two words
should be abolished. One does not
enter or exit: one continues.
> Antonio Gramsci, in
> *Avanti!* (1917)

This work has described the reproduction of daily life over a century-long period. I have charted the history of daily customs, whose rationales were rooted in a specific class outlook. It was a perspective beautifully described by Herbert Gutman, who ended his story at the beginning of the twentieth century. I have proposed that Italian-American workers continued to create their own world long after that historical juncture. Theirs was a pattern of behavior which began before that time as well; indeed, before their entrance into the very different social relations of New Jersey and New York.

My central emphasis has thus been that of cultural continuity. The heroic days of radical labor confrontations were few when compared with the relative quiet of daily life. It was nonetheless in the construction of that life that we see the sustained attacks and counterattacks of class struggle. It was in that cultural arena that conflicts periodically exploding in dramatic confrontations between labor and capital were played out, and played out on a sustained basis. In general, that world developed outside of trade unions and radical organizing. Instead, it flourished in the institutions of civil society. In the lives of the workers I have studied, it tended to perpetuate a classically conservative view of the world which rejected both liberalism and radicalism. An hierarchical, cautious view of life remained the norm, a product of the harsh social relations in which peasants, and then workers, always found themselves.

Their conservatism always emphasized the subordinate position of the individual. Accordingly, liberal and radical exhortations about human potentialities fell on deaf ears. Their values, first formed in rural Italy, were reformulated in America within the context of new demands and modified desires. It was this initial rural view, which was later manifested as an urban "blue-collar" one, which situated the Italian-American within the historical reality of a capitalist social structure and demographic concentration. The social reproduction of culture thus took place outside of the initial class relations which helped to generate its early forms.

The culture of these workers was always embodied in their institutions and institutional rituals. Culture was a conscious perpetuation of a distinct class view, one which needed to be translated because it assumed so many forms. The workers producing this culture only emerged as fully human when they themselves became the object of what they had made. Theirs was a consciously purposeful endeavor which generally rejected both radical solutions and liberal perspectives. While their culture was often designed within materialist constraints, it also sometimes gave rise to those very constraints.

The effort of the lower middle class to design the labor process, a process which was the product of other concerns, is a case in point. Between 1880 and 1980, the pervasive lure of small-scale entrepreneurship remained profound.[1] In this context, the dynamics of family relations explain far more than a conception of labor drawn from classical political economy. Relationships between parents, children, and assorted relatives up to and including cousins had a special intensity—a fundamental bond which, among the shopkeepers, was kept alive in the workplace. America's "work ethic" was never a central concern for the lower middle class. Instead, work was viewed as a way of meeting other desires—such as allowing family members to be together in the workplace.

The view of labor as an inherently alienating experience did not arise upon entrance into the capitalist infrastructure of New Jersey and New York. Indeed, it was evident in the attitude of the peasants viewed by such scholars as Anne MacDonnell. Accordingly, the concept of continuity has remained a paramount concern in this study, as I have turned my attention repeatedly to what Georg Hegel spoke of in the *Science of Logic*:

> What is transcended is also preserved; it has only
> lost its immediacy and is not on that account annihi-
> lated.[2]

It was upon such views that Hegel propounded his much noted negation of the negation. From Hegel's perspective, a negation operated on two levels. First, and most easily grasped, is the obvious destruction of past trends. It is this aspect of historical change which has most concerned scholars engaged in immigrant and ethnic studies.[3] What they fail to see, however, is that this one-sided conception of historical development does not take into account the analogous reality of preservation. To put it another way, the rationales behind past practices can indeed survive surface abolitions. This is what Hegel was suggesting when he wrote of the preservation of the properties of extinct entities within the reality of latter developments—"the other of the first."

This continuum was, for Italian-American workers, the result of purposeful, voluntary action. They fashioned their lives within obvious social boundaries. But this preservation was always a double-edged sword, for it also retained some characteristics which the worker would just as soon leave behind. Andrew Rolle has written of the emotional turmoil which this often created for Italian-Americans and, by implication, other groups in the working and lower middle class as well:

> Mangione, though deeply respectful of his roots,
> explained that "for all their wisdom, none of the
> Italian immigrant parents I knew grasped the dilem-
> ma of their children, who from early childhood were
> pulled in one direction by their parents' insistence on

Old World traditions and in the opposite direction
by what their teachers told them in the classroom."
The result was children with confused impressions of
identity that were never resolved.[4]

Regardless of whether a particular level of this culture has been
consciously perpetuated or involuntarily dragged along, a pervasive motif
which continuously surfaced was that of classical conservatism. Novelists
emerging from this mileau typically stressed this theme.[5] Surprisingly,
labor historians have not generally examined this rich vein of working class
perceptions. As a result, they have sometimes misread key elements of
working and lower middle class life. Feasts thus become examples of
working class "community," strikes assume the embryonic forms of socialist
revolution, and leisure time activities reveal fundamental "alienation."
While it may be appropriate to read radical socialist intentions into other
working class people at other historical moments, it is a real strain on the
evidence to do it here.

What these Italian-Americans strove to maintain, most of all, fell
outside of both liberal and radical objectives. Apart from some early
Paterson and New York anarchists, there has existed little in the way of
critical social analysis among Italian-American workers. Their view of
society as hierarchical remained intact, drawn from experiences in southern
Italy, and confirmed later on in America. Individualism captured their
imagination only within certain pre-approved boundaries, e.g., family
cohesiveness. Consequently, their reactions to social change were steady
and predictable. Authority and tradition on the local level, not individual
initiative or critical awareness, have been the guides.[6]

Views of human nature also proved decisive. The older peasant focus
on the imperfectibility of human beings has been particularly noticeable in
the areas of sexuality and Roman Catholicism. This stands in stark contrast
to the faith in human perfectibility displayed by liberals and radicals alike.[7]
As a result, radical proposals for class solidarity have historically been
rejected. The liberal emphasis on Hooverian "rugged individualism" has
also been generally ignored or, at best, greatly modified. The local
community remained culturally insulated, and it rested on the premise of
hierarchy.[8]

This study, however, is in no way suggestive of Italian-Americans on similar class levels in other parts of America.[9] Italians in areas such as San Francisco, or even Los Angeles, present distinct methodological problems, not the least of which is their very different demographic history.[10] Such trends make a study of the Northeast all that more intriguing. This is because it is in New Jersey and New York that Italian culture has never been merely what Stephen Steinberg has called the "symbolic plane."[11] Such an argument ignores the often vivid cultural continuity which I have tried to suggest. To argue that Italian-American culture has, historically, developed into only a leisure time pursuit is to overlook the daily manifestations of a complex and purposeful culture. On the eve of the 1980 presidential election, the *Italian Tribune* of Newark, New Jersey expressed the reality of that lived culture:

> ...Be aware that discrimination, exclusion, depriva-
> tion—which have all been visited upon Italian
> Americans at one time or another because of their
> ethnic origins—are a consequence of [a] lack of
> political power. Your heritage is a tradition that
> embraces a whole set of values, and elections are a
> good opportunity to stop and think about what these
> values are and how prospective candidates measure
> up to them.[12]

Thus the creation of a "whole set of values" has been one directed against a dominant culture convinced of its legitimacy and seemingly assured of its supremacy. Italian-Americans consistently organized their culture in order to subvert the discourse of the dominant. The horizon of the middle class was always undergoing change, its boundaries always in need of patrols to protect its integrity. The stakes in this struggle are high. As we move into the twenty-first century, this cultural frontier, if anything, is becoming more complex. It is also becoming more crucial, for what is at stake is the issue of domination itself.

CONCLUSION NOTES

1. Representative accounts include Michael Parenti, "The Blessings of Private Enterprise: A Personal Reminiscence," in *Studies in Italian American Social History*, ed. Francesco Cordasco (Totowa, New Jersey, 1975), pp. 81–83; John J. D'Alesandre, "Occupational Trends of Italians in New York City," *Casa Italiana Educational Bureau, Bulletin Number 8,* 1935, unnamed Italian shopkeeper's ledger book (1920–1926) in New Jersey, in the William L. De Yoe papers, Rutgers University Library (New Jersey Room), pp. 1–30; Colleen L. Johnson, *Growing Up and Growing Old in Italian-American Families* (New Brunswick, New Jersey, 1985), pp. 32–33, and 77–78; Charles W. Churchill, "The Italians of Newark: A Community Study" (Ph.D. dissertation, New York University, 1942), pp. 28–42, and 53–75; James A. Testa, "The Italians of Newark: The Process of Economic Victory and Social Retreat, 1910–1940" (B.A. thesis, Princeton University, 1970), pp. 22–68, and for a wider geographic consideration of my point, see George Herrmann, Samuel Patti, and William Simons, "Bloomfield: An Italian Working Class Neighborhood," *Italian Americana*, Fall/Winter 1981, pp. 102–116. This last article deals with a community in the Pittsburgh, Pennsylvania area. Also refer to the results of an oral interview with Leo Frodella of Oakland, New Jersey, in the summer of 1984.

    For attendant theoretical concerns, see Frank Bechhofer and Brian Elliott, "An Approach to a Study of Small Shopkeepers and the Class Structure," *European Journal of Sociology*, 9, 1968, pp. 180–202; Bechhofer and Elliott, "Persistence and Change: The Petite Bourgeoisie in Industrial Society," *European Journal of Sociology*, 17, 1976, pp. 74–99; Geoffrey Crossick, ed., *The Lower Middle Class in Britain* (London, 1977); Bechhofer and Elliott, *The Petite Bourgeoisie: Comparative Studies of the Uneasy Stratum* (New York, 1981); Nicos Poulantyas, "Part Three: The Petty Bourgeoisie, Traditional and New," in *Classes in Contemporary Capitalism* (London, 1975), pp. 191–336; John H. Bunzel, "The General Ideology of American Small Business," *Political Science Quarterly*, March, 1955, pp. 87–101; Martin Trow; "Small Businessmen, Political Tolerance and Support for McCarthy," in *Political Sociology: Selected Essays*, ed. Lewis A. Caser (New York, 1967), pp. 181–203; C. Gerry,

"Petty Production and Capitalist Production in Dakar: The Crisis of the 'Self-Employed,'" *World Development*, 6, 1978, pp. 1,147–1,160; and Bechhofer and Elliott, "The Voice of Small Business and the Politics of Survival," *Sociological Review*, 26, 1978, pp. 57–88.

2. *Science of Logic* (London, 1929), p. 120.

3. See James A. Crispino, *The Assimilation of Ethnic Groups: The Italian Case* (Staten Island, New York, 1980); Herbert J. Gans, "Symbolic Ethnicity: The Future of Ethnic Groups and Cultures in America," *Ethnic and Racial Studies*, January 1979, pp. 1–20; Alba, "Social assimilation among American Catholic National-Origin Groups," *American Sociological Review*, December 1976, pp. 1,030–1,046; and, especially, Stephen Steinberg's *The Ethnic Myth: Race, Ethnicity, and Class in America* (Boston, 1981).

4. Rolle, "La Famiglia: Defending the Old Ways," in *The Italian Americans: Troubled Roots* (New York, 1980), p. 122. The writings of Jerre Mangione reiterate this theme time and again. See *Mount Allegro: A Memoir of Italian American Life* (New York, 1981); *Reunion in Sicily* (New York, 1984); and *An Ethnic At Large: A Memoir of America in the Thirties and Forties* (Philadelphia, 1983). Also view the poignant lamentations of Mario Puzo's Lucia Santa, in *The Fortunate Pilgrim* (New York, 1985).

5. Along with the novelists cited throughout this work, there is the literature of Mario Pei. His *Swords of Anjou* (1953) focuses on several themes historically paramount in this culture. There is the treacherous brother-in-law Ganelon, who suggests the untrustworthy character of non-blood relatives. Honor, loyalty, and rigid hierarchical relations are all embodied in the novel's main characters, especially Roland. His *Sparrows of Paris* (1958) celebrates the ritualistic meal and traditional sources of authority. It also features a virulent anti-communism which is not necessarily the product of late McCarthyism. More profoundly, it is rooted in a view of human nature which denies the possibility of rationality, high ideals, and an equal distribution of wealth.

6. For example, see Colleen L. Johnson's *Growing Up and Growing Old in Italian American Families* (New Brunswick, New Jersey, 1985); and Anthony L. LaRuffa, *Monte Carmelo: An Italian-American Community in the Bronx* (New York, 1988).

7. Even though Karl Marx never really addressed the issue of "human

nature" per se in a systematic fashion, there are numerous passages in his writings which give rise to his observation that human beings are basically rational (at least if we ignore the French peasantry in *The 18th Brumaire of Louis Bonaparte*). In *Capital*, Volume I, he spoke of "human nature in general." When one considers this statement in light of his belief that the working class will inevitably revolt as the crisis of capitalism deepens, then his faith in the rational person, one who always understands the world in all of its complex processes and manifestations, becomes clear.

This preoccupation with the quest for universal understanding is also detectable in the writings of such liberal theorists as Louis Hartz. Like Marx and a plethora of liberal and Marxian scholars, Hartz focuses on a vision of an emotionally sterile humanity; he consequently speaks of the bourgeois "quiet, matter of fact quality" in *The Liberal Tradition*.

The classically conservative view expressed by the Italian Americans in this study, however, was not compatible with either brand of rationalism.

8. The psychologist Paul R. Cassarino suggests how such perceptions of the world are individually maintained over time:

> ...the argument is developed that perceptions of self are in part formulated from the perception of oneself as being ethnic or having a particular ethnic heritage. These ethnic perceptions include belief systems, patterns of emotions, expectations, perceptions of the environment, sense of reality, interpretive schemes for interacting in the world, etc. In the development of self-perception or self-concept, these perceptions that are ethnic in origin are incorporated into the self-concept and no longer are ethnic perception *per se*, but become part of the individual's perception of himself or herself. In that way, ethnicity becomes a psychological dimension, passed on from generation to generation through the psychological constructs which are responsible for the development of self-concept.

See Cassarino's "The Relationship Between Ethnicity and Self-Concept in Italian-Americans" (Ph.D. dissertation, University of Rhode Island, 1982), p. ii.

9. Introductory overviews include Andrew Rolle, *The Immigrant Upraised: Italian Adventurers and Colonists in an Expanding America* (Norman, Oklahoma, 1968); Paolo Giordano, "Italian Immigration in the State of Louisiana: Its Causes, Effects, and Results," *Italian Americana*, 5, 1979, pp. 160–177; Anthony V. Margavio, "The Reaction of the press to the Italian-American in New Orleans, 1880 to 1920," *Italian Americana*, 4, 1978, pp. 72–83; Hans C. Palmer, "Italian Immigration and the Development of California Agriculture" (Ph.D. dissertation, University of California, Berkeley, 1965); Rolle, "Dispersal," in *The Italian Americans: Troubled Roots*, pp. 16–27; Barbara Botein, "The Hennessy Case: An Episode in American Nativism, 1890" (Ph.D. dissertation, New York University, 1975); and Dino Cinel's *From Italy to San Francisco: The Immigrant Experience* (Stanford, 1982). Also see Rudolph J. Vecoli's "Change and/or Continuity in the Immigrant Experience," *Reviews in American History*, March 1984, pp. 109–114.

10. For example, consult Paul Radin's *The Italians of San Francisco: Their Adjustment and Acculturation* (San Francisco, 1970). The popular Italian-American perception of California has been graphically portrayed by Lucas Longo, in his novel *Family on Vendetta Street*:

> One summer afternoon while teaching me the finer points of boccie in our back yard, he stopped to wipe his brow. "I should never have come to New York. Never. This damn city. Filthy. A dirty hell. I should have done the right thing. I should have saved more money and taken a boat for California. That's the place for human beings. Farmland. Sun. Space. They say the land is so beautiful there. And that the earth brings forth lovely things.

See Longo, *The Family on Vendetta Street* (New York, 1968), p. 55.

11. Steinberg, *The Ethnic Myth: Race, Ethnicity, and Class in America*. Arthur M. Schlessinger, Jr., in *The Disuniting of America: Reflections on a Multicultural Society* (New York, 1992), agrees with Steinberg but does not appear to question the evidence Steinberg uses.

12. "Editorial," *Italian Tribune*, 31 October 1980, p. 4.

A Bibliographical Note

I was led to most of the primary sources used in this book by outstanding bibliographical guides. Dennis J. Starr's *The Italians of New Jersey: A Historical Introduction and Bibliography* (Newark, 1985), was indispensable. His bibliography led me to the collections of numerous antiquarian and local historical societies. Francesco Cordasco's bibliographies were also important. See *The Italian-American Experience: An Annotated and Classified Bibliographical Guide* (New York, 1974). Along with Salvatore La Gumina, Cordasco also compiled *Italians in the United States: A Bibliography of Reports, Texts, Critical Studies and Related Materials* (New York, 1972). Also useful is another work by Cordasco, and Michael V. Cordasco, entitled *Italians in the United States: An Annotated Bibliography of Doctoral Dissertations Completed at American Universities* (Fairview, New Jersey, 1981).

There were other important reference tools which helped me to locate material at local libraries and in university special collections. Cordasco's *Italian Mass Emigration, The Exodus of a Latin People: A Bibliographical Guide to the Bollettino Dell 'Emigrazione, 1902–1927* (Totowa, New Jersey, 1980), is the only guide to the voluminous *Bollentino* which began as a result of Italian legislation in 1901. It is a guide to articles, investigations, and consular reports all concerned with the plight of Italian immigrants. Another useful source was the Center for Migration Studies in Staten island, which has an organized and extensive collection of Italian-American sources. A guide which proved helpful in the location of anarchist newspapers was the *Italian American Collection: A Brief Description*, published by the University of Minnesota's Immigration History Research Center. Edward J. Miranda and Ivo Rossi edited an excellent guide to census data and public health issues in *New York City's Italians* (New York, 1976). Also advert to Ferdinando P. Alfonsi's *Dictionary of Italian-American Poets* (New

York, 1989.)   At UCLA's Ethnic Folkways Library there is an interesting collection of sound recordings entitled *Calabria bella: dove t'hai lasciate; Italian Folk Music Collected in New York, New Jersey, and Rhode Island*, edited and recorded by Anna L. Chairetakis.

INDEX